# SPIRIT WORKS

# SPIRIT WORKS

## CONTEMPORARY VIEWS ON THE GIFTS OF THE SPIRIT AND THE BIBLE

JERRY · VINES

BROADMAN
& HOLMAN
PUBLISHERS

Nashville, Tennessee

© 1999
by Jerry Vines
All rights reserved
Printed in the United States of America


0–8054–1996–9


Published by Broadman & Holman Publishers, Nashville, Tennessee
Acquistions and Development Editor: Leonard G. Goss
Page Design: TF Designs, Mt. Juliet, Tennessee

Dewey Decimal Classification: 277
Subject Heading: CHARISMATIC PRACTICES
Library of Congress Card Catalog Number: 99–11262

Unless otherwise noted, Scripture quotations are from the Holy Bible, New International Version, copyright © 1973, 1978, 1984 by International Bible Society. Passages marked NASB are from the New American Standard Bible, © the Lockman Foundation, 1960, 1962, 1963, 1968, 1971, 1972, 1973, 1975, 1977; used by permission. Passages marked The Message are from *The Message,* the New Testament in Contemporary English, © 1993 by Eugene H. Peterson, published by NavPress, Colorado Springs, Colo.

**Library of Congress Cataloging-in-Publication Data**
Vines, Jerry
    SpiritWorks : charismatic practices and the Bible / by Jerry Vines.
        p.   cm.
    Includes bibliographical references.
    ISBN 0–8054–1996–9 (pbk.)
        1. Pentecostalism—United States. I. Title.
BR1644.V56    1999
277.3'082—dc21

99–11262
CIP

1 2 3 4 5 03 02 01 00 99

# Contents

# Preface

His name was Sammy. He was the center on my high school football team. Sammy was nothing but good! And could he make plays!

Sammy's father always stood outside the field house after our games. He would wait for Sammy there. With his overcoat and dark hat, there was a serene dignity about him. Sammy's father was a Church of God pastor. Something about him intrigued me. It seemed to me, a teenager, that Sammy's dad must be very spiritual. I knew he was different. He wasn't like my own pastor, but I really respected him. In fact, I admired many Pentecostal Christians in our little town because they were so godly and Christlike.

Then there was Olin, an Assembly of God pastor in the town where I pastored a church. We were friends, and we enjoyed talking over coffee. Olin and I disagreed in some areas, but we never argued. Our fellowship with the Lord wasn't hindered at all. I have known many folks like Olin throughout the years.

But the fact is, there are differences and that's what this book is all about. I'm not writing this book because I'm mad at Pentecostals or Charismatics. I don't feel I'm better or that I have the final answers on what the Bible teaches. My purpose is to look at some of our differences in the light of my best understanding of the Scriptures.

The Introduction gives some perspective on the history of the Charismatic movement. You will also see differences between Charismatics and Pentecostals. Throughout the book, however, I use the Charismatic movement to refer to both groups.

Soon into my research for this book, I realized that I would not be able to complete an exhaustive treatment of all the current Charismatic manifestations. I have written this book in the midst of a busy schedule as pastor of First Baptist Church, Jacksonville, Florida. Many interesting aspects of the study are not as complete as I would desire. I simply ran out of time. I also realized that each of my chapters dealing with the manifestations could and should be the subject of an entire book. My hope is that I have at least opened the door through which our scholars will go to provide us thorough, definitive studies.

I wanted to present several areas of Charismatic doctrine in more depth. There are other areas I didn't deal with at all, such as the latter rain movement, prophecy and the nature of Scripture, the guidance of the Holy Spirit, the laying on of hands, the feast of tabernacles, and the similarities between modern Charismatic teaching and second-century Montanism. I am aware some of the examples I have used are extreme forms of the various manifestations. I did this for two reasons. First, it's what rank-and-file Christians encounter as they listen to the radio, watch TV, and read books on these areas. Second, I want you to see how what appears to be minor deviations from Scripture can lead to huge errors.

Basically, I have arranged the book into three sections: foundations, manifestations, and exhortations. The first section seeks to lay the basic foundations which give us a basis for a correct approach to Charismatic issues. The second section deals with several current Charismatic practices. The last section gives closing impetus to the work of the Holy Spirit in the life of the church and in individual Christian lives today.

As in my first book on the Holy Spirit, *SpiritLife*, I have sought to write in down-to-earth language. I want to thank Nancy Smith for her superb help in making my language a little less "preachy" and a lot more current and for helping me rework and edit my text. At times, my language is loose and light-hearted. I do not mean this to indicate I am making fun of or minimizing the importance of this subject. I'm really just trying to give relief from this heavy-duty subject matter.

Many people have helped me with this book. Thanks to Shirley Cannon, who worked on the manuscript while winning a bout with cancer. Thanks to Jacki Raulerson and Kathy Murray for their assistance. Drs. Al Mohler, Paige Patterson, and Daniel Akin allowed me to bounce my interpretations off them from time to time. Dr. Phil Roberts pointed me to competent scholars who have written on Charismatic subjects. My pastor buddy, Fred Wolfe, listened to some of my conclusions and provided helpful advice.

I am especially thankful to Dr. Chuck Lawless and his students who researched several areas of Charismatic doctrine for me. They provided me with an abundance of material. The reader will profit from their invaluable assistance.

Finally, I am grateful to my friends at Broadman & Holman Publishers who graciously agreed to publish this work: Len Goss, my editor, has been encouraging and helpful, as have others at Broadman & Holman, including John Landers, Sandy Bryer, and Bucky Rosenbaum. I am grateful to them.

None of the above-mentioned people are to be blamed for any mistakes which may appear here. Nor does their mention suggest they agree with every conclusion I have drawn.

Now let's move out and seek to understand how the SpiritWorks.

# Introduction: Watch the Waves!

I live only ten minutes from the Atlantic Ocean, and I love to watch the waves. Waves have a dynamic nature. They are a constant force of energy, changing and rearranging the sand and shells on the shore. Waves are also extremely dangerous. They can hide unseen dangers like rocks, sharks, or riptides. Waves can also wear down the hardest rock into grains of sand.

Waves can also be gentle. Children often play in the shallow water, letting the calm waves push them safely to shore. Yet these waves can also turn and toss a person helplessly out to sea.

"It's more fun to ride them," John says as we talk about ocean waves. He is a chef at a restaurant at the beach. John is a surfer who loves the waves and the challenges they represent. Sometimes, he tells me, the urge to surf just hits him, and he has to drop everything and ride.

"It's a thrill," John says, "but you have to be careful. If you catch the wave just right, it gives you a fabulous ride. But you've got to watch the waves. They can totally wipe you out!"

Remember Gamaliel in Acts 5:34? He was no surfer, for sure. He was a leading teacher of the Jews. Early Christians were going everywhere telling the good news of the resurrection of Jesus Christ. The age of the Holy Spirit had begun, and his power was moving like a mighty ocean wave.

In other words, there was a change. People were disturbed. There was controversy and debate. In the midst of all this, Gamaliel gave some interesting advice. Much of it is true. He said, "Leave these men alone! Let them go! For if their purpose or activity is of human origin, it will fail" (Acts 5:38). Manmade movements ultimately come to nothing. Then Gamaliel said, "But if it is from God, you will not be able to stop these men" (v. 39). He was saying that a person must not fight against God or what he ordains.

Gamaliel's words are true, but his advice is bad. If a matter is indeed of God, then we want to take part in it. We want to be involved in whatever God is doing in this world. So Christians must watch the waves. These waves may be unpredictable, extremely powerful, and even dangerous; but if we don't determine whether to ride them (the way John does), we may miss out on what God is doing—just as Gamaliel did.

The Charismatic movement is a source of great controversy and difference of opinion among Christians. Some describe it as a mighty moving of God in our day. If you don't catch the wave, they warn, you will miss out on what God is doing. Others take the opposite view. They believe the movement is satanic in origin and is a counterfeit movement that will produce not an end-time revival but will be part of the end-time apostasy. The Bible predicts a departure from the true faith in the time before Jesus returns.

The purpose of this book is to study what is taking place in the Charismatic movement. Using the Bible as our criteria, we will study especially the different manifestations or evidences that are a part of the Charismatic movement.

Our study will not be an attack on Charismatic people. The vast majority of them believe the Bible, love Jesus, and live as our brothers and sisters in Christ. Our intention is to examine this movement, not make fun of anyone.

Years ago, Pentecostals were subjected to a great deal of ridicule. They were called "Holy Rollers" and other names because of their lively physical manifestations in worship services. Of course, there are some funny aspects. One leading woman in the movement talked about her pet chicken being raised from the dead. That struck me as humorous. But my purpose is to speak the truth in love (Eph. 4:15). By using names, I will not be attacking the individuals or questioning their Christian faith or sincerity. I will be using names to reference certain points in history and to define more clearly some of the manifestations with which these individuals are associated.

Who is a Baptist? Who is a Charismatic? Charismatics and Baptists are not the same, and there are reasons. Most of our differences revolve around our understanding of the person and work of the Holy Spirit.

I believe this is the age of the Holy Spirit because the Holy Spirit is active and at work in the world today, convicting the lost, making Christians like Jesus, and restraining evil in the world. Therefore, this supernatural aspect is not the primary issue with me. To believe in the Bible is to believe in the supernatural. I am, however, curious if what we are seeing today in some aspects of the Charismatic movement is actually supernatural. And, if it is supernatural, is it of God or of some other source?

Let's look at current and past waves historically, culturally, and biblically. I want you to get a good view of the Charismatic movement as we surf the waves of man's quest for an understanding of God.

Look at the waves historically. The "wave" terminology referenced here was coined by Peter Wagner, a professor at Fuller Seminary in California. Professor Wagner says we have witnessed three distinct movements of the Holy Spirit worldwide. The first wave is "Pentecostalism," which started in the early 1900s. The religious world in America was taken totally by surprise. Pentecostalism's focus was on the baptism of the Spirit, evidenced by speaking in tongues.

Charles Parham, a teacher in a small Bible college in Topeka, Kansas, became convinced that the baptism of the Holy Spirit was the next step after salvation. He was considered by his students a latter-day Elijah who would usher in the Lord's return. The prophet Malachi predicted Elijah would be sent before the coming of the day of the Lord (Mal. 4:5; see also Luke 1:17). Parham assigned his students to find evidence in Scripture that one had been baptized by the Holy Spirit. His students concluded that speaking in tongues was that evidence. One of his students, Agnes Ozman, spoke in tongues. Many said she was speaking Chinese.

Parham later moved to Texas. There he influenced a young African-American student, William Seymour. Seymour moved from Texas to Los Angeles. At the Azusa Street Mission in Los Angeles in 1906, under Seymour's leadership, there was an outbreak of tongues. This phenomenon received national publicity. Like the Toronto Revival at the Airport Vineyard and the revival at the Brownsville Assembly of God in Pensacola, Florida, people flocked there from all over the world.

This spawned a movement that resulted in the mainline Pentecostal denominations: the Church of God, the Assemblies of God, the United Pentecostal Church, and others. Initially, the movement appealed to the poor. Small, struggling Pentecostal churches appeared all over America. Pentecostals emphasized personal holiness and living a separated life. Most of the women believers did not wear any makeup. They did not cut their hair.

I believe that this first wave was based on an incorrect interpretation of the baptism of the Spirit. This teaching is incorrect because the baptism of the Spirit is presented as a kind of "delayed honeymoon." While this Spirit baptism may happen at a person's salvation, most often it does not, according to their interpretation. The teaching that an additional experience is needed to reach a new level of spirituality is not true, in my opinion. A chapter of the book is devoted to this subject.

I call the second wave "ecumenism." I mean by *ecumenism* a uniting of Christian denominations around certain Charismatic themes. The stage was set for this second wave by the Full Gospel Business Men's Fellowship, the healing crusades of Oral Roberts, and the healing services of Katherine Kuhlman. Today's Charismatic movement actually began in the 1960s.

People were attracted to religion during this wave because emotion was emphasized. The mainline churches were strongly influenced by liberalism, and liberalism left people spiritually starved and emotionally unsatisfied.

People were hungry for a real and satisfying experience with God. Liberalism, with its denial of the inerrancy of Scripture and its surrender to secular culture, robbed people of the truth of God and the Word of God.

In 1959, Dennis Bennett, rector of an Episcopal church in Van Nuys, California, announced that he had been baptized by the Holy Spirit and that he had spoken in tongues. Another Episcopalian, John Sherrill, made a similar announcement and wrote a book entitled *They Speak with Other Tongues*. These two events precipitated the movement that brought the walls of the mainline denominations tumbling down.[1] This new Charismatic movement was interdenominational. Every major denomination, including Roman Catholicism, was affected. New denominations were not created, but people in established denominations became a part of this Charismatic movement. This is why I call the second wave "ecumenism."

The focus of the second wave was on spiritual gifts, especially the more sensational gifts such as miracles, healings, words of knowledge, etc. Also, the Charismatic movement was less legalistic than the old-line Pentecostals. Standards of conduct were relaxed. Long hair was out, and makeup was in! Therefore, the movement was more readily accepted by the population at large. Many Pentecostals have been uncomfortable with certain aspects of the Charismatic movement possibly for this reason. There are differences between Pentecostalism and the Charismatic movement, and we should keep this in mind. In addition, I believe that the Charismatic movement misreads the Scripture on the matter of spiritual gifts.

I call the third wave "evangelism." The emphasis was placed on the New Testament mandate to make disciples worldwide (Matt. 28:18–20). There appeared on the scene two men who were used to inaugurate and to promote this third wave activity at about the same time the second wave was dying. Peter Wagner, the professor whom I previously mentioned, coined the term "the third wave." He was strongly influenced by John Wimber (now deceased), founder of the Vineyard Fellowship in California, and also a visiting teacher at the seminary.

Now the thrust would be an end-time restoration of signs and wonders that would result in a mighty ingathering of unsaved people before Jesus returns. Wimber used the term "power evangelism" to describe this. He taught that signs and wonders would provide the right atmosphere for people to hear the gospel. The signs and wonders would be the "bait" which would draw the fish.

Miracles, healings, and other supernatural phenomena would convince the unsaved of the reality of the gospel.

Several other phenomena have taken front stage during the third wave, including prophetic revelation, visions, and unusual manifestations in worship services. Some churchgoers speak in tongues. Others fall. Still others dance. In some settings people bark like dogs and roar like lions. They believe these are evidences of the presence of the Holy Spirit. Some in the movement claim that if you don't have these kinds of manifestations your efforts to win the lost will be ineffective. Others go so far as to say this wave will be far greater than anything that has been seen before, will be irresistible to people, and will engulf everything.

Third wave teaching proposes that apostles and prophets will be restored to the church. This is troubling. Some even say that modern-day apostles and prophets will do greater works than the Old Testament prophets, the apostles, or Jesus himself. Some go so far as to claim that revelations will be received as additions to surpass what we have available in the Bible.

I believe third wave teaching is based on an incorrect understanding of where the power lies. The gospel is the power of God unto salvation (Rom. 1:16). God's power has been supremely manifested in the death, burial, and resurrection of Jesus Christ.

Pentecostalism and the Charismatic movement are now the fastest-growing segments of Christianity. David Barrett of Regent University estimates there are 20,000,000 Charismatics in the United States and as many as 460,000,000 Christians involved in the movement worldwide.[2] An article in the *Florida Times-Union* entitled "The Ultimate Revival" states that the fastest-growing religious group in the United States in the last 30 years has been the Pentecostals. Jehovah's Witnesses have grown 162 percent; Mormons have grown 90 percent. But the Assemblies of God have grown 267 percent.

*Newsweek* also makes an interesting observation: "Whenever the kinds of things that are now appearing in the Charismatic Movement have developed throughout the history of Christianity, they tend to get out of hand, disrupting the peace and the harmony of the church. Hyper-emotionalism, bizarre heretical revelations have thrown Bible doctrine out of balance."[3] This is also one of the aspects of the third wave that has caused old-line Pentecostals to be concerned. Watch the waves! Remember the nature of waves. There are dangers out there.

Now, let's watch the waves culturally. The Old Testament tells us about the children of Issachar who were men "who understood the times and knew what Israel should do" (1 Chron. 12:32). Jesus said, "You know how to interpret the appearance of the sky, but you cannot interpret the signs of the times" (Matt. 16:3). In other words, it is important to know what is going on in the culture. We need to know because we want to impact our culture spiritually. But we also need to understand how the culture impacts us.

Christians are meant to be thermostats—changing our culture; too often we are thermometers—merely registering the temperature around us. The big question is, Are we changing the world or is the world changing us? Consider modern American culture. Intellectually, we are experiencing a radical change in the way our society views the world, reality, and truth itself. There is broad rejection of the notion of absolute truth. Truth is whatever is true to you, the world would have us believe. If I believe Jesus Christ is my Savior, and that works for me, then that's my truth. But if someone else believes Ronald MacDonald is his savior and it works for him, and he gets Big Macs, then that is his truth. Truth is whatever works for you. Not!

The perception of truth is changing in our society. Dr. Chuck Lawless, professor at Southern Seminary, says (speaking of spiritual warfare), "In a culture where two out of three persons reject the notion of absolute truth, an unquestioned, uncompromised commitment to the Scriptures as the guide for living is . . . imperative."[4] As believers committed to the lordship of Jesus and to His authority, we must affirm, "Your word is truth" (John 17:17). It's not what the culture says, not what other people believe about it, but truth is what the Bible says.

Also consider what is happening to us emotionally. The failure of science to answer the deeper questions: Why is there a universe? Why do people have a yearning for God? has caused a real search for religious experience in America. Think about the phenomenal interest in angels. Sophia Burnham's book, *A Book of Angels*, is now in its thirtieth printing with more than half a million copies sold. Have you seen the Angel-watch Network on TV? Professor Robert Elwood says, "With angels around, people feel they don't have to bother Almighty God in order to get help."[5]

Today's emphasis on psychics also indicates a hunger for spiritual, emotional experience. The Psychic Friends Network 900 line debuted in 1991 with singer Dionne Warwick as host. Seventy-five hundred to ten thousand calls come in daily at a cost in excess of three dollars per minute. A twenty-three year-old bride of a U. S. Navy officer ran up a forty-five-thousand-dollar phone bill to psychic lines while her husband was out to sea.[6] I'm sure her husband wondered what was up with that!

In such an emotionally starved atmosphere, experience-oriented religion has become very popular. Vinson Synan, dean of divinity at Regent University, says, "Pentecostalism matches most people's genuine belief in the supernatural. It fills a hunger for the miraculous that transcends anything intellectual."[7] One Charismatic leader said, "Personal experience is what Pentecostalism is all about."[8]

Many leaders in the Charismatic movement have a background in rock music. One pastor of a Missouri church that is experiencing ongoing revival formerly played in a rock band. John Wimber was a part of the rock group, The Righteous Brothers. Perhaps this is why many Charismatic services and crusades utilize rock music.

Perhaps the Charismatic movement is growing because we live in a rock, experience-centered, culture. Our generation wants to "feel it" or to "just do it." Some religious services seem more like rock concerts than places where a person can enter the presence of a holy God.

Many of these services are not as spontaneous as they may seem. There is often a kind of audience buildup, usually reserved for rock stars. Services can be lengthy. Long jam sessions often occur. Guitars, keyboards, lights, and high-tech sound systems are used. There is a sermon. Then comes the power surge when people rush forward.[9]

The tendency in our culture is to test everything by experience. *Has it happened to me? If I can feel it, it must be good.* But think about it. Bible truth is not tested by experience; rather, experience is tested by Bible truth. Frederick Bruner put it right, "The test is truth."[10]

An "anything goes" mentality opens the door for any experience at any time. It also opens the door to deceptive mystical experiences. Eastern religions report visits from their gods. New Age enthusiasts report contact with spirit beings through mediums and spirit-buddies. If anyone discourages you from examining any movement by Bible truth, be immediately suspicious.

When I was a young Christian, someone made the following distinction for me, and it has been helpful. Three words need to be kept in the proper order: facts, faith, and feelings. Facts—find out what the Bible says; faith—by faith believe what God has said in his Word; feeling—then God will give whatever feeling he wants us to have. But in an experience-centered culture, the order

**17**

is reversed. It becomes feeling, faith, then facts. When you rely on individual emotional experience rather than on God's truth, you are headed for some dangerous waves.

Look at what is happening in our culture socially. People are desperate for answers and for help. Many of them "don't have a clue." They want to belong and to be accepted. They desire to be a part of something, yet many are extremely isolated. There is an emphasis on power, bigness, and material prosperity in our society. Anything that caters to or promises success, especially instant success, gets America's attention.

People have real needs, and they need real help. One very appealing part of Charismatic services is the ministry time. People come forward to have a hands-on time of ministry where their needs can be met. In a sense, this is what our church does in the invitation time. There is a difference, however. We take people to a counseling room, where a trained counselor uses the Bible to deal with the person's need from a scriptural perspective.

Americans desire "instant" solutions. We want everything immediately. If we are hungry, we want fast food. If we want information, we hit the Internet. If we want to get fit, we order a workout machine from a television commercial. Too many people are looking for instant spirituality.

People want God to solve their problems instantly. Of course, God can certainly do that. He is not restricted by time or the complexity of our problems. But many times God's work is slow. You may not get it all instantly.

Just where is American culture religiously? It's obvious that there is a growing tolerance for all forms of religious expression. It is certainly good to tolerate the views of others. But today we often hear that all religions should be tolerated because they are all equally true. Diana Eck, professor of world religions at Harvard University, confirms this by saying, "Cultural pluralism is changing America's religious life. It is making our spiritual tradition much richer and broader."[11]

The cafeteria approach to religion is becoming quite popular as well. People pick the best from all religions to make a religion of their own. A *Florida Times-Union* newspaper article says, "With so many new elements influencing the nation's spiritual life, a growing segment of Americans have started to *custom-blend* their faith."[12] The big word for this is *syncretism*—putting together elements from a number of religions. That's just a fancy word for hash!

The idea of syncretism is that doctrine doesn't matter. The Charismatic movement is doing what has been attempted unsuccessfully before. It is bringing together people from all denominations around a common experience. On the surface, this may seem good. But does doctrine matter? Does it matter whether you believe Jesus is the Son of God? or that the Bible is the inerrant truth of God? Doctrine does matter.

The Charismatic movement is the fastest-growing segment of Christianity. Does this prove it is of God? Not necessarily. The three fastest-growing religious groups in the world are Mormonism, Jehovah's Witnesses, and Islam. Size and growth do not necessarily prove anything. Some people believe the Charismatic movement will become the dominant expression of Christianity. In any event, the Charismatic movement does seem to fit our modern culture perfectly. But watch the waves!

Now let's briefly watch the waves biblically. In this book, I will consider the place of the Bible in the Charismatic movement. The vast majority of Charismatics affirm the inerrancy of Scripture and its final authority in matters of faith and practice. More recently, however, some in the movement are teaching that there is new, ongoing revelation. The danger here is that some not only affirm what the Bible says, but they also affirm *more* than what the Bible says. I will attempt to help you know how to find out what your Bible says. Ask these questions: What does the Bible say? How do you know what the Bible says? Are you saying more than what the Bible says?

My friend John, the surfer, says that while you are out surfing you need to wear a leash. This is a kind of tether line, a rope tied to your board and your ankle. If you get knocked over by a wave, you don't lose your board. As we watch the waves of the Charismatic movement, we need to be sure we are leashed to the Scriptures.

A number of Charismatic Christians come regularly to our church. Some have been caught by waves. Others have been wiped out. They want to know what the Bible says. In this book I will attempt to examine claims made in the Charismatic movement and interpretations given of certain Scriptures. I will try to help us watch the waves and keep us from getting separated from our boards (the Bible) lest we be taken under into dangerous waters. The Bible is our surfboard, and we need to stay connected to the Bible in order to overcome the waves.

Finally, I will list some positives and negatives about the Charismatic movement. It has brought attention to certain neglected truths of the Bible, including the personal work of the Holy Spirit, spiritual gifts, the power of God, the experience of God in one's life, and the importance and value of worship. It has sent us to our Bibles. In the spirit of Acts 17:11, the movement has caused us to "search the Scriptures every day to see if what Paul said was true." Also, when the gospel is preached and people are saved, we can rejoice in the spirit of Philippians 1:18, "Christ is preached. And because of this I rejoice. Yes, and I will continue to rejoice."

In addition, from the beginning, the Charismatic and Pentecostal movements have been interracial in nature. Their openness to all people shames many mainline denominations. They have consistently ministered to common people. The conversion testimonies of many alcoholics who came to Christ in Charismatic churches thrill our hearts.

There are some negatives. The decline in the importance of doctrine is certainly a cause for concern. Acceptance of some of the more questionable aspects of our culture into the life of a church is another cause for examination. To place more emphasis on "feeling" in worship than on systematic Bible teaching is a cause for concern. To place experience over truth can certainly cause people to be susceptible to satanic counterfeits.

Watch the waves and remember their nature. We want to be part of anything God desires for us. We know God wants us to win the lost and to help Christians grow in their faith. For those who have been "wiped out" by some tricky waves and are now barely treading water looking for solid ground, I have good news. Jesus said we should build our lives upon a rock, not upon the sand (Matt. 7:24–27). If we build on Jesus and his Word, we are on solid rock. Who needs waves when you're on the Rock?

## Tips for Wave Watchers

1. The popularity of a movement doesn't mean it is right. What does the Bible say?

2. We do not determine the correctness of any matter by experience. What does the Bible say?

3. Just because an inviting wave comes by, it doesn't mean we must ride it. What does the Bible say?

Just how do we know what the Bible says? We will discuss this question in chapter 1.

# PART 1

# FOUNDATIONS

The first three chapters of this book are foundational in nature. Before we seek to understand and evaluate current Charismatic manifestations, let's realize that true activity of the Holy Spirit will always be consistent with the authority of Scripture and the centrality of Jesus Christ.

# CHAPTER 1

# FLY BY THE INSTRUMENTS!

It was the biggest Bible I'd ever seen. When he wasn't reading it, Troy propped it on the shelf alongside his combs and scissors behind his tattered leather barber's chair. You could see the letters, H-O-L-Y B-I-B-L-E, embossed in gold on the spine, reflecting bits of light from anywhere in the small, dim shop. I first noticed it in the mirror as I sat having my hair cut in the chair next to Troy's.

Troy was also a Pentecostal preacher. He was a faithful and direct witness for the Lord. Few sat in his chair without hearing a clear explanation of how to know Jesus as personal Savior. When he didn't have a customer, he would sit in his own chair with his feet propped on the metal footrest and read that big Bible. He called it "the good book."

I have never forgotten Troy, his large Bible, or that two-chair barbershop. He was a wonderful preacher, and it was obvious to me that he believed the Bible and lived a fulfilling Christian life.

Do you remember when you learned to read books? I do. I was so excited. My first book was a Hardy Boys mystery. I read it many times. I almost became a detective!

As I progressed through school, I realized that people interpret and comprehend books differently. Five people reading the same book may develop five distinct interpretations. Their prejudices, upbringing, and worldview color their take on the books they read or the movies they see. In similar fashion, many religious groups today interpret the Bible—Troy's "good book"—differently.

The Charismatic movement supports the inspiration of the Bible. Their statements of faith indicate an understanding of the Bible very similar to the statements of other evangelical Christians. Charismatics believe in the complete authority, inspiration, and accuracy of the Word of God. Charismatic Christians believe what the Bible says is true.

It is vital for Christians to approach the Bible as the final source of authority. There is a tendency today to elevate one's personal experience above truth as revealed in the Bible. Our culture tends to place trust in one's feelings as the prominent feature in making decisions about truth. Our feeling-oriented society wants to go by how it feels about a matter in determining what the truth of a matter is.

Do you like to fly in airplanes? The pilots have the best job—to control all that jet power! Yet it can be very dangerous. One of the leading causes of plane crashes is flying by VFR (Visual Flight Rules) and depending solely on what can be seen. There are no problems on a clear day; but if the pilot steers his plane into clouds or passes through a storm, he or she must rely on the flight instruments.

When we can't see, our brain sends us confusing signals. Imagine what happens to a pilot flying a plane. Vertigo may set in. The pilot may have feelings he or she is inclined to trust, yet the feelings don't correspond to reality. He or she may feel that the plane is completely upside down, and it's not. A pilot must trust his or her instruments, not the feelings that seem so real. It could mean the difference between life and death.

The same thing is true in our understanding of the Bible. We must not let our experience, or someone else's, be the final authority. We must always go by what our instrument, the Bible, has to say instead of what we feel we have experienced.

The apostle Peter shares with us the wonderful experience he had on the Mount of Transfiguration. He tells about it in 2 Peter 1:19 and following. He saw Jesus Christ transfigured. What Jesus was on the inside was manifested on the outside. His clothing became white as light. His face was shining as the sun. There was a visit from Moses and Elijah, both of whom had been dead for hundreds of years. Pretty sensational stuff, wouldn't you say? Imagine seeing headlines about this event on some of those tabloid newspapers in the grocery checkout line. Peter refers to this experience in verse 18. Then in verse 19 he says, "We have the word of the prophets made more certain."

To what does he refer? He is referring to the Word of God, the Bible. Peter is affirming that the truth of God's Word is more reliable than anything we humans may experience.

If the Bible says it, it is so. If the Bible does not say it or affirm it, it is not so. When we get away from what the Bible teaches and rely on our own experience, we move in the direction of mysticism and fanaticism, not biblical Christianity. Such an approach changes truth into what happens to you, not what God says in his Word.

Remember that the Holy Spirit will never contradict what is in the Bible. The Holy Spirit inspired the Bible. The Holy Spirit will always be consistent. He will not contradict in manifestation what he has given in revelation. Or, more simply put—the Holy Spirit's works will never contradict his words.

John White quotes Martin Lloyd-Jones, "Fanaticism is a terrible danger which we must always bear in mind. It arises from a divorce between Scripture and experience, where we put experience above Scripture claiming things that are not sanctioned by Scripture, or are perhaps even prohibited by it."[1]

So, how do we find out what the Bible says and what it means by what it says? Which interpretation of the Bible do we believe? We want to learn how to fly by our instrument (the Bible) and not depend on our feelings. That's what this chapter is all about.

## The Inspiration of the Bible

The Bible towers above other books like a bright star above the flickering lights of earth. There is simply no other book like it. Why do I say this? I say it because the Bible is supernaturally inspired.

Second Timothy 3:16 is one of the clearest statements in the Bible about its own inspiration. Note the phrase, "All Scripture is God-breathed." It takes several English words to convey the meaning of a single word in the original language. It is the Greek word *theopneustos,* which means "inspired" or "God-breathed." Every word of Scripture was breathed by God. He authored the Bible. Man could not have written it if he would and would not have written it if he could.

The Bible is not merely words of humans. It is the Word of God. This means that the Bible is infallible. The Bible does not mislead or deceive us. There are no contradictions. God doesn't change his mind.

So we affirm the supernatural inspiration of the Bible, but we do not eliminate the human authors. In a sense, there is a dual authorship of Scripture. The Holy Spirit used people to write Scripture. Just as you may recognize the work of your favorite author, the personalities of the Bible's human authors are apparent everywhere. Remember the burning sarcasm of Isaiah? the pathos of Jeremiah? the deep philosophy of John? the crisp logic of Paul? Amos writes like a farmer. Peter writes like a fisherman. Paul writes like a scholar and theologian. Luke writes like an artist and a physician. Inspiration does not mean human writers were uninvolved. It means that the Holy Spirit breathed into them what God wanted them to write in the Bible.

How did this happen? "For prophecy never had its origin in the will of man, but men spoke from God as they were carried along by the Holy Spirit" (2 Pet. 1:21). The words "carried along" are used to paint a picture of a vessel being gently carried by the wind. The wind of the Holy Spirit gently blew over these Bible writers so that their writings are the very Word of God.

For example, Simon Peter quotes an Old Testament psalm in Acts 1:16: "Brothers, the Scripture had to be fulfilled which the Holy Spirit spoke long ago through the mouth of David." He said the Holy Spirit spoke the Scripture by the mouth of David. David spoke; but he spoke as inspired by the Holy Spirit. The Holy Spirit is the author of the Bible. So the Bible is God's message to humanity. This gives the Bible its authority. Therefore the Bible is our final authority.

Second Timothy 3:16 also teaches that the Bible's words are inspired by God. Look at the word *scripture*. It means "to write." Our words *graph* or *graphite* come from this. The reference is to the words of Scripture.

"What are you doing?" my buddy at school would ask as I stared out the classroom window before class began.

"I'm thinking," I would reply somewhat dreamily.

"Thinking?" he would ask increduously, and I knew he wondered what was up.

Do you like to think? Do you ever *think* about *thinking*? How exactly do we humans think? The process is complex, but one thing is sure: Thought cannot exist without words. You simply cannot think a thought without words. They are vital. Words are the vehicles of thought, and God uses words to communicate his truth to us.

First Corinthians 2:13 says, "This is what we speak, not in words taught us by human wisdom but in words taught by the Spirit, expressing spiritual truths in spiritual words." This verse refers to the words the Holy Spirit teaches. Where can we find these words from God? In the Bible.

Did Jesus teach this? Yes. He said, "It is written: 'Man does not live on bread alone, but on every word that comes from the mouth of God'" (Matt. 4:4). Actually, Jesus went further. He also declared, "I tell you the truth, until heaven and earth disappear, not the smallest letter, not the least stroke of a pen, will by any means disappear from the Law until everything is accomplished" (Matt. 5:18). Jesus referred to the smallest letter in the Hebrew alphabet. It is a breathing mark, just the stroke of a pen. Jesus was saying that all Scripture will be fulfilled, even to the smallest letter of the alphabet.

In the King James Version of this verse, the word *tittle* appears. So what is a tittle? It is an extension on a Hebrew letter, just a fraction of an inch. What difference does that make? It makes quite a difference. That little tittle on a letter determines what it is. A tittle can change a letter, and a letter can change a word, and a word can make a world of difference!

When I took Hebrew in seminary, I discovered that the tittles were very important. "Don't forget your tittle! You might flunk the Hebrew test," we would remind one another. Jesus is saying that even the smallest part of a letter will be fulfilled. In fact, Jesus uses a double negative for emphasis. He means under no circumstances—never. Let me give my own translation of his statement: "Until heaven and earth pass away, the smallest letter of the Hebrew alphabet and the smallest part of the letter shall under no circumstances never pass from the law until all be fulfilled." Sounds to me like the words are inspired.

The whole Bible is inspired. Second Timothy 3:16 says, "All." Herschel Hobbs was one of Southern Baptists' great pastor-teachers. I have heard him say many times, "*All* means that every single part of the whole is God-breathed." He was exactly right.

What did Jesus say about total inspiration? He said, "How foolish you are, and how slow of heart to believe all that the prophets have spoken!" (Luke 24:25). Verse 27 of this same passage says, "What was said in all the Scriptures concerning himself."

The poet got it right:

> I know the Bible was sent from God,
> The old as well as the new;
> Divinely inspired the whole way through,
> I know the Bible is true.

Therefore, the Bible is our only absolute authority—not the Bible plus church dogma, not the Bible plus what Christians experience, not the Bible plus our feelings. When a new teaching comes along or when someone tells you about an experience, immediately ask yourself what the Bible says about that? Chapter and verse. Jot and tittle. Where is it in the Bible?

## The Intention of the Bible

What is the Bible's purpose? What is it intended to do? Why is it here? We must know why the Bible was given to us if we are really to understand it.

The Bible is not meant to be an encyclopedia or a reference book. Of course, when the Bible speaks on a subject, it does so accurately. The Bible speaks on scientific subjects, and we know it is scientifically correct. But the Bible is not intended to be a science book. When the Bible touches on a matter of finances, we know it is correct. But the Bible was never intended to be a CPA manual or a tax guide. When the Bible discusses the matter of nutrition, it is correct. But the Bible is not intended to be sold on the health and beauty row at the bookstore.

The Bible has a much more specific purpose than to catalog every conceivable subject: "From infancy you have known the holy Scriptures, which are able to make you wise for salvation through faith in Christ Jesus" (2 Tim. 3:15). This verse indicates the two purposes of the Bible. One purpose is to present the Lord Jesus Christ.

John 20:31 says, "But these are written, that you may believe that Jesus is the Christ." The Bible points us to Jesus Christ. Luke 24:27 declares, "And beginning with Moses and all the Prophets, he explained to them what was said in all the Scriptures concerning himself." Jesus is the central theme of the Bible. We learn in Acts 10:43, "All the prophets testify about him." The vehicle of the written Word drives us to the living Word.

The Old Testament predicts him; the New Testament presents him. The Old Testament anticipates him; the New Testament announces him.

> I find my Lord in the Bible
> Wherever I choose to look.
> He is the theme of the Bible,
> The center and heart of the book.
> He is the Rose of Sharon,
> He is the Lily fair.
> Wherever I open my Bible,
> The Lord of the book is there.

Ulysses is the hero of the *Odyssey*. Alice is the heroine of *Alice in Wonderland*. Rocky Balboa is the hero of the "Rocky" flicks. The Jesus of the Bible outshines these and all other heroes. He is no hero of fiction. Who is this Jesus? He is the One in whom all fullness dwells and in whom we are complete (Col. 2:9–10).

There is a second purpose of the Bible. The Scriptures are to "make us wise for salvation." Paul is speaking to Timothy, recalling Timothy's childhood. Paul reminds him that he was taught the Scriptures at an early age. His godly mother Eunice and his godly grandmother Lois must have faithfully told him the truths of the Old Testament. I can picture them carefully guiding him into the way of salvation. Then one day young Timothy went to church. The visiting preacher, Paul, told the good news of Jesus Christ. Young Timothy went forward, giving his hand to the preacher and his heart to Jesus. Through the preaching and teaching of the Word, he was "made wise for salvation."

The Bible shows people how to be forgiven of their sins and how to go to heaven when they die. People are changed through the message of this book.

> The law of the LORD is perfect,
>> reviving the soul.
> The statutes of the LORD are trustworthy,
>> making wise the simple (Ps. 19:7).

It is the only book that can change lives. Have you ever heard a thief give testimony that he discovered that two plus two equals four in a math book and it transformed his life? Yet, through the Bible, drunks have been made sober; harlots have been made pure.

The Bible not only brings us to the initial experience of salvation, but it also helps us grow in our salvation, and it fully equips us with the necessities for Christian development and maturity. Second Timothy 3:17 talks about this. John White, a Charismatic psychiatrist, studied a number of groups involved at his church. "I have noticed that in many smaller home and kinship groups that while lip service is paid both to the importance of studying Scripture and of intercessory prayer, nobody does either in such gatherings . . . In some groups nobody brings Bibles. And having conversed with many of the people I found that few people know how to study it."

Unfortunately, this could be said of groups from all denominations of Christians. God has given us a guidebook, which plays a crucial role in helping Christians mature in their Christian life.

### The Interpretation of the Bible

Move now to 2 Timothy 2:15. What does the Bible say? We must read it to answer that question. This is investigation. What does the Bible mean? This is interpretation. "Do your best to present yourself to God as one approved, a workman who does not need to be ashamed and who correctly handles the word of truth" (2 Tim. 2:15). "Correctly handles" means to cut along a straight line. The word referred to a priest slicing sacrificial animals according to divine instructions. It was used to describe a farmer cutting straight furrows in a field. It was also spoken to refer to a tent maker cutting cloth according to pattern. [2]

It is, of course, possible to misuse the Bible either by design or unintentionally. All of us have. I look back over the years of my own teaching and preaching ministry. I have said some things along the way that misinterpreted the meaning of the Bible. This can be dangerous. Second Peter 3:16 talks about distorting the Scripture or twisting its meaning to our own destruction. Misinterpretation of Scripture is a very serious matter.

Jim Bakker is back in the pulpit again. He spoke recently to about four hundred worshipers at Way of Life Church in Anaheim, California. In that message, he preached against "the gospel of money."[3] He said, "If you fall in love with the things of this world, you will be disappointed."

During his prison term, Jim Bakker, the central figure of the PTL scandal, came to understand he had misinterpreted one verse of Scripture. Third John 2 says, "Dear friend, I pray that you may enjoy good health and that all may go well with you, even as your soul is getting along well." He misused this verse to teach that it is God's will for every Christian to prosper materially. This was the basis for his lavish lifestyle and the extravagant display of materialism at PTL. He twisted the Scriptures and destroyed himself and many other people. It is crucial not only to know what the Bible says but also to understand what the Bible means by what it says.

How do we get to the meaning of the Scripture? Think about flying again. When pilots land a plane, they use lights located on the runway. These lights enable them to make a safe landing. Let me give you three guide lights. These lights, if applied, will help you illuminate the runway of correct interpretation and meaning of the Bible. Some of the teaching in the Charismatic community, when evaluated by these principles of interpretation, will help you understand.

### Context

Have you ever heard the statement, "Text without context is pretext"? I believe it is true. If you take the Bible out of its context, you can make it teach anything. False teaching almost always ignores context. For instance, I can show you where the Bible says you should never cut your hair. It says, "Top not come down." Of course, the entire verse says, "Let him that is on the housetop not come down." (Find the Scripture yourself!) I can show you that you should commit suicide. One verse in the Bible says, "Judas went out and hanged himself." Another says, "Go thou and do likewise." (Find those for yourself, too!)

There are three circles of context that must be kept in mind if you are to understand what the Bible says. The inner circle is the *immediate* context, the verse itself, and the verses before and after it. Find what the thought is before the verse. Find what the thought is after the verse. Give attention to the meanings of the words. What did they mean to the original author? Who was being addressed? How are the words used in the sentence? Normally, we take the words for their literal meaning. Someone said if the plain sense of Scripture makes sense, then seek no other sense.

If the literal meaning of a passage is absurd and is not in harmony with what is said, however, realize that there could be a figurative interpretation. The Bible is filled with figures of speech. A figure of speech is a poetic means of conveying a literal idea. Remember those English classes? Our language is full of figures of speech. We say, "He gives me a pain in the neck." That may be literal! Or we may be speaking figuratively. We say, "She had on a drop-dead outfit." We mean by that that the outfit was very attractive, not that it caused anyone to drop dead.

Cults go astray because they do not understand the use of figures of speech in the Bible. For instance, Mormons believe God has a physical body. Isaiah 59:1 mentions God's hands and ears. Mormons conclude that this means God has hands and ears; he has a physical body. Psalm 91:4 refers to God's feathers and wings. Does this make God a chicken?

We must also keep in mind the setting of the verse or verses we are reading. The Bible was written in a certain cultural setting within a specific history and custom. We must ask what these words meant to the first readers. Yet none of this means that Scripture is bound or limited to one particular time in history. It simply means that God gave truth in a cultural setting from which we can draw eternal and timeless principles that can be applied today.

America is oriented toward material prosperity. We should be very careful that we do not read back into the Bible our contemporary system of values. Is the prosperity gospel (the teaching that God intends for every Christian to be materially prosperous) really taught in the Bible? How would this go over in countries like India or Bosnia or Kenya?

The second circle, outside the immediate context, is the book of the Bible where the passage is located. The Bible has a variety of books. There are books of poetry and proverbs. There are books of history and doctrine. Some public schools today are teaching the Bible as literature. I'm sure English teachers love this. The Bible has every plot, every type of character, and every theme imaginable.

Solomon said, "The dead know nothing" (Eccl. 9:5). He said this at the end of his life, looking back regretfully on his wasted years. Solomon lived with no heaven-reference guiding his life. To him death meant knowledge of this world would cease. He would no longer know about his material possessions and successes. This is not what Jesus indicated about the rich man in hell (Luke 16). The rich man certainly had knowledge after death—probably far more than he wanted.

It is possible for Christians to interpret the Bible in a cultic way. That is, they interpet it in ways similar to the ways cults do. How? By interpreting a passage of Scripture without consideration of the book where it is found. John Phillips is one of the finest Bible teachers in the world today. I have heard him say many times, "It is an axiom that you don't get your doctrine from the Book of Acts." We get our doctrine from the teaching of the apostles, not the experiences of the apostles. More about this in later chapters.

The third circle of context, outside the immediate circle and the secondary circle, is the whole Bible. If your interpretation of a passage of Scripture contradicts the whole message of the Bible, it is incorrect. Never let an obscure passage overthrow the clear, definitive passages of the Bible. This is a very helpful principle to remember when looking at passages which seem to teach that a person can lose his or her salvation. One of the clearest teachings in all the Bible is that the salvation God gives us is eternal. No obscure, out-of-context passage should cloud this truth.

It is often helpful to cross-reference subjects in the Bible. Take a concordance and follow a word or subject throughout the entire Bible. This often yields a great deal of information. But remember, stringing verses together without looking at the immediate context, the book context, and the context of the whole Bible can lead you astray.

### Culmination

There is a progress of revelation in the Bible. God gave his truth as people were able to receive it. We are told that Jesus spoke to people "as they were able to receive or hear it." We do not teach calculus to six-year-olds. We teach them two plus two equals four; three times two equals six. Then when they are eighteen we may teach them calculus. Hebrews 1:1–2 indicates this progress of revelation: "In the past God spoke to our forefathers through the prophets at many times and in various ways, but in these last days he has spoken to us by his Son, whom he appointed heir of all things, and through whom he made the universe." In the Bible, God brings the human race along gradually to the full revelation that we have in the New Testament. It has been well said that in the Old Testament men were learning the ABCs of God and in the New Testament, they learned the XYZs.

This does not mean that the Old Testament is not true, has errors, or is on a lower level of inspiration than the New Testament. It just means that Old Testament truth moves forward to New Testament truth. It's linear; it follows a line and the ultimate end is the Lord Jesus Christ. Books are linear. We start at the beginning and read to the conclusion. Audiocassettes are also linear. We begin listening at the front and continue listening until the end of the tape. Here is my point: *Do not interpret the New Testament in light of the Old Testament, but interpret the Old Testament in light of the New Testament.* To go to the Old Testament to build doctrine without finding the culmination of that doctrine in the New Testament is to stop short of the correct Bible interpretation. When you find an Old Testament truth, check it in the New Testament. Is it stated again in the New Testament? Is this particular teaching fulfilled in Jesus?

First Corinthians 10:32 indicates that there are three divisions of humanity: the Jews, the Gentiles, and the church. All Scripture is addressed to one of these three groups. This does not mean that we cannot draw profit from any verse of Scripture anywhere in the Bible. It just means that all Scripture is written *for* us (Rom. 15:4), but not all Scripture is specifically written *to* us. Some passages are *specifically intended* for a particular group. For example, in the Old Testament numerous promises are made to Israel about the land of Palestine. God specifically promised this land to the Jews.

It is also helpful to keep in mind the dispensational aspect of the Bible, realizing that a person can go to extremes in this area. Dispensations are specific periods of time during which God related in different ways to humanity in general and to his special people in particular. It is true that some practices commanded in earlier dispensations are no longer applicable today.

Don't go to seed over this. It can rob you of blessing and help from certain portions of your Bible. Vance Havner used to say that he enjoyed his Bible more before he met so many Bible scholars! But it is clear in the Bible that the Old Testament was the dispensation of law and that the New Testament is the dispensation of grace. This is why we do not offer animal sacrifices in our worship centers. Those sacrifices, commanded in the dispensation of the law, have now been fulfilled in the person of Jesus Christ in the dispensation of grace.

## Canon

Do you know the word *canon*? It means "measuring rod" or "standard." The canon of Scripture is the sixty-six books in your Bible. This is all the Bible there is. It is the Word of God. It is all God has revealed to us. What we have in our Bible was completed by the second century after the time of Christ. God has completed his revelation in the Bible.

One of the more troubling aspects in the Charismatic movement is the claim by some that the Holy Spirit is giving new revelation today. Some say that their teachings are just as inspired as what is found in the Bible and that this gives an added authority to what these teachers say. Thus, whatever some "self-proclaimed prophet" claims God gave him or her opens the floodgate to false teaching, bizarre behavior, and weird activities. I will discuss this in a later chapter.

God has closed the canon of Scripture. There is no new revelation today. If God were giving new revelation now, we should be putting it in books and adding it to our Bibles. This belief opens the door to anything anyone wants to claim as being from God. Whatever you hear, ask yourself, Where is that in the Bible? Give me the specific chapter and verse.

Revelation 22:18–19 warns against adding anything to the Bible. I am aware that this statement could be interpreted as referring only to the Book of Revelation. Jude 3, however, makes it plain. "Dear friends, although I was very eager to write to you about the salvation we share, I felt I had to write and urge you to contend for the faith that was once for all entrusted to the saints." The "faith" refers to the entire body of God's truth. Where do we find that? In the Bible. "Once for all" means there will be no additional revelation. "Entrusted" is in perfect tense. It means it was delivered and it stands completely delivered now. The verse teaches that the faith, God's truth, has been once for all entrusted or delivered to us and it stands complete. There is no new revelation.

How do we know a teaching or an experience is of God? It must be approved or validated by the Bible. Don't bring the Bible to your experience; bring your experience to the Bible. The disciples of Jesus had listened to Jesus show himself to them from the Scriptures. They said, "Were not our hearts burning within us while he talked with us on the road and opened the Scriptures to us" (Luke 24:32). Notice that experience came from the Bible. Their experience did not produce the Bible. Your authority must not be what happens to you or to someone else but what God says in the Bible. If experience becomes the basic court of appeal, then the Bible is no longer our guide for determining truth.

Though the Holy Spirit does not reveal new revelation today, he does help us understand the revelation that God has already given us in his Word. This is called the illumination of the Holy Spirit. First Corinthians 2:10–12 puts it very clearly: "But God has revealed it to us by his Spirit. The Spirit searches all things, even the deep things of God. For who among men knows the thoughts of a man except the man's spirit within him? In the same way no one knows the thoughts of God except the Spirit of God. We have not received the spirit of the world but the Spirit who is from God, that we may understand what God has freely given us."

## Cross-check

1.  Sometimes life gets into cloudy, turbulent weather. Make your decisions by your instrument (the Bible), not by how you feel. *Fly by the Instrument!*

2.  Your feelings may tell you to veer to the left. Your instrument (the Bible) says, keep the straight course. *Fly by the Instrument!*

3.  "But a lot of pilots are flying by what their ears hear and their eyes see. They are experiencing some pretty sensational sights." *Fly by the Instrument!*

4.  "My instrument (the Bible) doesn't say it, but I'm not going to deny what is happening to me." You are headed for a crash landing. *Fly by the Instrument!*

# CHAPTER 2

# I'M A
# JESUS MAN!

"I'm a soul man! I'm a soul man!" A few years ago you could have heard this song on the radio. I've always thought that phrase was fitting for Christians because we are concerned with people's souls. There's another song with a similar phrase that I like even more.

When I was a young preacher, I loved to listen to radio preachers like John Rawlings of Landmark Baptist Temple in Cincinnati, Ohio. (I still love to listen, but there aren't as many radio preachers these days, and they aren't nearly as exciting!)

I remember one preacher who started his broadcast with a song including the words, "I'm a Jesus man." His voice wasn't very good, and it sounded like he made up the song as he went along, but that phrase always appealed to me.

"I'm a Jesus man." I guess I liked it so much because it stated in song form how I felt in my heart. The desire of my heart was then and is now to be a Jesus man. I want him to be the focus of my faith and the center of my life. I am a soul man, but more importantly I am a Jesus man. Are you a Jesus man? Are you a Jesus woman?

One of the ways to evaluate any Christian movement is to find the place it gives to the Lord Jesus Christ. The primary role of the Holy Spirit is to call attention to Jesus, according to several statements Jesus makes in the Bible.

"He [Holy Spirit] will testify about me" (John 15:26); "he will convict the world of guilt in regard to sin and righteousness and judgment: . . . because men do not believe in me" (John 16:8–9); "he will not speak on his own; he will speak only what he hears, and he will tell you what is yet to come. . . . All that belongs to the Father is mine. That is why I said the Spirit will take from what is mine and make it known to you" (John 16:13, 15).

Jesus could not be clearer. Jesus gives us the "411," as the kids like to say, on the role of the Holy Spirit. The role of the Holy Spirit is to call attention to Jesus. His words make it apparent that the Spirit's work is not to be independent of Jesus or to replace Christ. Frederick Bruner says, "The Spirit's real evidence is His power to connect men with and remind them of Jesus Christ, not carry men beyond Him."[1]

Similar statements are made in other places. Acts 1:8 specifically says that when the power of the Holy Spirit is upon believers, they will be "my witnesses," referring to the Lord Jesus. Unto whom? We are to be witnesses unto the Lord Jesus Christ, not unto the Holy Spirit.

First Corinthians 12:3 teaches us that the Holy Spirit, not in a pop psychology way, but in a very personal and meaningful way, is our Enabler. He enables us to affirm the lordship of the Lord Jesus. The most spiritual affirmation a

Christian can make is to say, "No one can say, 'Jesus is Lord,' except by the Holy Spirit." With the Holy Spirit enabling my mind, I see that Jesus is Lord.

In these first chapters I am placing some important foundation stones. These stones will help us better understand and evaluate current manifestations in the Charismatic movement. These manifestations or physical phenomena are said to demonstrate the presence and power of the Holy Spirit. We will study the manifestations in the next section of the book.

The first foundation stone we have laid is the authority of Scripture. The Holy Spirit will never work in contradiction to the Bible. His works and his Word will not cancel out each other.

In this chapter we must lay the foundation stone of the centrality of Jesus Christ. Any movement which claims to be of the Holy Spirit will put Christ in the center place. If the movement magnifies the Holy Spirit to the detriment of Jesus Christ, it is not of the Spirit. Likewise, any Christian who claims to be Spirit filled, yet does not give Jesus first place, is not actually a spiritual Christian.

Think of a telescope. What is its purpose? It is not intended to call attention to itself. A telescope brings into sharp focus the beauties of the universe. It calls attention to the beauties of the heavens, not to itself. Imagine someone at a planetarium getting caught up with the intricacies of the telescope, never using it to view the stars, the planets, and the galaxies of our universe. Wouldn't you think he was foolish? Even so, we must not get caught up with the Holy Spirit and miss the beauties of the Lord Jesus Christ.

You may be wondering where Jesus stands in the doctrinal statements of the major Charismatic groups. Without exception, they affirm the same teachings about the Lord Jesus Christ which evangelical Christian groups do. They believe in the virgin birth of Jesus; his sinless life; the substitutionary death of Jesus on the cross; his literal bodily resurrection from the dead; and his personal, visible return. In doctrinal statements the centrality of Jesus Christ is clearly set forth.

Yet many within the Charismatic movement itself have cautioned that there is a tendency in the movement for many people to become preoccupied with the Holy Spirit, thus taking attention from the Lord Jesus. The unintended result is that Jesus is not central and foremost.

I have heard my friend Warren Wiersbe say many times, "Blessed are the balanced." Christians, as well as other overcommitted, overworked Americans today, have the tendency to live life out of balance. We can become preoccupied with certain aspects of Christian truth to the exclusion of others. Preachers do this. One area of truth, like the second coming of Christ or particular facets of Bible prophecy, can become the focal points of their preaching. Jesus is coming again, but other truths are also taught in the Bible.

Perhaps you heard the fictitious story about the preacher who was preoccupied with the account of the woman at the well. His text for the Sunday sermon was Numbers 22:21, "Balaam got up in the morning, saddled his donkey and went with the princes of Moab." The preacher said, "Beloved, I want to speak about three matters this morning. First, the ancient craft of saddle making. Second, the life and habits of donkeys. Finally, I want to say a word about the woman at the well."

The centrality of Jesus Christ is far more important than saddles, donkeys, or wells. It touches the very heart of the gospel. All Christians must remain true to the gospel teaching and keep Jesus Christ in the preeminent place in theology and in Christian living.

In the Bible, which the Holy Spirit inspired, many references to the Holy Spirit are made. For example, Jesus says, "He will bring glory to me" (John 16:14). In the previous verse he says, "He will not speak on his own." This does not mean the Holy Spirit would seldom, if ever, refer to himself. The point is, this is not his primary purpose. His primary purpose is to call attention to the Lord Jesus Christ—the incarnate Son who glorified the Father on the earth. Look at John 8:50, "I am not seeking glory for myself"; or John 8:54, "If I glorify myself, my glory means nothing"; or 17:4, as Jesus concluded His ministry, "I have brought you glory on earth." Hebrews 5:5 specifically says, "Christ also did not take upon himself the glory of becoming a high priest."

The role of the Holy Spirit is to exalt Christ. John Phillips, in his commentary on John 16:15, confirm this. He said, "All that the Father was had been interpreted by the Son. [All the purpose and work of Jesus Christ.] All that the Son was would be interpreted by the Spirit. . . . The Holy Spirit is here to teach us great thoughts about the Son. If anything calling itself Christian teaching makes its approach to us and does not exalt and glorify Christ, it is not of the Holy Spirit."[2]

The Holy Spirit is here to magnify the beauty of our Lord's character and the redemption he secured for us at the cross. Joseph Parker said, "What light is to the earth, the Holy Spirit is to Christ."[3]

As you listen to preachers, ask yourself what place the preacher gives to the Lord Jesus. Is Jesus the center of his preaching? Is Jesus the focus of any

Christian book you read? If you listen to an audiotape, ask yourself what place this teaching gives to the Lord Jesus. If the Holy Spirit is in the spotlight and not Jesus, immediately raise questions about the validity of the teaching and the balance of the movement.

Let's spend a little time understanding the Holy Spirit's role in exalting the Lord Jesus Christ.

## The Holy Spirit Exalts Christ by Composing a Book

The author of the Bible is the Holy Spirit. As we saw in the previous chapter, the Holy Spirit inspired men to write the various books of the Bible. It's a book all about Jesus. It is indeed a "Him Book"! The whole Bible points to him: "All the prophets testify about him" (Acts 10:43).

Additionally, Jesus said, "He will guide you into all truth" (John 16:13). Which truth did Jesus mean? Geology or genetics or physics truth? No—Jesus truth.

As we read the Bible, we can ask the author of the Bible, the Holy Spirit, to reveal Christ to us. Ephesians 1:17–18 reads, "I keep asking that the God of our Lord Jesus Christ, the glorious Father, may give you the Spirit of wisdom and revelation, so that you may know him better. I pray also that the eyes of your heart may be enlightened in order that you may know the hope to which he has called you, the riches of his glorious inheritance in the saints." First Corinthians 3:18 says, "Do not deceive yourselves. If any one of you thinks he is wise by the standards of this age, he should become a 'fool' so that he may become wise." Every part of the Bible points to Jesus; and with the help of the Holy Spirit, we can see Christ revealed as we read it.

The Old Testament prepares us for Jesus. In the New Testament, after the coming of the Holy Spirit, preachers teach truth which had been often obscured in the Old Testament. Promises which had puzzled Old Testament readers for centuries now blaze forth to completion in the Lord Jesus. It was now obvious that the Old Testament sacrifices pointed to Jesus.

For example, the tabernacle, where God dwelt among human beings, is now fulfilled in Jesus who dwelt among us (John 1:14). The lamb laid on Jewish altars is now fulfilled in Jesus, the Lamb of God, who takes away the sin of the world (John 1:29). The Old Testament proclaims one central message: He is coming!

The Gospels present Jesus to us. In these four Holy Spirit-inspired books we see a beautiful full-length portrait of the Lord Jesus. We see the life he lives. We hear him speak the very words of God. We follow him as he goes outside Jerusalem to a hill called Calvary. We weep as we see him crucified between two thieves, dying for our sins. Then we follow these Gospel accounts to the tomb. On the third day we shout the Easter victory message: "He is not here; he is risen as he said."

The Old Testament predicts him. The Gospels present him. The Old Testament says he is coming. The Gospels say he is here!

In the New Testament epistles, the resurrection life of Jesus, lived in the daily life of believers, is expressed. We understand that the life Jesus Christ lived is now to be reproduced in the lives of believers. Take three verses from just one of the epistles, Colossians. Jesus is set forth as our life (Col. 3:4). He is all and in all (Col. 3:11). We are complete in him (Col. 2:9–10).

In the last book of the Bible, Revelation, the final dominion and authority of Jesus is displayed. Jesus is walking in the midst of his churches. The Holy Spirit unveils the future in this gripping book, and it is obvious that Jesus is the sum and substance of all future history. The book concludes with Jesus the Lamb on the throne (Rev. 22:3). Jesus, not the Holy Spirit, is the goal toward which all human history and human kingdoms move. The hero of the Bible is not the Holy Spirit. Jesus is. Hebrews 12:2 does not say, "Let us look unto the Holy Spirit," but rather, "Let us fix our eyes on Jesus, the author and perfecter of our faith."

The purpose of the Bible is to focus our faith on Jesus. Remember the telescope? Focus on the Holy Spirit instead of Jesus, and you miss the central message of the Bible. It's not the Holy Spirit and his gifts, but Jesus and his resurrection. Look for Jesus in your Bible. Wherever you look, Jesus is there. As a gospel song expresses it, "Standing somewhere in the shadows you will find Jesus." This will change Bible study for you. The Holy Spirit has exalted Jesus by giving us a book in which he is the hero. The Bible's presentation of Jesus should prompt us to say to Jesus, in the words of the popular song, "Did you ever know that you're my hero?"

## The Holy Spirit Exalts Christ by Changing a Believer

The Christian life is intended to bring glory to Jesus. Philippians 1:20 says, "So that now as always Christ will be exalted in my body." Verse 21 continues,

"To live is Christ." The beauty of the Christian life should make Jesus beautiful to the world.

The Holy Spirit brings a person to salvation in a thrilling way. This person sees a new and searching standard for the human condition, for human sin, and for one's relationship to the Lord Jesus. The Holy Spirit adds another component in his work of exposing the lostness of the human soul. In other words the Holy Spirit is responsible for conviction. In discussing the Holy Spirit's role in conviction, Jesus said, "He will convict the world of guilt in regard to sin and righteousness and judgment: in regard to sin, because men do not believe in me" (John 16:8–9).

We do know that God gave the law to show us we are sinners. It makes us aware of the nature of sin. Galatians 3:19 says of the law, "It was added because of transgressions." The law is not what makes us sinners, but it shows us we are sinners. The law also shows us our vast need for a Savior, for Christ.

The King James Version of Galatians 3:24 says of the law that it is our schoolmaster bringing us to Christ. A schoolmaster was a child guardian who took a child from the house to the school. The law takes us by the hand and brings us to him.

Just what is sin? It's not just violating the law; it is also refusing the Savior. Rejecting the Lord Jesus Christ is the worst possible sin. Jesus, with nail prints in his hands, stands before the human heart and pleads. To reject the Jesus who died on the cross and paid the enormous price for our sins is sin to the lowest degree. We are able to see sin more graphically and seriously because the Holy Spirit has come.

But when people respond positively to this convicting work of the Holy Spirit concerning Jesus Christ, they open their lives and allow Jesus Christ to come in. Christ comes into a life and suddenly becomes central and decisive for that person. Once this happens in a life, we see the next exciting phase of the Holy Spirit's work.

What is the purpose of it all? What is the Holy Spirit's goal? His goal is to make us like Jesus, to help us live a Christlike life. Romans 8:29 says that we have been predestined "to be conformed to the likeness of his Son." Jesus put it this way, "He will bring glory to me by taking from what is mine and making it known to you" (John 16:14). The Holy Spirit takes the various relationships we have to Christ and makes them real to us. The Holy Spirit teaches us that Jesus is our strength for life's burdens, our wisdom for daily decisions, our assurance for the fears of the future. He shows us how Jesus, our High Priest, prays for us and he shows us how Jesus, our example, teaches us the right way to live.

The work of the Holy Spirit is not to make you like the Holy Spirit but to make you like Jesus. In other words, the real test of the Holy Spirit in my life is not, Do I speak in tongues? Can I perform miracles? Is my preaching powerful? The real test is, How much like Jesus am I? The Holy Spirit's work is much more internal than external. Charles Spurgeon was London's marvelous preacher. There was another great preacher in London. A visitor attended the other preacher's service on Sunday morning, and he walked away saying, "What a wonderful preacher!" He attended Spurgeon's service that Sunday night. He walked away saying, "What a wonderful Savior!" When Spurgeon preached, it was Jesus, Jesus, and more of Jesus! That's the way our lives should be. His likeness should be seen in my life. I should be becoming more Christlike. If I am showing Christlike traits, the Spirit is at work in my life. Christ was loving. I am to be more loving. Christ forgave others. I am to be forgiving.

Unfortunately, some people who claim to be led by the Holy Spirit do things contrary to the example of Jesus. Jesus is the truth (John 14:6). The Word of God is the truth (John 17:17). The Holy Spirit is the Spirit of truth (John 16:13). Where the Holy Spirit is at work, there will be truth. The Holy Spirit will never lead anyone to do anything contrary to the Word of God or inconsistent with the Son of God.

Colossians 2:10 also teaches us that we are complete in him. The Gnostics (first-century teachers who spread error about Christ and claimed to know special secrets not available to others) taught that the early Christians needed some experience beyond and in addition to Jesus Christ. Unfortunately, this old error has been revived. But Jesus said, "All that belongs to the Father is mine" (John 16:15). Think about it. If the Father gave all he has to the Son, all to whom Christ is given have been given all as well.

Perhaps you have heard the old story about the Roman master who had a rebellious son and a very faithful slave. He told his son, "I'm so displeased with you I'm giving everything I have to Marcellas except one gift. You can pick one gift. Marcellas gets the rest."

The shrewd son quickly replied, "I'll take Marcellas." When he got Marcellas, he got it all. When we come to Christ, we are complete in him.

Paul expresses the great desire of the Christian life: "I want to know Christ" (Phil. 3:10). What is the evidence of the Holy Spirit in our lives? Is it being laid out for hours or spending time reading the Gospel of John? Is it jumping up and down or using our energy to make a visit for Jesus? How does the Holy Spirit make us more like Jesus? Second Corinthians 3:18 and Colossians 3:10 seem to indicate God generally uses the ordinary means of grace rather than some of the extraordinary means people clamor for today. A daily quiet time of Bible reading and prayer is certainly more effective for growing in Christ-likeness than shouting in a high-energy service or loudly applauding a Christian performer.

I want to be a Jesus man. I want to be more like Jesus every day. Are you a Jesus man? Are you a Jesus woman?

## The Holy Spirit Exalts Christ by Claiming a Bride

Look at a beautiful Bible picture which explains how the Holy Spirit intends to give Jesus the central place. Two times in John 16:14–15 Jesus uses the terminology that the Holy Spirit would take the things of Christ and "make it known to you." This New Testament truth is beautifully illustrated in an Old Testament story in Genesis 24.

This chapter of Genesis chronicles the story of Abraham's sending his servant to seek a bride for his son Isaac. This Old Testament story is an allegory showing us how the Holy Spirit brings Christ into clear focus for us.

Do you remember allegories from English class? An allegory can be very helpful in teaching and learning. It's a symbolic representation used to explain an abstract or difficult concept. Galatians 4:24, for example, indicates that the two sons of Abraham, Ishmael and Isaac, can be considered an allegory. Ishmael represented the bondage which law brings. Isaac represented the freedom that comes by grace. In the Genesis 24 allegory, Abraham is symbolic of God the Father, Isaac represents God the Son, the servant represents God the Holy Spirit, and Rebekah symbolizes the sought bride.

In this account, the servant remains unnamed. Jesus said, "He will not speak on his own" (John 16:13). He is leaving the village, and he carries with him ten camels loaded with treasure belonging to his master. Jesus said, "The Spirit will take from what is mine and make it known to you" (John 16:15).

When the servant meets Rebekah, he shows her a portion of his master's wealth. It seems to me that Rebekah was more excited to learn more about her future husband Isaac. On the other hand, Laban, her brother, could not take his eyes off the gifts. John Phillips says, "It often happens that those who neglect the heart and core of the message nevertheless manifest interest in the 'fringe benefits' of the faith. . . . Laban's present-day counterparts are taken up with the Holy Spirit or the sign gifts . . . the sole purpose of the gifts given by the servant was to authenticate his story and draw Rebekah's heart away to Isaac."[4]

So the allegory is clear. The purpose of the work of the Holy Spirit is not to call attention to himself but to point to the Lord Jesus Christ.

Rebekah is invited to become the bride of one whom she had never seen. She accepts! She is going to see one whom, not having seen, she loves (see 1 Pet. 1:8).

She must have had all kinds of questions, just like we do about the Lord Jesus. What does he look like? Is he kind? Where will we live? Will he love me? I can imagine the servant stopping the camels, taking out some of the treasures, showing them to Rebekah, and saying, "See these? They belong to my master. You will be his bride. They all belong to you." Then he would tell her again how Isaac was the heir of all the possessions of his father Abraham. He would thrill her with the story of how Isaac was laid on the altar on Mount Moriah.

As we journey through life, the Holy Spirit delights to show us the things of Christ. Jesus said, "All that belongs to the Father is mine. That is why I said the Spirit will take from what is mine and make it known to you" (John 16:15). He delights to glorify Him (John 16:14). He always testifies of Him (John 15:26). J. Sidlow Baxter said, "Science glorifies knowledge; philosophy glorifies reason; history glorifies great men. But the Holy Spirit comes to glorify 'Jesus only.'"[5] The Holy Spirit tells us of the fullness of our Lord's person and the glory of his work. Just as Isaac became more and more real to Rebekah, the Holy Spirit turns our attention to Jesus and he becomes more and more tangible to us.

The journey is almost over. Isaac is in sight. The servant says, "It is my master." The servant is then just phased out of the picture! "He will not speak on his own; he will speak only what he hears, and he will tell you what is yet to come" (John 16:13). Rebekah is not looking at the gifts or the servant now. She only has eyes for Isaac. This is how the Holy Spirit brings us to Christ. Our eyes should only be on him, not on the Holy Spirit or his gifts.

The Charismatic movement must carefully evaluate the place it gives to the Lord Jesus Christ. All Christian groups should do the same. Bob Hunter, who spent some time studying the recent manifestations at Toronto's Airport Vineyard Church, makes an interesting observation. Over a three-month period he did a computer database of sermons preached in the nightly meetings. He found 372 references to prophecy, 383 to the Holy Spirit, but only 143 to Jesus. All preachers should analyze their preaching. Hunter says it is obvious that the "content of the sermons clearly concentrated more on the Spirit than on Jesus Christ." Then he continues, "This is no picky point about word games. It is about lost opportunity in the preaching to give clear focus on the Son of God."[6]

This does not mean that those who are involved in the Charismatic movement do not love Jesus or talk about Jesus. They do. But we must consider whether the Holy Spirit is overemphasized to the neglect of Christ.

One of the key reference books in the Charismatic movement is the *Dictionary of Pentecostal and Charismatic Movements*. This dictionary says, "The more of the Spirit pervading one's total experience, the more one will have a preoccupation with Jesus as the object of adoration."[7] I'm sure all Charismatics as well as all groups of Christians will agree with this statement.

Care must also be taken that we do not become so in love with the things of the Holy Spirit, his gifts and manifestations, that we take away from the simple gospel of Jesus Christ. Paul says, "So that your faith might not rest on men's wisdom, but on God's power" (1 Cor. 2:5). But, he has just said in I Corinthians 2:2, "I resolved to know nothing while I was with you except Jesus Christ and him crucified." I have a good preacher friend who has a unique way of putting the emphasis of this chapter: "If you see a parade and the Holy Spirit is leading it, Jesus ain't in it!"

The mother of the great preacher Andrew MacLaren advised him before he preached his first sermon, "Make much of Jesus." That's good advice for all of us. We should daily sing in our hearts,

> More about Jesus let me learn,
> More of His holy will discern;
> Spirit of God, my teacher be,
> Showing the things of Christ to me.

The Holy Spirit exalts Jesus. The Holy Spirit glorifies Jesus. The Holy Spirit testifies of Jesus. Shouldn't we? I'm a soul man. I'm a Jesus man too! Are you a Jesus person?

About the only thing I could agree with the radio preacher about was his song. He was too extreme for any of the established Pentecostal or Charismatic groups. He made numerous prophecies that never came to pass. Worst of all, the mother of one of my young church members sold her house, gave the money to the radio preacher, and moved to his compound in Alabama. It takes more than singing a song to make you a Jesus person.

## Rehearsal for Jesus People

1. If you are a Jesus person, you will love to study about him in the Bible.
2. If you are a Jesus person, you will be caught up with him and not with the Holy Spirit.
3. If you are a Jesus person, you will magnify Jesus in your daily life.
4. If you are a Jesus person, you will not spend time trying to get people to have some "beyond Jesus" experience but will be seeking to bring them to Jesus.
5. If you are a Jesus person, he will be the focal point of your life and work.

   I'm still a Jesus man. What about you?

# CHAPTER 3

# GOT FRUIT?

I admit it! I'm in a rut. Every Saturday morning I do the same thing. I jog. I eat breakfast. I read the paper. I lift my weights. And then I go get my bananas—my quick fix.

I go into the store for my quick fix, and I pick up the first clump of bananas I see. No produce guy, no wife picking them out—just me and my bananas.

I love bananas and other fruit, but the fruit I am most concerned with is spiritual fruit. The Holy Spirit is able to produce his fruit in the lives of Christians. In fact, the evidence of Christ's influence in a life is shown in the fruit that life produces.

So are you supposed to eat bananas every Saturday morning like me? Should you have ecstatic utterances or fall and run and shout? No. The real, indisputable evidence that the Holy Spirit is working powerfully in me is that my life bears the fruit of the Spirit. When our lives are transformed as the love of God is poured into our hearts through the Holy Spirit, others will see and know that the Holy Spirit is indeed working in our lives. In other words, *get fruit!*

The Trinity is quite a concept! The Holy Spirit is the third person of the Trinity, and he has many functions. He is God the Holy Spirit. He cooperated with the other members of the Trinity in the creation of the universe, inspired the writing of the Bible, and conceived the Lord Jesus Christ in the womb of Mary. He also convicts unsaved people of their condition and of their need for Christ, and he restrains the insidious power of evil in the world today.

But we are interested in the work of the Holy Spirit as it relates to Christian believers. (Some of what I will say in this chapter will be somewhat repetitious. In my previous book *SpiritLife*, especially chapter 8, you will find a discussion of these matters.) Let's study his work in three main divisions: salvation, his work *for* us; service, his work *through* us; sanctification, his work *in* us. Let's look at these three areas, keeping in mind the ideas of the *gift*, the *gifts*, and the *graces* of the Holy Spirit.

## The *Gift* of the Holy Spirit

Salvation is presented in the Bible as a gift. How do we know this? Jesus said to the woman at the well, "If you knew the gift of God and who it is that asks you for a drink, you would have asked him and he would have given you living water" (John 4:10). Romans 6:23 says, "The gift of God is eternal life in Christ Jesus our Lord." Ephesians 2:8–9 makes it even clearer: "For it is by grace you have been saved, through faith—and this not from yourselves, it is the gift of

God—not by works, so that no one can boast." When we are saved, we receive the gift of the Holy Spirit in our lives.

Jesus promised the Holy Spirit would be given. In John 7:39 we are told, "By this he meant the Spirit, whom those who believed in him were later to receive." The Father had promised the gift of the Holy Spirit. John 14:16 says, "And I will ask the Father, and he will give you another Counselor to be with you forever." Acts 1:4 adds, "On one occasion, while he was eating with them, he gave them this command: 'Do not leave Jerusalem, but wait for the gift my Father promised, which you have heard me speak about.'"

We are also told that Jesus gives the Holy Spirit. In John 16:7 he says, "I tell you the truth: It is for your good that I am going away. Unless I go away, the Counselor will not come to you; but if I go, I will send him to you." Also, in John 15:26 he said, "When the Counselor comes, whom I will send to you from the Father, the Spirit of truth who goes out from the Father, he will testify about me."

Well, who is it? The Father or the Son? Actually, both. Acts 2:32–33 clears up any confusion: "God has raised this Jesus to life, and we are all witnesses of the fact. Exalted to the right hand of God, he has received from the Father the promised Holy Spirit and has poured out what you now see and hear." The resurrected Lord Jesus received the promise of the Holy Spirit from the Father. He gives the Holy Spirit at salvation as his resurrection gift to you and to me.

What does *gift* mean to you? Think about it. To Christians it means that salvation is a free gift of God's grace. It's not something we do. Our efforts and activities alone can't bring the Holy Spirit to us. At salvation the Holy Spirit comes to dwell in a life. Remember in the Old Testament the Holy Spirit was *with* people. Now, it's different. Since Pentecost the Holy Spirit is *in* believers. John 14:17 says, "The Spirit of truth. The world cannot accept him, because it neither sees him nor knows him. But you know him, for he lives with you and will be in you." The Holy Spirit will never be withdrawn. He is in a Christian's life forever.

Have you ever watched a series on TV? My grandchildren are now watching the reruns of the shows my kids watched years ago. I like to watch the *Andy Griffith Show*. Each episode places the characters I know so well in different situations. I can watch their lives unfold in installments.

The Holy Spirit is not like a TV show entering our lives each week with a new plot or character struggle. The Holy Spirit comes into a life in the totality of his person. So we don't say we can get more or a little less of the Holy Spirit.

When he is received as the love gift from the Lord Jesus, he comes as a whole package, and we should yield our lives completely to Him.

The Book of Acts depicts salvation as receiving the gift of the Holy Spirit. This was true in Jerusalem on the day of Pentecost. In Acts 2:38, Peter said, "Repent and be baptized, every one of you, in the name of Jesus Christ so that your sins may be forgiven. And you will receive the gift of the Holy Spirit." There is an order—repentance, baptism for the remission of sin, and receiving the word, then the gift of the Holy Spirit comes into a life.

Later, in Samaria, salvation is also seen as a gift, but the Holy Spirit is received immediately. Acts 8:17 says, "Then Peter and John placed their hands on them, and they received the Holy Spirit." Later, verse 20 says, "Peter answered: 'May your money perish with you, because you thought you could buy the gift of God with money!'" When the Samaritans were saved, they received the gift of the Holy Spirit. In Acts 10:44–48, Cornelius, a Gentile, and his household were saved. Acts 11:15–17 makes clear that their salvation experience involved receiving the Holy Spirit.

Do the New Testament epistles teach that the Holy Spirit is a gift? You bet! Romans 5:5 says, "And hope does not disappoint us, because God has poured out his love into our hearts by the Holy Spirit, whom he has given us." First Thessalonians 4:8 says, "Therefore, he who rejects this instruction does not reject man but God, who gives you his Holy Spirit." Salvation is a gift. When we are saved, we receive the gift of the Holy Spirit. He is not something we obtain as time goes by. He is Someone we receive.

How do we receive this gift? As the accounts in the Book of Acts are studied, there are four words clustered together: *promise, gift, give,* and *receive.* At least one of these four words, and usually more, is present every time the gift of the Holy Spirit is described. Bruner says, "The Holy Spirit is the promise-present of the Father and as such, is a perfect free gift given to believers who simply receive (never obtain) Him . . . together (these four words) spell the freedom of grace."[1]

How is a gift received? We do not pay for it or work for it. It would be embarrassing and insulting. Romans 4:4–5 says, "Now when a man works, his wages are not credited to him as a gift, but as an obligation. However, to the man who does not work but trusts God who justifies the wicked, his faith is credited as righteousness." If you work for something, it is not a gift.

Picture this. Next payday your boss comes to your desk with a beautifully wrapped package. You unwrap it while he stands there beaming at you. Your paycheck is inside. He says, "I want to give you this present out of the goodness of my heart." You say, "Gift? I earned every dime of it and more!" If you put in the hours and do the work, you can go to the office and demand your paycheck. If necessary, you can even go to court to collect it.

But the Holy Spirit is a gift. We receive him into our hearts by simple faith. As Jesus said in John 7:39, we receive him by believing in Jesus. The gift of the Holy Spirit at salvation is to make real in us what Christ has done for us. So get the Holy Spirit and get real!

## The *Gifts* of the Holy Spirit

When the Holy Spirit comes into our lives, he brings gifts. Notice an interesting connection between two statements of Jesus. In Luke 11:13, he says, "If you then, though you are evil, know how to give good gifts to your children, how much more will your Father in heaven give the Holy Spirit to those who ask him!" Then in Matthew 7:11, he says, "If you, then, though you are evil, know how to give good gifts to your children, how much more will your Father in heaven give good gifts to those who ask him!" The gift of the Holy Spirit brings good things into our lives. He brings God's love into our lives. Peace with God is now ours. A joy we've never known comes in. James 1:17 teaches, "Every good and perfect gift is from above, coming down from the Father of the heavenly lights." The Giver brings gifts.

In my previous book, *SpiritLife*, I gave a rather extensive survey of spiritual gifts. A little review: Every Christian has one or more spiritual gifts, and it is through these gifts from the Holy Spirit that he is manifested in our lives. These gifts are not to be used for our own enjoyment but to be a blessing to others. No Christian has all of the gifts.

The Holy Spirit's gifts are divinely given. Check out 1 Corinthians 12:11: "All these are the work of one and the same Spirit, and he gives them to each one, just as he determines." Notice 1 Corinthians 12:18, "But in fact God has arranged the parts in the body, every one of them, just as he wanted them to be." Look at 1 Corinthians 12:28, "And in the church God has appointed first of all apostles, second prophets, third teachers, then workers of miracles, also those having gifts of healing, those able to help others, those with gifts of administration, and those speaking in different kinds of tongues." The gifts of the Holy Spirit are given solely by the divine choice. First Corinthians 12 makes plain that not all Christians have all the gifts.

First Corinthians 12:7 teaches us that these gifts are given for the common good. As we exercise these gifts in the power of the Holy Spirit, there is a manifestation of the Spirit in our lives that benefits others. Some look to the more spectacular gifts as evidence of Holy Spirit manifestations. But any spiritual gift is a manifestation of the Spirit. Think about the gift of encouragement. When we encourage others in the power of the Holy Spirit, he is manifested. The gift of helps may seem dull and insignificant. Taking a meal to someone? Filling a behind-the-scene role in the church? These actions are manifesting the Holy Spirit as much as a person who stands to preach the gospel with Holy Spirit power.

The Holy Spirit energizes these spiritual gifts for service. He must provide the power if these gifts are to be used effectively. In other words, for our service to count as a blessing to others, his power must be present.

The Charismatic movement has focused a spotlight on the gifts of the Spirit. For too long the Christian community neglected these gifts and failed to show their importance to the body of Christ. But first, there must be an understanding of the proper place of the spiritual gifts. Don't place these gifts in the forefront of Christian experience. This leads to the misunderstanding that the presence of the Holy Spirit in a life is proved by activities. Lawrence Wood says, "The gifts of the Spirit in Corinth, such as prophecy and healing, were not distinctly Christian."[2] He goes on to say, "Seers, magicians, witch doctors and divine healers in other religions are common, as in ancient pagan religions and in Islam, Hinduism, and Buddhism."[3] Spiritual gifts are not essential to the gospel message. These are separate entities. The fundamental truths of the gospel are the death, burial, and resurrection of Jesus Christ. Keep a Jesus center. Talk about being energized! This is what having Jesus as the center of your life will do for you. When the gifts become too prominent, the spotlight is taken off Jesus.

Yet, remember that the spiritual gifts are manifestations or visible evidences of the presence and power of the Holy Spirit. Whenever and wherever we serve in the power of the Holy Spirit, he is manifested.

Gifts deal with service and action or what we do. Graces concern character and influence or what we are. Spiritual graces, like spiritual gifts, are manifestations of the Holy Spirit. They are shown by what we are and how we live our lives.

So what is this all about? It's about fruit. It's about the fruit (or the graces) of the Holy Spirit. It's about learning to live a life that bears fruit so that others see and know we are Christians.

The first fruit mentioned in the Bible is love. Look at verse 31 of 1 Corinthians 12: "But eagerly desire the greater gifts. And now I will show you the most excellent way." Tie in the statement from verse 31 to the first verse of chapter 13 and you're getting the picture of the graces of the Holy Spirit: "If I speak in the tongues of men and of angels, but have not love" (1 Cor. 13:1). From that point on, the entire chapter is devoted to love.

Get the picture? Galatians 5 points out the fruit or the graces of the Holy Spirit. This fruit is manifested in our lives by the work of the Holy Spirit inside each Christian.

## The *Graces* of the Holy Spirit

Three words will help us understand what's going on here: production, intention, and examination. The first word is *production*. A process is involved in producing fruit. It's not instant. Today we have a "quick fix" mentality. We want everything instantly. But you don't get fruit that way. You don't get instant Christlikeness or spirituality by one quick experience. Wood says again: "To focus attention on an emotional overdose, as if one could bypass the ordinary means of grace and secure a quick fix through a self-validating ecstatic experience is patently fanaticism. This is not at all to suggest that emotion should be repressed. Indeed, one fruit of the Spirit is joy. . . . But to promote, to program and to expect certain emotional responses as the decisive evidence of the Holy Spirit is to detract from the true meaning of revival."[4]

In John 15, Jesus used the same fruit analogy. He mentions fruit seven times. He also indicated a progression of fruitfulness. Fruit and more fruit (v. 2). Much fruit (v. 5). Fruit that remains (v. 16). He also gave us the key to the production of fruit. What is it? It is found in the phrase "abide in me." This phrase is used eleven times. To abide in Christ is to stay in the atmosphere of Christ as a person stays in a home. Jesus is saying, "If you want fruit in your life, you must maintain a heart-to-heart relationship with me." The point is we cannot produce the Christ-life or the spiritual life on our own. What's on the tree is caused by what's in the tree. The same is true in our lives. The fruit is produced *in* us, not *by* us. The kind of life we live on the outside is directly related to what is going on inside.

The second word is *intention*. What is up with the fruit? What is its goal? The purpose of the fruit is to reproduce the identity of the tree. Apple trees are intended to produce apples. The purpose of an apple tree is not to produce grapefruit but apples. Look at the nine graces in the fruit of the Spirit (See *SpiritLife*, p. 189). Whom do you see as you look at these graces? Jesus, of course. They give us a full-length portrait of the Lord Jesus. They show us how Jesus lived, the things he did, and what he said.

What is the purpose of the Holy Spirit in our lives? To make us like Jesus. Second Corinthians 3:18 indicates that as we read the Bible and see the Lord Jesus the Holy Spirit transforms us, making us more like Christ. I read about the love of the Lord Jesus and realize I'm not as loving as I ought to be. "Holy Spirit, help me be loving like Jesus." I read about the deep, settled peace of the Lord Jesus and know I need peace in my life. "Holy Spirit, fill my life with peace like the peace of Jesus." As I live in love, joy, peace, etc., the Holy Spirit is manifested in my life.

How do we know the Holy Spirit is working in our lives? What is the evidence? It's not the gifts!

Many have pointed out that the gifts of the Spirit may be counterfeited. In the first century, mystery religions were prominent. Believers were converted from these mystery religions in Corinth. These mystery religions had all kinds of ecstatic manifestations. Some even cursed Jesus in tongues (1 Cor. 12:3)! These religions were a powerful threat to Christianity because of their emotional appeal. Eventually, Christianity won out over the mystery religions because the Christian faith is grounded in God's truth as revealed in Scripture. But it was possible for spiritual gifts to be counterfeited by cheap, emotional extremes in the mystery religions.

Fruit, like God's truth, can't be counterfeited. A counterfeit fruit is recognizable upon close examination. So the third word to help us understand these concepts is *examination*. When you go to the store, don't you feel the tomatoes and plunk the cantaloupes? As fruit in the produce section is examined, so are our lives as Christians. The fruit of the Christian life can be produced only by the Holy Spirit, and its manifestation cannot be counterfeited. Wood says again, "Any manufactured fruit is only inedible plastic decoration. The fruit of the Christian life can only be produced by the Holy Spirit, and that is the final test of Christian character . . . final proof of truth of the Christian faith is demonstrated in the holy lives of the people of God."[5]

This is essentially what Jesus says in Matthew 7. He pictured people who will one day offer certain manifestations as proof of the reality of their life: "Many will say to me on that day, 'Lord, Lord, did we not prophesy in your name, and in your name drive out demons and perform many miracles?'" (v. 22). Jesus adds the solemn word, "I never knew you. Away from me, you evildoers!" (v. 23).

According to Jesus, if these spectacular works are no evidence, what is the evidence? Fruit! "Watch out for false prophets. They come to you in sheep's clothing, but inwardly they are ferocious wolves. By their fruit you will recognize them. Do people pick grapes from thornbushes, or figs from thistles? Likewise every good tree bears good fruit, but a bad tree bears bad fruit. A good tree cannot bear bad fruit, and a bad tree cannot bear good fruit. Every tree that does not bear good fruit is cut down and thrown into the fire. Thus, by their fruits you will recognize them" (Matt. 7:15–20).

Remember, the Holy Spirit is called holy. His work is to make us holy by producing in us and through us the likeness of the Lord Jesus. Any emphasis on the Holy Spirit that does not make clear this sanctifying work of the Spirit misses the point of the Holy Spirit's work in our lives.

## Got Fruit?

1. The Holy Spirit comes into our life to make real what Jesus has done for us. Are we becoming more like Jesus?

2. Spiritual gifts are manifestations of the Holy Spirit in our life. But these may be counterfeited.

3. The fruit of the Spirit produced in us by the Holy Spirit will cause our lives to be Christlike in our attitudes, actions, and winsomeness to those who do not know Christ.

4. As we daily study the Bible and pray, we must ask the Holy Spirit to make us like Christ. Look at your life to see if it is becoming more like the image of Christ as we read it in the Bible.

5. As we live our life daily in the home, school, or workplace, we should be aware of this fact: Those around us are checking to see if we have fruit.

# P A R T  2

# MANIFESTATIONS

This section contains a chapter on the general subject of manifestations. Then the main Charismatic manifestations seen today are surveyed. We will observe them, search the Bible concerning them, and then give some evaluations of these manifestations.

## CHAPTER 4

# THIS IS ONLY A TEST

"This is only a test. The Emergency Broadcasting System is conducting a test in your area. In the event of a real emergency. . . . This is only a test."

Does that sound familiar? Have you ever turned on your radio or TV during that long beep, only to freeze in fear for a second or two? Is this a real emergency or what? You then realize it's another test and it is not a real emergency. But the test is necessary.

There are other tests in life. Think of high school and college. Even on the job, closing that big business deal or making the sale can be considered a big test.

The purpose of a test is to define what is real and true. I remember those true/false tests asking questions about the Civil War in my ninth-grade American History class. Those tests instantly indicated a student's knowledge of the subject matter.

In the same way, tests are needed today in the religious realm because there's a lot of false teaching out there. Many people are saying their messages are from God or from the Holy Spirit. Tests can help us discern what's real and true from what's false and wrong.

At the Vineyard Church in Toronto, Canada, in January 1994, Randy Clark, now assistant to the pastor of the church, shared his experiences at a

Rodney Howard-Browne meeting he had attended. After Clark spoke, people rushed forward. Some were knocked to the floor. Others just started laughing. Some experienced other unusual manifestations. This was the beginning of what is known as the "Toronto Blessing."

People have rushed to the Toronto Vineyard Church from all over the world. The meetings have continued nightly since 1994. The visions and healings have attracted worldwide attention. Some who have attended have described the experience like being at a zoo. People bray like donkeys, cackle like chickens, roar like lions, and oink like pigs. The "Toronto Blessing" has been called by many evidences of a great move of the Holy Spirit. Is it?

In Pensacola, Florida, at the Brownsville Assembly of God, sensational spiritual services have been going on since Father's Day of 1995. On that day, evangelist Steve Hill preached. People began to fall, weep, dance, and shake uncontrollably. The pastor felt wind blowing through his legs that he described as something like that of the rushing wind described in the Book of Acts. He was laid out and could not get up from 12:30 until 4:00 P.M. Some men had to drive him home. Since 1995, hundreds of thousands have visited Brownsville. The services continue four nights a week. People arrive as early as 4:00 P.M. to get a seat and the services sometimes go on until 3:00 A.M. Is this a genuine work of the Holy Spirit?

As people visit Toronto and Brownsville, they experience similar phenomena and take them back to their churches. This has created a series of similar manifestations in churches all over America and the world. Some people report great blessing, while others report disruption and conflict in the churches. Some churches have been split over these manifestations.

Physical manifestations like these are happening everywhere in the Charismatic movement. People report having visions of Jesus. Others experience uncontrollable laughter. Some fall to the floor unable to get up, caught in what some refer to as "Holy Ghost glue." This time spent on the floor is referred to by some as "carpet time" (like maybe our after-lunch nap in kindergarten). What about these physical manifestations? Are they for real? Do they show the presence of God?

Actually, these manifestations are not new. They have been a part of Pentecostalism since the beginning. This could explain why Pentecostals were made fun of as "Holy Rollers" in the past. Perhaps we know more about the manifestations today because of our modern means of communications. Television, radio, and even the Internet make the physical manifestations more accessible to a larger number of people.

Some believe the Bible predicts an end-time revival before Jesus returns. This revival will bring about the greatest ingathering of lost souls in the history of the world. A part of this revival, they believe, will be a restoration of the New Testament manifestations of signs and wonders, such as miracles and healings. To these people, these physical manifestations provide on-the-spot, instant evidences of God's presence and power.

Those who believe these manifestations are evidence of genuine revival point out that these types of phenomena are not new. They mention that in the history of revivals, unusual physical outbreaks often occur. For example, in the Great Awakening in America in the 1700s (a mighty revival which swept through the American colonies, bringing thousands to Christ) such physical phenomena occurred. Jonathan Edwards, perhaps America's greatest theologian and president of Princeton University, wrote extensively about these phenomena. His wife experienced some of them—hopping or swooning. Jonathan Edwards was sympathetic to the physical phenomena that occurred.

Similar physical manifestations occurred in America's Second Great Awakening (another mighty revival which brought many to Christ), the camp meetings of the 1800s. In Kentucky, Tennessee, and North Carolina thousands of people were brought to Christ through these camp meetings. Many physical manifestations occurred at that time. People shouted, wept aloud, and fell out.

So what is up with all of this? Is what we are seeing today a genuine evidence that God is manifesting himself to his people? What does it mean? How can we explain these manifestations? I can see only four possible tests for them. The first is that they may be self-created. We know that either consciously or unconsciously people are able to create certain physical responses. It is possible that because of deep inner needs or tensions people act in certain ways. Maybe they do it to get attention. Jeremiah 17:9 reminds us that "the heart is deceitful above all things and beyond cure. Who can understand it?"

Secondly, physical manifestations may be the result of the influence of others. Either by example or by suggestion, people can encourage others' physical behavior. The power of suggestion is very strong. It is possible for some to manipulate others to do certain things. Anyone who has worked with youth groups for a period of time knows that manipulation and suggestion can cause young people to do many things. I have seen many young people stirred to unusual behaviors by a rock star. Preachers and Christian singers should take warning. We must be very careful never to produce or to manipulate people to do certain things, then claim what they do as evidence of God's presence.

A third test: Satan himself may be the cause. He can produce certain manifestations. Virtually all false religions and cults report phenomena similar to the kinds of manifestations that are pointed to as evidences of a genuine move of God. (In later chapters I will give some examples.) The Bible clearly indicates that the antichrist will show himself (2 Thess. 2:4). More about this in a later chapter.

Lastly, it is possible that God is the source of certain physical phenomena. The question to remember is, How do we know that these manifestations are of God and not from one of the other three sources? We need a test. This calls for the exercise of discernment. Discernment is the ability to examine a matter and determine whether it is acceptable. We must not automatically accept anything that happens as being from God. First Thessalonians 5:21 says, "Test everything. Hold on to the good." Peterson paraphrases it, "Don't be gullible. Check everything out, and keep only what's good" (1 Thess. 5:21, The Message). The Bible, one of our tests, teaches us to exercise discernment.

The yellow light is flashing—CAUTION! If someone suggests that you turn off your mind and just go with the flow, be wary. If anyone discourages your praying about a matter or checking it by the Bible, run up the red flag. The Bible tells us we are to love God with all our mind (Luke 10:27). The Holy Spirit does not rob us of the use of our rational faculties. So use your brain.

We know that God does manifest his presence in the world. This is sometimes referred to as the "manifest presence" of God. God is everywhere or omnipresent. But at specific times, in certain situations and places, God reveals his powerful presence. God "comes down." Charismatics call this a "power encounter." When God manifests his presence in this way, we can expect the unusual. But remember, outward manifestations in and of themselves do not prove God is the source of the encounter. Blindly accepting whatever happens as being from God sets up self-deception.

Two verses in the Bible indicate genuine manifestations of God among people. In 1 Corinthians 2:4, Paul talks about his preaching: "My message and my preaching were not with wise and persuasive words, but with a demonstration of the Spirit's power." The next verse is 1 Corinthians 12:7, where Paul talks about spiritual gifts: "Now to each one the manifestation of the Spirit is given for the common good." *Manifestation* is the key word. Taken from the word *manifest*, which means "to make visible" or "to make known," it conveys the idea of exposing to view. The word is used again in 2 Corinthians 4:2, "We have renounced secret and shameful ways; we do not use deception, nor do we distort the word of God. On the contrary, by setting forth the truth plainly we commend ourselves to every man's conscience in the sight of God."

Let's focus on three statements about genuine manifestations.

## A Genuine Manifestation Reveals God's Presence

God did not create the world and then walk away from it. He is transcendent (above his creation), but he is also present (within his creation). I like the story about the atheistic science teacher who was trying to impose his atheism on the minds of his young students. He asked one of his students to go to the board and write, "God is no where." The young child went to the board but didn't know how to group the syllables together correctly. Instead of writing, "God is no where," the child wrote, "God is now here." Amen! God is here.

In the Old Testament there are occasions where God manifests his presence. Remember Moses and the burning bush? In Exodus 3, God manifests himself in the bush, which is burning but is not consumed. Out of the bush, God speaks to Moses. God's presence is manifested to him.

When Moses was on Mt. Sinai, God came down (or created a power encounter), giving the Ten Commandments. Exodus 19:16–19 mentions thunder, smoke, shaky ground, and even the sound of trumpets (my favorite instrument). God's presence was known there.

Often when God reveals himself to his people in the Old Testament, the word *glory* is used. Just what does this mean? Glory is the outward manifestation of God's presence among his people. During the days when Israel was wandering in the wilderness, God manifested himself by a visible pillar of cloud in the day and a pillar of fire in the night. The pillars indicated that God was present with his people. They knew God was with them.

Individuals in the Old Testament also experienced the presence of God. For example, Daniel experienced some unusual revelations from God, including the meanings of dreams which in reality foretold the future of the world. Unusual physical phenomena occurred to Daniel. Maybe an episode of *The X-Files* should center on him! When God revealed to Daniel the answer to a strange dream, he was astonished (or struck dumb) for a time. Daniel also had a vision of Gabriel the angel. He was afraid, and he fell on his face. "I, Daniel, was exhausted and lay ill for several days" (Dan. 8:27). He saw such evidence of divine happenings that he was overcome and became sick. Unusual phenomena did occur to certain people in the Old Testament.

The New Testament also records outward manifestations of the presence of God. The unique manifestation of God's presence is the incarnation of Jesus. In Jesus God manifested himself. First Timothy 3:16 says,

> Beyond all question, the mystery of godliness is great:
>> He appeared in a body,
>>> was vindicated by the Spirit,
>> was seen by angels,
>>> was preached among the nations,
>> was believed on in the world,
>>> was taken up in glory.

God showed himself in the person of Jesus Christ. John 1:14 says, "We have seen his glory, the glory of the one and only, who came from the Father."

Throughout the life and ministry of Jesus, God's presence was uniquely demonstrated. His miracles, for example, manifested God's presence. After his first miracle of turning the water into wine, we are told, "This, the first of his miraculous signs, Jesus performed at Cana of Galilee. He thus revealed his glory, and his disciples put their faith in him" (John 2:11). Also remember that before he healed the man who had been blind from birth Jesus said, "Neither this man nor his parents sinned, . . . but this happened so that the work of God might be displayed in his life" (John 9:3). God's presence was shown in Jesus. In the Old Testament, God's glory shines in a cloud. In the New Testament God's glory dies in living color on a tree, then walks on two feet out of a tomb. We see God's glory on a tree and coming out of a tomb.

Groups of Christians, as well as individuals in the New Testament, sometimes experienced God's presence in an unusual way. Jesus promises, "For where two or three come together in my name, there am I with them" (Matt. 18:20). There are times when God's presence is more real in our public worship. Sometimes our church congregation sings, "Surely the presence of the Lord is in this place," and God's presence is felt.

Look at two examples of this in the New Testament. When the apostles were threatened about preaching the resurrection, they gathered for prayer, asking God for boldness, and we are told, "The place where they were meeting was shaken" (Acts 4:31). Or consider Paul and Silas in the Philippian jail: "About midnight Paul and Silas were praying and singing hymns to God, and the other prisoners were listening to them. Suddenly there was such a violent earthquake that the foundations of the prison were shaken" (Acts 16:25–26). I have often thought that the Lord got so happy with the prayers and praises of his preachers that he started patting his foot to the music. The results were a great earthquake and broken prison chains!

But remember these were phenomenal experiences unexplainable in human terms, and they did not occur every time New Testament Christians gathered for worship. Remember the culmination principle from chapter 1? The New Testament shows no evidence that preachers touched people and caused them to fall to the floor or to lose control over themselves. In Toronto and in Pensacola, the people were prepared for certain manifestations. They were not as spontaneous as they might have seemed. Randy Clark, assistant pastor at Toronto, shared his experience of laughing while attending a service led by Howard Rodney-Browne. This seemed to prepare the people for what followed. There does not seem to be any indication in the New Testament manifestations that certain outward responses were set up.[1]

Don't forget the authority of Scripture. When any manifestation is presented as being from God, always ask, "Where is this in the Bible?" Yet you don't want to use the Bible as an accessory after the fact, trying to find a passage in the Bible to prove any experience. To try to prove uncontrollable laughing with a passage like "inexpressible and glorious joy" (1 Pet. 1:8) is laughable! This verse of Scripture cannot remotely be tied to uncontrollable laughter.

## Genuine Manifestations Reveal God's Power

When God's power comes down, things happen! In the previous chapter, we saw that God's power is shown in the graces produced by the Holy Spirit in the life of the believer. The graces are demonstrations of the life of Christ in the life of a Christian (see again 2 Cor. 4:10). We have also previously seen that the exercise of spiritual gifts manifests the power of God. This brings us again to 1 Corinthians 12:7 and spiritual gifts.

It's easy to see power manifested in the more spectacular gifts. When a person is healed, for example, God's power is obvious. When miracles occur, no one questions the power of God. In the preaching of the gospel and the resulting conversion of lost people, God's power is there. But God's power is also manifested in the less spectacular gifts. Even the neglected gift of helps shows God's power. When we encourage others, God's power must be present. Showing mercy is also a demonstration of the power of God.

Remember 1 Corinthians 12:7: "Now to each one the manifestation of the Spirit is given for the common good." Remember that the context is vital to understanding the Bible. Look at 1 Corinthians 12:2: "You know that when you were pagans, somehow or other you were influenced and led astray to dumb idols."

Before the Corinthians were saved, they had been carried away by demonic pagan influences. Many were involved in mystery religions that were characterized by ecstatic outbursts. Worshipers shook, fell to the ground, and burst into unintelligible babbling. Demons worked them into a frenzy. Some worshipers were carried away by powers they could not understand or resist. The center of their pagan religions consisted of experience and emotion. Their mental reasoning was out the window. Think of many eastern religions and cults today, and you can see how this would happen.

Just look at our culture. It's about experience. Rock concerts are experiences. They are felt. When Marilyn Manson assaults his audience with ear-splitting sound, shocks with his lewd apparel, and spits on the audience, that is an experience which is felt! Drugs can control a person's emotional life. It's dangerous to make the worship of Jesus the same kind of experience. During the years of the Jesus Movement (when many hippies embraced Christianity in the 1970s), I was troubled by the phrase, "Get high on Jesus." It may be an attempt at engaging the culture as a Christian, but Jesus is not a drug. He is a person.

Look at 1 Corinthians 12:3, "Therefore I tell you that no one who is speaking by the Spirit of God says, 'Jesus be cursed,' and no one can say, 'Jesus is Lord,' except by the Holy Spirit." This verse indicates that believers in Jesus are to be controlled by the divine. Paul seems to be saying that spiritual Christianity is one totally different ball game! In 1 Corinthians 11:34, Paul says when he comes to them he will "give further directions," meaning to arrange or to give order to something. First Corinthians 14:33 says, "For God is not a God of disorder but of peace. As in all the congregations of the saints." The word *disorder* here means instability or a state of disturbance and confusion. Peterson paraphrases, "When we worship the right way, God doesn't stir us up into confusion; He brings us into harmony . . . this goes for all the churches— no exceptions" (1 Cor. 14:33 The Message). Finally, 1 Corinthians 14:40 says, "Everything should be done in a fitting and orderly way." The word *fitting* carries the idea of "in a proper manner" or "graceful and elegant." "Orderly way" means right or correct order. Paul compliments the church at Colosse when he makes reference to "your order."

When the Holy Spirit is in control, the worship service will not be a wild frenzy. We must remember that one of the fruits of the Spirit is self-control (Gal. 5:22–23). You will not be out of control when the Holy Spirit is in control!

First Corinthians 12:7 also indicates that the manifestation will be "for the common good." The Corinthians had become selfish. They were interested in having a good time. This is why Paul specifically introduces measures to restore a sense of consideration for others and a selflessness in the Corinthian church.

While spiritual gifts are evidences of the power of God, they are primarily for the purpose of equipping us to serve others. While a spiritual gift may manifest the power of God, it does not indicate that the person exercising the gift is necessarily a spiritual person. The Corinthian church had all the gifts (see 1 Cor. 1:7). But Paul said they were not spiritual (I Cor. 3:1).

## Genuine Manifestations Reveal God's Purpose

Why does God reveal himself? What is his purpose in manifesting his presence and power among his people? Here are two reasons God manifests himself to us today.

Look at Paul's statement about the demonstration of the Spirit in 1 Corinthians 2:4. He refers to the preaching of the Word. When he preached the gospel, miracles occurred. The greatest miracle, of course, is the salvation of people. "It took a miracle to hang the stars in place, /It took a miracle to hang the world in space, /But when He saved my soul,/ Cleansed and made me whole, /It took a miracle of love and grace" (John W. Peterson).

Paul wants you to know that when he preaches there is a demonstration of the Spirit and power of God. This is what happened when Peter preached on the day of Pentecost. People were "cut to the heart" (Acts 2:37). When Paul preached in Thessalonica, he says, "Our gospel came to you not simply with words, but also with power, with the Holy Spirit and with deep conviction" (1 Thess. 1:5). In other words, there was a demonstration of God's presence and power in his preaching.

The word *demonstration* has been defined as a most rigorous proof of spiritual power that produces results which can't be denied. The same happens today when preachers preach the Word in the power of the Holy Spirit. The preacher becomes aware of another power beyond himself. He is a channel for the Holy Spirit to use in reaching the lost. The same is true for Christians as they witness. As they claim the power of the Holy Spirit, they become aware that God is using them to witness to others in their daily existence.

When the Holy Spirit is present, the people involved know it. Something miraculous happens when the Holy Spirit takes the eloquent language of the preacher or the simple language of a schoolgirl. Many are convicted and converted. One of the sweetest testimonies I have ever heard in our church is about the two middle-school girls who visited an adult lady one Saturday morning. With simple, childlike language the girls explained to her God's way of salvation. The Lord touched her, and she invited Jesus to come into her heart. How can middle-school girls convince a grown woman? It can happen only through the demonstration of the presence and power of God.

Over and over again I have seen God's presence and power manifested in witnessing situations. I have shared the simple gospel plan of Jesus Christ in people's homes. I have been aware of the presence of God as we pray on our knees together.

So this is what Jesus meant when He said, "Go and make disciples of all nations. . . . And surely I will be with you always, to the very end of the age" (Matt. 28:19–20). But remember the manifestation of God's presence and power may not always be spectacular, exploding like a fireworks display. Yet, in these very special times when we are used of God to lead someone else to the Lord Jesus, God manifests himself.

At other times, God manifests himself to Christians in very personal and special ways, and these experiences may be sensational. Charles Finney, the nineteenth-century American evangelist, told of an experience when God manifested himself to him in an experience he described as "waves of liquid love." Perhaps more familiar is the experience of D. L. Moody, the famous evangelist. He says, "One day in the City of New York, Oh what a day!—an almost too sacred an experience to name . . . I can only say that God revealed Himself to me, and I had such an experience of His love that I had to ask Him to stay His hand."[2]

A manifestation of God's presence in our lives may not be as dramatic. There is a beautiful passage in John 14. Jesus talks about the coming of the Holy Spirit. He says, "Whoever has my commands and obeys them, he is the one who loves me. He who loves me will be loved by my Father, and I too will love him and show myself to him" (John 14:21). Then in verse 22 Judas (not Iscariot) asks the Lord, "But, Lord, why do you intend to show yourself to us and not to the world?" Jesus answers, "If anyone loves me, he will obey my teaching. My Father will love him, and we will come to him and make our home with him."

So how will Jesus manifest himself? Will he appear to you in physical form? Not likely. In 2 Corinthians 5:16, Paul says, "So from now on we regard no one from a worldly point of view. Though we once regarded Christ in this way, we do so no longer." Paul is saying that believers sustain a faith relationship to Jesus, just as athletes sustain their muscle tone through exercise and workouts. When you come to Christ, God gives you a new set of eyes. In other words, God gives you a new perspective. You realize, once you start exercising, just how out of shape you are. Once God gives us the new set of eyes and we realize we must exercise our faith, we also realize how unconditional our faith was before.

Paul said in another verse, "We live by faith, not by sight" (2 Cor. 5:7). How does God manifest himself to us? Through our eyes of faith. As we grow in love and obedience, we experience (or tone those spiritual muscles) a deeper relationship with the Father, the Son, and the Holy Spirit.

My daily quiet time is one way I condition my faith. Many times in my Bible reading and prayer devotional, the Lord Jesus becomes very real to me. It is not always dramatic. Usually it is not. The psalmist says, "Be still, and know that I am God" (Ps. 46:10). Think about Elijah's experience. He was alone, discouraged, and ready to quit, but God manifested himself to his prophet. There was a great wind, but the Lord was not in the wind; there was an earthquake, but the Lord was not in the earthquake; a fire, but God was not in the fire. Then after the fire, "a gentle whisper" (1 Kings 19:11–12). God came to Elijah in a gentle whisper.

Are these current-day manifestations real? Are they genuine or fake? Where do we draw the line? The Toronto church was a part of the Vineyard Fellowship movement started by founder John Wimber. Feeling that the animal sounds were not genuine and calling them "exotic phenomena," he felt it was best to cut all ties with the Toronto church. Wimber said there was no biblical or doctrinal framework for any of it.[3] In the New Testament, you will not find Jesus or the apostles encouraging or promoting manifestations which result in animal sounds. Wimber drew a line.

Howard Rodney-Browne, the laughing evangelist who was the inspiration for the phenomena which began in Toronto, said about animal sounds, "We don't have any barking or roaring in our meetings. If you bark like a dog, we'll give you dog food. If you roar like a lion, we'll put you in a zoo. If you cluck like a chicken, we'll give you birdseed."[4] Rodney-Browne drew a line.

John Arnott did not draw a line. The pastor of the Toronto Church did not object to a man barking like a dog. If the Holy Spirit led a man to bark, Arnott would not forbid it. But when the same man stepped in the aisle, lifted his leg, and pretended to urinate, the pastor did finally draw a line.[5] Where do we draw the line?

Where is Jonathan Edwards when you need him? Edwards wrote extensively about the physical phenomena which occurred in the First Great Awakening. Those who approve and those who disapprove of current manifestations quote him on these manifestations matters, and it's easy to understand why. In some places, he seems to support all kinds of physical phenomena. In other places he seems to be critical of them. But he did give what he called his "distinguishing marks," which would help people to evaluate physical phenomena. So let me be your Jonathan Edwards and give you some "distinguishing marks" so you can test religious experience or physical phenomena today.

## The Five Tests

1.  The Bible Test. Where is it in the Bible? Bible teaching, not feelings, must be the test of truth. "It's not in the Bible, but I know it happened to me." That's not enough. Does it add to, take away from, ignore, or violate the Bible? Don't seek some experience not promised in the Bible.

2.  The Jesus Test. Does it bring glory and honor to the Lord Jesus? Is Jesus exalted? or a movement? or the Holy Spirit? Roy Fish has said it well. "The Holy Spirit is to lift us to the level of Christ, not to lower us to the level of animals."[6]

3.  The Character Test. Is the fruit of the Spirit evident? Does it change and make a person better? Some unusual outward expression is not the litmus test of God working in a person's life. Jesus says, "By their fruit you will recognize them" (Matt. 7:20). The most important evidence of God in one's life is a change. God wants to work in and through us so he can change the world around us.

4.  The Decency and Order Test. Joy and spiritual excitement in public worship is one thing. Chaos and frenzy are totally different. God is not honored by confusion and turmoil. Ask questions like these: Is there order to the service? Is the service understandable? What about lost people? Will they be drawn to Christ as a result of what occurs? Is this reasonable? Does it violate common sense?

5.  The Evangelism Test. Is the purpose and goal to win people to the Lord Jesus? We are not here just to enjoy ourselves. We are here to win lost people to Christ and to glorify God. Will this result in lost people being won? If so, there's not a problem!

Remember, these are only some tests. God will guide you to the Bible—and to the truth.

# CHAPTER 5

# FIRST-CLASS UPGRADES

You know about upgrades? They move you from coach to first class on the plane. Believe me, first class is definitely better. There is more legroom, wider seats, and better service. They even hang up your coat for you. And the food! You arrive at the same time, but the flight is more comfortable. Upgrades are great.

Is there anything like an upgrade in the spiritual realm? Is there an experience you can have that will move you to a higher level of spiritual life? Some Charismatic groups say yes. The experience, they say, is the baptism of the Holy Spirit. Charismatics teach that the baptism of the Holy Spirit is a distinct work of the Holy Spirit beyond, separate from, and in addition to salvation. They also believe that certain physical manifestations show that a person has experienced this baptism. Initially, the proof was speaking in tongues. Now, a variety of other physical manifestations—such as shouting, physical jerks, electric currents in the limbs, and sometimes falling into trances—are considered proof of the baptism.

One current Charismatic statement of faith that is typical of most Pentecostal and Charismatic statements says, "All believers are entitled to and should ardently expect and earnestly seek the promise of the Father, the baptism in the Holy Ghost and fire, according to the command of our Lord Jesus

Christ. This was the normal experience of all in the early Christian Church. With it comes the endowment of prayer of power for life and service, the obtainment of the gifts and their uses in the work of the ministry. This experience is distinct *from* and subsequent *to* the experience of the new birth."[1]

It continues, "With the baptism in the Holy Ghost come such experiences as an overflowing fullness of the Spirit; a deepened reverence to God; an intensified consecration to God and dedication to His work; and a more active love of Christ, His Word, and for the lost. Then . . . the baptism of believers in the Holy Ghost is witnessed by the *initial* physical sign of speaking with other tongues as the Spirit of God gives them utterance. The speaking in tongues in this instance is the same in essence as the gift of tongues, but different in purpose and use."

This is a fairly comprehensive statement of the Charismatic position on the baptism and the evidence of tongues.

The teaching here is that a person can be saved and go to heaven without the baptism of the Spirit; but if you have it, you can move to a higher level of Christian living and service. This is really the linchpin doctrine for the Charismatics. By *linchpin,* I mean it holds all the other Charismatic teachings together. It is at this point where the Charismatic movement differs from other evangelical groups. Keep in mind several aspects of this linchpin teaching: The baptism is a manifestation that happens *after* the salvation experience. The evidence of it is speaking in tongues. Christians must seek this baptism.

As always, ask, "What does the Bible say?" Remember, go to the authority of Scripture, not to our experience or to anyone else's, to determine the truth of the matter. Let's consider this doctrine of the baptism of the Spirit from several angles.

## Observing

Let's look at this manifestation the way Charismatics do. The baptism can happen *at* salvation, but usually it happens *after* salvation. The idea is that a person is saved at one point, and he or she receives this Spirit baptism at a later point. They cite the experience of the apostles in Acts 2 as proof. They correctly point out that the apostles were believers before the day of Pentecost and that they were to wait for this promise of Spirit baptism.

Speaking in tongues is the initial evidence that a person has had the Spirit baptism experience, according to Charismatics. Again, they go to the experience of the apostles on the day of Pentecost. Acts 2:4 clearly states, "All of them were filled with the Holy Spirit and began to speak in other tongues as the Spirit enabled them." They also point to the experience of Cornelius in Acts 10. Here we read that while Simon Peter was preaching, "The Holy Spirit came on all who heard the message. . . . For they heard them speaking in tongues and praising God" (Acts 10:44, 46). According to Charismatic teaching, how do people know they have received the baptism? They speak with tongues they do not know or in an ecstatic utterance known only to God.

Recently some Charismatics have added other manifestations as indications of the baptism: falling to the floor, being immobilized for a period of time, crying, shaking, jerking, etc.

Charismatic Christians testify that this Spirit baptism experience has brought great blessing to their lives. They say prayer and Bible study have become more enriching, and they experience a new freedom and greater joy in worship. They have been given spiritual gifts they didn't have before. These gifts could be a new prayer language or gifts of healing and prophecy. They also confirm that they are able to serve the Lord more effectively since their baptism.

Some Pentecostals compare this to working a garden. Though all Christians can work effectively in their gardens, some Christians have a bigger hose (the baptism of the Spirit). This bigger hose provides more water for the garden. The fruit grows bigger and better. They claim a person can serve the Lord without the baptism of the Spirit, but this person reaches only a certain level of spiritual ministry. With the baptism comes the full expression of service. Sounds like a booster shot for the Christian life—an energy pill that invigorates a believer's spiritual activity.

Charismatics also believe that Spirit baptism is an experience a person must seek. Read again the statement of faith at the beginning of this chapter. The statement clearly says that Jesus commands us earnestly to seek the baptism. Having sought it and received it, one moves to a higher level of spirituality.

Charismatics take this belief very seriously. In Charismatic services, special altar calls are given for people to receive the baptism. At times, this appeal is stronger than the salvation appeal. People share testimonies about the baptism; and they are encouraged to pray until they receive it by repenting of sin, by humbling themselves, and by being patient. Sometimes it is conveyed to people by the laying on of hands or even by blowing on people. Preachers and teachers give all kinds of explanations and guidelines for receiving this baptism.

There are problems with the Charismatic position on Spirit baptism. First, it is taught that the Christian life happens in two stages. In stage one, a person is born again. In stage two, he or she receives the baptism of the Holy Spirit. How does this square with such statements as "you have been given fullness in Christ" (Col. 2:10)? How can a new Christian be complete if he or she has only experienced stage one?

Teaching about Spirit baptism also creates two levels of Christians: first class and coach class, just like accommodations on an airplane. Christians are divided into the haves and the have-nots. Though some Charismatics don't take this position, the question, Have you received the baptism of the Holy Spirit? places Christians on two levels of Christian experience.

### Searching

It's about time for some Bible study. Let's check the Scriptures on the subject of the baptism of the Holy Spirit. Remember, we must go to our Bible, not to the experiences of ourselves or of others. What does the Bible say? We must be guided by revelation, not by experience.

When matters of Bible doctrine are disputed, we must be careful and precise about the terminology we use. Words are very important. Words make a difference. Would it make any difference to you if I said, "This dessert I'm serving you is filled with ambrosia," or if I said, "This dessert I'm serving you is filled with arsenic"? Words are vehicles of thought. They communicate ideas. We must be extremely particular about our terminology when Bible doctrine is in dispute.

The phrase "the baptism of the Holy Spirit" is not in the Bible. We use other phrases that are not specifically used in the Bible, but they correctly indicate something the Bible says. For instance, the phrase "the substitutionary atonement of Jesus" is not found in the Bible. But this truth is clearly taught there in the Scriptures.

There are very few references to Spirit baptism in the Bible. In the New Testament, there are only seven clear references to Spirit baptism. Four are in the Gospels. Two are found in Acts. Only one is found in the rest of the New Testament.

Before we look at these references, we should remember that the word *baptize* is used in two different ways. We frequently use literal and figurative terms. "I slept eight full hours" is literal. "I could sleep for a year" is probably figurative! Sometimes *baptism* is used literally, with the meaning of "to immerse in water." John the Baptist baptized people in water. Both Jesus and the Philippian jailer were immersed in water. This is literal baptism.

At other times, the word *baptize* is used figuratively, with the meaning of "to identify with." For instance, Jesus referred to his death as a baptism in Matthew 20:22–23. He said to James and John, "Can you drink the cup I am going to drink?" Jesus was saying, "Are you able to be baptized with the baptism that I am baptized with?" He was not talking about water baptism, but his baptism of death on the cross. We use similar terminology today. Rookies at NFL football camp get their "baptism."

Let's examine the references. The first five are in the form of a promise. Four of them refer to the words of John the Baptist (see Matt. 3:11; Mark 1:8; Luke 3:16; John 1:33). The phrases are almost identical, but there are two small differences. Matthew and Luke add "with fire." What does that mean? John is addressing believers and unbelievers. His point is that everyone will experience a baptism by Christ, whether by Holy Spirit baptism or by a future baptism of judgment fire. Also, in John 1:33, John the Baptist says that he was told about the Spirit baptism by the Father.

Jesus makes one statement about the Spirit baptism. In Acts 1:4–5 he says, "Do not leave Jerusalem, but wait for the gift my Father promised, which you have heard me speak about." Note that Jesus ties Spirit baptism to the promise of the Father. The apostles are told to "wait for the promise."

These first five references look forward to what would happen at the day of Pentecost. They also clearly show Jesus as the baptizer and the Holy Spirit as the agent—the One by whom he baptizes. Jesus was the primary agent; the Holy Spirit was the immediate agent. A similar example is found in John 4:1–2, where we are told that Jesus baptized. But the verses explain that Jesus did not actually baptize. His disciples did. Jesus was the primary agent of that water baptism; the disciples were the immediate agents. The same is true in this baptism by means of the Holy Spirit. Jesus is the originator; the Holy Spirit carries it out.

The disciples desperately needed power. Jesus had given them the first impossible mission—preaching the gospel to the whole world. They needed the power of the Holy Spirit. Jesus promised the power in Acts 1:8: "But you will receive power when the Holy Spirit comes on you; and you will be my witnesses in Jerusalem, and in all Judea and Samaria, and to the ends of the earth."

There is only one reference to Spirit baptism that we can consider historical. In Acts 11:15–17 Simon Peter talks about what happened at the household of Cornelius the Gentile. He describes the Holy Spirit falling on Cornelius and his family and says he remembers the promise of Jesus about being baptized by the Holy Spirit. In verse 17 he says that God gave them (the household of Cornelius) the like gift (Holy Spirit) as he did unto us (those apostles on the day of Pentecost in Acts 2). Simon Peter is referring to two separate times when people were baptized by means of the Holy Spirit: the day of Pentecost in Acts 2 and at the house of Cornelius in Acts 10. Let's examine these further.

In Acts 2, the apostles received Spirit baptism after salvation. They were already saved. They had waited in an upper room for ten days for it to happen. On the day of Pentecost, they were filled with the Holy Spirit, obviously baptized by the Holy Spirit, and they spoke with tongues. The people heard the apostles speak in their own languages and as a result, three thousand people were saved. However, it does not say these converts spoke with tongues.

Look at Acts 10. These Gentiles were baptized by means of the Holy Spirit *at the time* of salvation. They spoke with tongues on this occasion, but it is not said that the apostles did or that the apostles received another baptism.

Two other times are mentioned by Charismatics as occasions when people received Spirit baptism. The first is in Acts 8 in Samaria. These people were believers. Peter and John came to Samaria, prayed, laid hands on them, and they received the Holy Spirit (Acts 8:14–17). The Holy Spirit was received after they believed (see Acts 8:17). However, it is not said that they spoke with tongues.

The second time is mentioned in Acts 19. Paul came to Ephesus and was immediately aware something was missing in these disciples. He asked, "Did you receive the Holy Spirit when you believed?" They had never even heard of the Holy Spirit! Upon further questioning, Paul realized they had been baptized by John's baptism, which was a baptism indicating they had repented of their sins. Paul explained the meaning of believing on Christ. Then they are baptized in the name of the Lord Jesus. When this occurred, Paul laid his hands on them, the Holy Spirit came upon them, and they spoke with tongues and prophesied (Acts 19:1–6). Evidently, these disciples of John had not been born again. When they received the Holy Spirit, they believed. Paul laid hands on them and they spoke in tongues.

What do we learn when we add up all these accounts? They are all different! If we try to use what happened in Acts as a guide for our practice today, the question is, Which guide? Remember the rule: Don't build doctrine from the Book of Acts.

The only other reference to Spirit baptism in the rest of the New Testament occurs in 1 Corinthians 12:13. It is the most important of the seven references because Paul explains what Spirit baptism is. The King James Version says, "By one Spirit are we all baptized." Actually, the terminology is the same as the previous references. Think of it as "by means of one Spirit," and you'll have a better translation. We are handling the phrase consistently when we translate it this way in all of its references.

Also, it is better to translate "were" instead of "are" in this verse. The tense of the verb is a Greek aorist, meaning something that happened at a definite point in the past. Look at the word *all*. This is something that takes place not to just a favored few believers but to all believers. There is no separation of believers into the "haves" and the "have-nots." Consider the phrase "into one body." The reference is to the body of Christ, the church. At the moment of salvation, all believers are placed into the universal, invisible church, the body of Christ. Being made a part of the body of Christ clearly refers to the salvation experience.

Spirit baptism happens to all believers. It takes place at the moment of salvation, not at some later time. There is no mention of tongues anywhere in 1 Corinthians 12:13. No other physical manifestation is given as an evidence of the Spirit baptism. When you look at the big picture, you see there is no indication that this Spirit baptism will move one to a higher level of Christian living or to special holiness. Remember, Paul is writing to the Corinthians. They were baptized by means of the Holy Spirit, yet Paul said specifically that they were carnal, or worldly minded. Finally, there is no command in this verse or anywhere else in the whole Bible that one should seek the Spirit baptism.

## Evaluating

There are several explanations about Spirit baptism which I believe will clear up the confusion surrounding this matter.

What happened to the apostles on Pentecost is not the norm for us. Pentecost was a biblically promised historical event. It cannot be repeated. There can be no second Pentecost just as there cannot be a second Bethlehem. The day was planned by God at a specific time and a specific place. Just as God had promised, the Holy Spirit was given and the apostles were baptized by the Spirit into the body. This happens to us personally today when we trust Christ as Savior and are born again. At the moment of salvation, we receive the gift of the Holy Spirit (Rom. 8:9). And we are baptized by means of the Holy Spirit into the body (1 Cor. 12:13).

The apostles became believers before Pentecost, before the promised gift of the Holy Spirit was fulfilled. The way it happened was the only way it could have happened to them. But we become believers after Pentecost. This is why we should not expect the events of the early church necessarily to be the norm for today. For instance, do we choose leaders by lot? No. They did this in the Book of Acts. Do we pool all our possessions? No. They did this in the Book of Acts. The apostles of Acts had a special role in the founding of the church. Ephesians 2:20 says that we are built upon "the foundation of the apostles." Their roles and our roles today are completely different.

There are other examples. Neither the day of Pentecost nor the experience of the Gentiles (Acts 10) in the household of Cornelius is a norm for other conversion experiences in the Bible.

In Acts 8, the Ethiopian eunuch heard Philip preach Jesus from Isaiah 53, believed on the Lord Jesus, and was baptized. Did he need a Spirit baptism at a later point? No.

Consider Lydia and the jailer at Phillipi in Acts 16. Paul preached the gospel to Lydia, and the Lord opened her heart. She was saved. Did she need a Spirit baptism later? No.

The Philippian jailer was told, "Believe in the Lord Jesus, and you will be saved—you and your household." He did and was saved. Did he need a Spirit baptism later? No.

In Acts 18, Crispus, the chief ruler of the synagogue, heard Paul preach, believed, and was saved. Did Crispus need a Spirit baptism at some later time? No.

There is no indication any of these believers spoke with tongues. Does this mean they needed another experience later? No.

Spirit baptism is a part of the salvation package. When you are saved, you receive the gift of the Holy Spirit. The Spirit comes to live in you. You are sealed by the Holy Spirit. The Spirit is your down payment of more blessings to come. You are anointed by the Holy Spirit. The Spirit baptizes you into the body of Christ (the church). It's all part of the package. These sovereign acts of God are never repeated, never withdrawn, and they are guarantees that the believer is eternally secure and has a glorious standing in Christ. This is like a soldier entering the army. At the moment he becomes a soldier, he gets his gear. He gets a rifle, binoculars, combat boots—the whole package, everything he needs to be an effective and successful soldier. The same is true of salvation and the package we receive with it.

The Bible is full of many commands to us: abstain from, walk in, be filled, etc. We are never commanded to seek the baptism of the Spirit. In the seven references to Spirit baptism, not one is a command. The reason is obvious. Why ask God to do something he has already done? Suppose Dad buys Jake a bike for Christmas. What would Dad think if Jake started begging him for a bike on January 1 right after Christmas?

Believers do not need something more than Jesus and salvation. To teach a subsequent work of grace beyond the salvation experience is to tamper with the doctrine of salvation. Believers don't get Jesus now and the Holy Spirit later. When we are saved, we have all we need for spiritual life, service, and victory in Jesus Christ.

Paul wrote letters to many of the New Testament churches. Most of the churches had spiritual problems and difficulties. He never told a church or an individual Christian that the solution to his or her problems was an experience of Spirit baptism. Jesus sent letters to the seven churches of Asia Minor (modern Turkey). Most of them had serious problems. He never said to any that they needed a baptism of the Holy Spirit.

Perhaps the Charismatic movement confuses baptism with the filling of the Holy Spirit. Recently, theologians with Charismatic leanings have suggested that Charismatics might use the word *filling* instead of *baptism*. The suggestion is that this would be more acceptable.[2] Wayne Grudem says, "The divisiveness that comes with the term 'baptism in the Holy Spirit' could easily be avoided by using any of the alternative terms mentioned in this section (fullness of the Holy Spirit or a new empowering for ministry, etc.)."[3] An excellent suggestion. If it were taken, confusion might be lessened and the level of disagreement might be lowered.

There is a distinct difference between Spirit baptism and being filled with the Spirit. Baptism places us into the body of Christ. The filling gives us power for Christian living and service. Remember, there is no command to seek the baptism. There is a specific command to seek the filling (Eph. 5:18). However, let it be quickly said that we do not have to wait to be filled with the Spirit. The moment we yield to the Holy Spirit, we are filled or controlled by him. If we do wait, it is not because the Holy Spirit must be begged but because something in our life is not yielded.

Acts 2:1 in the King James Version says the believers were of "one accord." This was certainly not the case previously. Could this be part of what was going on in the ten-day upper room prayer meeting (Acts 1)? Maybe Martha and Mary put aside their differences. Or Peter and John, who had plenty of squabbles, may have put aside their differences and formed one accord.

Baptism is a once-for-all sovereign act of God. The filling of the Spirit may be and should be repeated. Every day we should ask the Holy Spirit to take control of our lives. A frequently used formula is still a good one: one baptism; many fillings.

How will we know we are filled with the Holy Spirit? Acts 1:8 says we will be witnesses to him. Ephesians 5 indicates our personal life as well as our family life will be affected. There will be greater joy and deeper peace in the inner life. Dads will be more Christlike, and moms will teach spiritual lessons more effectively in the family. That indeed is living the Christian life with a first-class upgrade!

## Testing, Testing . . .

1. The Bible Test. What does the Bible say about this manifestation? Is it clearly taught in the Bible?

2. The Jesus Test. Does it honor and glorify Jesus? Is Jesus, the Holy Spirit, or the Christian the focus?

3. The Character Test. Does it contribute to a more Christlike life?

4. The Decency and Order Test. Is this within the guidelines of decency and order?

5. The Evangelism Test. Does it place the focus on winning people to Christ?

   Does it pass?
   YES _____
   NO _____

## CHAPTER 6

# HEAVENLY LANGUAGE

Have you heard a phrase similar to this lately: "Talk to the Lord 'cause our ears ain't understandin'." I have. At the mall the kids often say, "Talk to the hand 'cause the ears ain't listenin'." They say this in response to what friends may say to them. This means they don't like what they are hearing, so they hold up a hand in the "stop" position while they utter these words.

Well, it may be a pop culture phrase, but as I thought about what I had heard, I realized that Christians could use this illustration to refer to the recent revival of the tongues movement. Many of our Charismatic friends are seeking experiences and special prayer languages to help move them along to a higher level of spiritual awareness. God gives these special and sometimes incomprehensible languages, many believe, so we can praise him more effectively. Is God hearing these attempts at holy communication? Perhaps some good advice (after hearing the kids in the mall) is to "talk to the Lord, 'cause our ears ain't understanding'."

## Manifestation

On the day of Pentecost in Acts 2:1–11, the disciples of Jesus were baptized by the Holy Spirit, filled with the Holy Spirit, and they spoke with other tongues. These tongues were languages they did not know. The word *glossa* means "recognizable language." The usage of the word *dialect* in verse 6 also indicates this. Finally, the references to the various nations represented at Pentecost shows this as well.

The second account of public tongues is mentioned in Acts 10 at the household of Cornelius. As Peter preached, the Holy Spirit came upon these new Christian believers, just like at Pentecost. They spoke with tongues (vv. 44–46).

Acts 19 also mentions tongues. Paul laid his hands upon disciples of John the Baptist, the Holy Spirit came upon them, and they spoke with tongues (Acts 19:6). Though tongues are not specifically mentioned in Acts 8, most Charismatics believe the Samaritans who received the Holy Spirit when Peter and John prayed for them and laid hands on them also spoke in tongues. They believe this because Acts 8:18 says, "When Simon saw that the Spirit was given at the laying on of the apostles' hands." They take the view that the fact Simon could see some outward evidence means they spoke with tongues.

Recently, many Charismatics have been emphasizing private prayer language. They believe this language is special and can enable them to pray more perfectly. Through this special prayer language, God is praised and petitioned in thought too deep for normal words. Romans 8:26 is one of their Bible texts for this practice. No interpretation of this gift is needed, in their opinion, because others are not present. Many Charismatic Christians claim to be greatly helped by this prayer language, saying it brings them peace, joy, and power. They are able to praise God more effectively and to obtain a level of prayer that exceeds praying in their own language. The result is refreshing spiritual enrichment.

Charismatic Christians often claim that all Christians should speak with tongues in their private devotions. When Paul asks, "Do all speak in tongues?" in 1 Corinthians 12:30, where the obvious answer is *no*, Charismatics believe this refers to the public use of tongues and not to private tongues. They say that private tongues is a heavenly language based on 1 Corinthians 13:1, which refers to the tongues of angels.

Speaking in tongues is not unique to Christianity. The phenomenon is found in Eskimo Shamanism, in the religion of the Caddo Indians of North America, among Buddhists, and in several cults in Japan. Also, it is found among Mormons. Remember that the practice of tongues speaking was found among the mystery religions in Corinth. To absolve sin, the worshipers of mystery religions had various ceremonies. Through ecstasies they sought contact with deity. They used drugs, cast spells, and promoted emotional excesses to induce their various states of bliss. Their normal mind and body functioning was suspended. This allowed their emotions to take over their rational mind. Through dancing, fasting, and rapid repetition of phrases, they worked themselves into a state of exhilaration.[1] This seems to be an ancient version of our modern idea, "If it feels good, it must be of God."

Prayer language is so big with Charismatics today that seminars are being held to help believers receive this gift. People are taught to utter praise to God in single syllables. Then they are instructed to go faster, not thinking consciously about what is coming from their lips. We should be cautious about seeking an experience that bypasses the mind. Jesus specifically says we are to love God with all our mind. But, some Charismatics say, "If you want to speak in a heavenly language, the intellect must be set aside." Does this seem like sound teaching to you? Just remember that we must always go back to the Bible as our guide.

## Exposition

Any casual survey of the New Testament on this subject will reveal that tongues is not one of the major truths taught there. Far more is said about

Christ and his salvation for us. If more time is spent in a religious service talking about tongues than teaching such matters as the cross of Christ and his shed blood for our sins, we should raise a red flag immediately.

In chapter 13 of my previous book, *SpiritLife*, there is a survey on the matter of tongues. I won't give a full repetition of that chapter, but I encourage you to get *SpiritLife* and read it. For now, let me give you the essential details on tongues.

First, in Acts, tongues is definitely a foreign language. The apostles are speaking languages they had not previously learned. What is the purpose of this gift of languages? First Corinthians 14:21–22 teaches it was a sign gift for unbelieving Jews. The spiritual gift of tongues in 1 Corinthians 12 is tied to interpretation. A foreign language is being talked about here. Everybody didn't share it (1 Cor. 12:30), so it cannot be the evidence of Spirit baptism (1 Cor. 12:13).

Think of it this way: Tongues is one of the temporary sign gifts. It authenticated the message of the apostles before the New Testament Scripture was completed. Once the canon of the New Testament was completed, the sign gifts were no longer necessary. First Corinthians 13:8 tells us that tongues would cease.

Tongues had become a problem in the Corinthian church. These Christians were trying to duplicate what happened at Pentecost. Paul is dealing gently with young Christians. In 1 Corinthians 14, he establishes guidelines to regulate and to eventually eliminate the use of the gift of tongues. It worked then. It works today.

But let's examine the matter of a prayer language. Is there a heavenly language believers may receive? Let's go to two verses in the Word. The first is Ephesians 6:18: "And pray in the Spirit on all occasions with all kinds of prayers and requests. With this in mind, be alert and always keep on praying for all the saints." The second verse is Jude 20: "But you, dear friends, build yourselves up in your most holy faith and pray in the Holy Spirit."

Note that no mention is made in these verses of any kind of special prayer language. The references indicate only prayer in the Holy Spirit. This means that prayer in the Holy Spirit is consistent with what has been taught in the Bible. Grudem says that praying in the Spirit is "to pray with the conscious awareness of God's presence surrounding us and sanctifying both us and our prayer."[2] There is no indication of a special heavenly language from these two verses.

In 1 Corinthians 13:1, Paul talks about the importance of love. He says, "If I speak in the tongues of men and of angels, but have not love, I am only a resounding gong or a clanging cymbal." What is this? Does it teach that we can have heavenly, angelic language? No! Paul is actually presenting a hypothetical case. The verbs used are in the subjunctive mood, indicating something that may be theoretical, but not actual. When angels speak in the Bible, it is with a language that people can understand (see Luke 1:11–20, 26–37; 2:8–14).

Charismatics also use Romans 8:26–27 to teach a heavenly prayer language. The context of the passage is important. Paul talks about our sense of helplessness and our lack of knowledge in prayer. He says, "We do not know." Our weakness as believers is certainly shown in prayer. Maybe Charismatics think a special prayer language helps us overcome this weakness.

While I was in college, a group of us believers decided to get up one hour before breakfast each morning for prayer. We picked a prayer place on the campus. At the first session I prayed for absolutely everything I could think of. I glanced at my watch and only five minutes had passed. I set in praying again. I went back over everything. I prayed a little bit longer on each item. I peeked again at my watch. Ten minutes! I learned my weakness and my ignorance in those early one-hour prayer times! I sympathize with the requests of the disciples, "Lord, teach us to pray" (Luke 11:1).

Paul also shares good news about prayer: "In the same way, the Spirit helps us in our weakness" (Rom. 8:26). He is talking about our inability to do anything for ourselves. We are weak. But the Holy Spirit can help. The Holy Spirit comes alongside us, gets underneath our weakness, and helps us.

Regarding prayer, Paul also says, "The Spirit himself intercedes for us with groans that words cannot express" (Rom. 8:26). "Groans" is also used in Acts 7:34, meaning "sighs" or "expressions of sorrow." The idea is that there are sighs and groans of the Holy Spirit which cannot be put into words. Sometimes our burdens are so great the Holy Spirit identifies with us by means of groans, expressing his compassion for us. But no prayer tongue is involved here. Divine communication between the Holy Spirit, the Son, and the Father can't be put into mere words (cf. 1 Cor. 2:11). True prayer consists of the Holy Spirit's praying in us through the Son and the Father.

I love old hymns. One has really helped me deal with the matter of prayer:

Prayer is the soul's desire,
Unuttered or expressed.
The motion of a hidden fire
That trembles in the breast.
It is the burden of a sigh,
The falling of a tear.
The upward glancing of an eye,
When none but God is near.

First Corinthians 14 is a vital passage because this is where many Charismatics turn to support their beliefs. The setting of the passage is Corinth. It is important to remember this because ecstatic speech was common here. Tongue speaking was a part of their previous pagan religions and customs. The effects of the pagan background remained in Corinth and its people. They were generally worldly and not very spiritual. In fact, the church at Corinth was plagued with incest, divisions, lawsuits between members, and, of course, tongues. Paul's goal in writing to the Corinthians was to discourage their use of tongues.

In addition, 1 Corinthians 14 talks about the use of tongues in public services. No private activity is even considered. The book also emphasizes the need for building up other church members, gaining understanding, and conducting affairs decently and in order. Lastly, Paul emphasizes the superiority of the gift of prophecy over the gift of tongues. All of this is important to keep in mind while examining tongues and its references here.

We know some Charismatics teach a private prayer language, but how? They use sections of 1 Corinthians 14 to teach this. First, consider verses 1–4. Before mentioning tongues in verse 2, Paul says in verse 1, "Follow the way of love and eagerly desire spiritual gifts, especially the gift of prophecy." After he mentions speaking in a tongue in verse 2, he continues in verse 3 by saying, "But everyone who prophesies speaks to men for their strengthening, encouragement and comfort." Isn't Paul teaching the superiority of the gift of prophecy? Yes. Because prophecy helps people. He says in verse 2 that one who speaks in a tongue is not speaking to men but unto God and there is no understanding by men who hear it because he is speaking "mysteries." We know spiritual gifts are to benefit others.

First Corinthians 12:7 specifically teaches that spiritual gifts are for the common good. God is not edified by our exercise of spiritual gifts. Is that news to you? The gifts are to be used to benefit people! There simply is no record in the Bible where anyone ever speaks to God in anything other than his own language. What is the point? If people don't know what is being said, they can't be helped.

First Corinthians 14:4 says that the person who speaks in tongue edifies himself. We know this is not the purpose of the spiritual gifts. Self-edification is selfish. Paul indicates their misuse of gifts for their own selfish purposes. First Corinthians 14:26 says, "All of these must be done for the strengthening of the church." He is criticizing them for the way they were exercising gifts in public worship services. His mention of the church in verse 4 makes this apparent. This is not about a private language.

Secondly, consider verses 13–15. If verse 14 is read by itself, it might cause one to think that to pray in a tongue is legitimate and that there may be some kind of special prayer language. But the key to the verse is the use of the word *interpretation*. If one prays in a tongue, Paul explains, his or her spirit is praying, but there is no understanding without interpretation. Verse 15 continues, "So what shall I do?" The point here is to pray with the spirit and with the understanding. Sing with the spirit and with the understanding. The reference is not to the Holy Spirit but to the spirit of the person praying. But the praying is not to be with the spirit alone. Paul says pray with both the spirit and the understanding.

Why the need for understanding? So people may be edified. He is talking about something that takes place in a public service as shown in verses 16–19. When someone doesn't understand what is going on in a worship service, he or she is not edified or built up. Paul says in verse 19 that he had rather speak five words with understanding so that others might be taught than ten thousand words in a tongue that no one understands.

Finally, consider verses 26–28. "All of these must be done for the strengthening of the church." A series of guidelines is given which eliminates most of the tongues used today. Remember, the discussion revolves around a public setting. Verse 28 specifically says that if there is no interpreter, the individual is to keep silent in the church.

From these sections we see that there is no clear-cut, easy-to-understand prayer language taught in the Bible, and there is no encouragement given that one should seek some kind of heavenly language.

## Explanation

Tongues is not a prominent subject in the New Testament. You never find mention that Jesus spoke in tongues. Perhaps the most intense prayer experience ever was our Lord's agony of prayer in the Garden of Gethsemane. If heavenly language was ever needed, it was then. But what happened? He prayed in his normal earthly language.

When Jesus made promises about the coming of the Holy Spirit, why didn't he talk about tongues (Acts 1:8)? When he started his own public ministry and indicated that he had been anointed by the Holy Spirit to preach, why didn't he talk about the need for tongues (Luke 4:18)? For us to emphasize any kind of tongues is to emphasize something Jesus did not. It's a self-centered activity. The focus is taken off the centrality of Jesus and placed on a minor area of Bible teaching.

It's extremely dangerous to switch off the mind and to allow the emotions freedom. Today I see the young people participating in these "extreme sports" like aggressive skating and ski-boarding. A sign reading "EXTREME DANGER" should be posted not just for those kids but also for anyone letting his or her emotions rule the mind. Such an approach can trap one in mysticism, and it completely disconnects a person from the clear teaching of Scripture.

George Gardner was a Charismatic pastor who left the movement. In his most interesting book *The Corinthian Catastrophe*, he discusses the danger of surrendering one's mind and self over to experience. This leads to an inevitable emotional letdown and opens one up to an attack from Satan. Such a letdown causes the individual to go back again and again to an experience for stronger doses of emotion. This, according to Gardner, becomes almost like a drug, requiring heavier and heavier doses to get the same emotional high. We are never told in Scripture to turn off our minds or to bypass rational thought. We are encouraged instead to renew our minds through the study of the Scriptures (Rom. 12:2; Col. 3:10).

Tongues could be considered a kind of backdoor ecumenism. Don't misunderstand. We should have fellowship with all genuine Christian believers, and we don't have to agree on certain minor matters (such as tongues) to have this fellowship. I try to follow the principle established in Psalm 119:63, "I am a friend to all who fear you, to all who follow your precepts." This is my basis for fellowship. If you love Jesus and believe the Word, I can fellowship with you.

But to establish a gift of tongues as a basis for breaking down all denominational distinctives creates some real problems.

The practice of tongues is found all over the place today. All kinds of denominational groups are exercising tongues. Some are practicing questionable doctrines. Basically, we're hearing that as long as we can unite around tongues, the doctrinal differences don't matter. One problem is that an experience of tongues, not Jesus and the Bible, can become a false center of fellowship.

The clear priority of our Christian life is evangelism. It permeates the message of the New Testament. The excitement of some kind of prayer tongue as personal edification takes the focus away from evangelism. Personal edification becomes more important than leading people to Jesus Christ. If you're in a worship service, ask yourself which is emphasized—inviting people to receive a spirit baptism and the gift of tongues or inviting people to come to Christ for salvation?

The practice of tongues-speaking provides no evidence for an advanced spirituality. Paul specifically says to the Corinthians, "Brothers, I could not address you as spiritual but as worldly—mere infants in Christ" (1 Cor. 3:1). Tongues is never listed as some requirement or proof of the presence of the Holy Spirit or that one is at a higher level of spirituality. There is no indication that any kind of tongues is evidence for the baptism of the Holy Spirit.

Basically, most people agree that what we're hearing in the Charismatic movement today are unknown languages. So what is going on? Where are the tongues in today's Charismatic movement coming from? Some may be satanic. Many in the Charismatic movement acknowledge this. For instance, in the *Dictionary of Charismatic and Pentecostal Movements* which is written by and for Charismatic Christians, we find this statement: "The impulse for glossolalia, not readily accessible to scientific determination, may rise from the speakers themselves, from a DEMONIC spirit, or from the Holy Spirit . . . the discernment of the community is essential."[3]

One Sunday morning during my message, a young lady stood and babbled sounds I had never heard. At the door, I looked her in the eye (her eyes looked like snake's eyes, jumping up and down) and said, "In the name of Jesus Christ, don't ever do that again."

She looked at me and snarled, "I am the Christ."

Later, missionaries from Nigeria who had been in the service told me she spoke in the same dialect they had heard used by witch doctors. She was involved in a satanic cult. We must watch out for "deceiving spirits" (1 Tim. 4:1) in the last days because we know the devil is behind all attempts to corrupt truth.

Some tongues may be psychological in nature. In times of great stress and need, people can have unusual experiences. People often seek an emotional release for this stress. Some find it in a tongues experience.

Sometimes tongues is learned. I don't believe we should view opinions from secular sources as necessarily authoritative in spiritual matters. "The man without the Spirit does not accept the things that come from the Spirit of God, for they are foolishness to him, and he cannot understand them, because they are spiritually discerned" (1 Cor. 2:14). But as in most controversial subjects, it is wise at least to look at the conclusions of research in these areas.

John P. Kildahl, a clinical psychologist, has studied the tongues phenomena. He concludes that tongues is not a real human language, known or unknown. He also states that the person speaking in tongues learns the method from someone else.[4] William J. Samaran, professor of linguistics at the University of Toronto, has also come to the conclusion that modern tongue-speaking is not a recognizable language.[5] This research, and the fact that seminars are held to instruct people in tongues, raises questions. When the pump is primed by giving people sample syllables, we do wonder what is supernatural? If a person can learn to speak this way, how is it a gift from God?

Neil Babcox was a Charismatic pastor who left the movement. In his study of the New Testament, especially Acts, he saw tongues as a miraculous language gift. He also learned to speak in tongues. He became aware that praying in tongues was not as edifying as he had previously thought. He says, "Praying in tongues was an evasion—a failure to grapple with the profundities of prayer."[6]

Prayer is profound. It brings a person to wrestle with his own heart, with the will of God, and with the tremendous problems of life. To turn off the mind and to speak some language that avoids all this may stop genuine growth and maturity in a Christian's life.

Perhaps a great deal of the current emphasis on tongues is a reaction to the deadness of many of our churches. There is a great hunger today for genuine spiritual reality. In Jesus Christ and in the power of the Holy Spirit, there is every emotional fulfillment and spiritual provision the heart could desire. Praise the Lord! Light fires for Jesus! "Fan into flame the gift of God, which is in you through the laying on of my hands" (2 Tim. 1:6). "Be . . . fervent in spirit; serving the Lord" (Rom. 12:10–11 KJV).

Use your native language to pray and to tell others about Jesus. Paul is right: "I would rather speak five intelligible words to instruct others than ten thousand words in a tongue" (1 Cor. 14:19). Here are five words: *Christ died for our sins.* Five words that can change a life. Five words that can deliver a soul from hell to heaven. That is heavenly language! That is talking to the Lord.

## Testing, Testing . . .

1. The Bible Test. What does the Bible say about this manifestation? Is it clearly taught in the Bible?

2. The Jesus Test. Does it honor and glorify Jesus? Is Jesus, the Holy Spirit, or the Christian the focus?

3. The Character Test. Does it contribute to a more Christlike life?

4. The Decency and Order Test. Is this within the guidelines of decency and order?

5. The Evangelism Test. Does it place the focus on winning people to Christ?

   Does it pass?
   YES _____
   NO _____

## CHAPTER 7

# THE UNCTION FUNCTION

I only recently bought a computer, and I really don't know how everything works. I know how to turn it on and off, and I've even learned how to E-mail my children who live across the country. My son, Jon, really knows computers, since he creates web pages. When I have a question about my computer, I either ask the tech people at my church or I call my son.

The other day I had a big question about my computer. I couldn't figure out how to change the format of the document I was writing. I looked and stared at the computer monitor, but it didn't help. The only thing moving was the cursor. It was a Saturday, and I knew my son would be home, so I called him and once again asked for his help.

"Dad," he said, "you've got to learn those function keys! F1 always means help."

As soon as he said it, I remembered. He had explained the role of the function keys on the computer to me at least two other times, and I had not remembered it. But the third time was certainly the charm, and as I continued to work on my document (an outline for an upcoming sermon), a thought struck me. What if we had function keys we could press for help on spiritual matters? What if we could learn a series of keystrokes to help us figure out how to live the Christian life? Maybe even software—SpiritWorks '99 compatible on Windows or Mac systems? Watch out, Bill Gates!

The fact is, the realm of the Holy Spirit is abstract. Aspects of the whole concept sometimes seem incomprehensible. The anointing, or unction, is one such abstract spiritual concept. Various beliefs are prevalent today regarding the anointing of the Spirit. Perhaps this chapter can be your F1 function key to help you understand this concept. In other words, I hope this chapter can be your *unction function.*

So, what is this anointing all about? Oil? Unction? Those who visit the church I pastor hear this terminology often. We pray that the singers will be anointed to sing and that the preachers will be anointed to preach their sermons. In my circle we use the term to refer to preaching. What is anointed preaching? I remember the country preacher who was asked to define *anointed preaching.* He thought for a moment, then said, "I can't say exactly what it is, but I sure know what it ain't!"

Is there more to it? Is it just preaching? Can all Christians share in the anointing? What's it all about? What is up with the oil?

The word is currently being used in Charismatic circles as an umbrella term to describe a variety of experiences of people. Some are slain by the anointing and they fall out. Others are healed as a result of a special healing anointing. Some people are delivered from demonic powers through the anointing.

The Charismatic movement teaches that a person can have a variety of experiences with the Holy Spirit beyond, after, and in addition to salvation. The anointing is one of those experiences. Some type of physical manifestation usually accompanies the experience. This is true in the matter of the anointing.

Let's turn on our computers and push our *unction function* (fun) key.

## Observing

Charismatic teaching about the anointing is not uniform. Some suggest that the anointing is identical to Spirit baptism. Others, perhaps the majority, teach that the anointing is an experience beyond salvation and Spirit baptism—that the anointing is another level of relationship with the Holy Spirit.

Kenneth Hagin is one of the most prolific writers concerning the anointing. Now in his eighties, Hagin is an advocate of the "Word of Faith" message (more about this later). He is the founder of the Rhema Bible Training Center, Tulsa, Oklahoma.[1]

Hagin's writings share his own experience in receiving the anointing. In a vision to Hagin, Jesus laid his right hand on each palm of Hagin's hands. As Hagin describes it, his hands began to burn like he was holding coals of fire. Jesus told him to kneel. Once Hagin was kneeling, Jesus laid his hand on his head and told Hagin that he would have a special anointing to minister to the sick. Then, Jesus told him, "However, this anointing will not work unless you tell the people exactly what I have told you . . . tell them that if they will believe that, then that power will flow from your hands into their bodies." He also says that his anointing will not work unless people believe that he (Hagin) is anointed.[2]

Hagin also teaches that there is a special anointing for each of the offices in Ephesians 4 (apostles, prophets, evangelists, pastors, teachers). Jesus, according to Hagin, is anointed to stand in all five offices. There is an additional healing anointing, according to Hagin. He says, "Electricity is God's power in the natural realm, and Holy Ghost power is God's power in the spiritual realm."[3] Interesting analogy. He also says that Holy Spirit power is better conducted through cloth, citing the use of handkerchiefs and aprons from Paul's body in Acts 19:11–12.

Further, Hagin says that the faith of the people makes the anointing work better. "I have noticed that when a crowd gets 'with' the preacher teacher or singer, then the Anointing is much stronger."[4]

The anointing can be transferred to other people, according to Hagin. He bases this on the passage in Mark 5:25–30, where healing virtue or power went from Jesus to the woman who was healed of an issue of blood. Hagin emphasizes the fact that the woman felt healed of the plague and that Jesus knew virtue had gone out of him upon her touch. The anointing is not mentioned in the passage, and Hagin points this out.

Obviously, there are differences among Charismatic teachers in this area. For example, Benny Hinn, who at times seems to teach that the anointing is transferred from one to another, also says this: "I can't wave a spiritual wand over your head and place an anointing on you. That only comes with a personal, deeply private encounter with the Spirit."[5]

Benny Hinn desired to have what Kathryn Kuhlman had. After attending one of her crusade services, Benny Hinn sought the same anointing which was upon her. After a time of prayer, he stepped out of the room into the hallway. His mom, who was there, was thrown against the wall. He says the presence of the Lord almost knocked her down. Now he has such a strong anointing upon him that at times he can blow upon people and they fall out. He describes the anointing that is upon him sometimes in terms of jolts of electricity. At other times he describes it as fire. Hinn believes there are levels of anointing. He says, "I am convinced there is a point in your relationship with the Spirit when the Anointing becomes so heavy on you that you can look up and see a vision of God."[6]

Let's talk about the basic teachings of the Charismatic movement on the anointing.

There is a special bestowal of Holy Spirit power beyond salvation described as the anointing. This anointing equips a person to minister in one of several offices, like preaching a sermon or teaching a Bible lesson. This anointing makes it possible for people to heal others. Sometimes, the anointing is used to break yokes of bondage, like a yoke of demon possession or a yoke of poverty. The anointing can be transferred from one person to another. Most often this is done by the laying on of hands. But other acts may convey it, such as blowing or even looking in the direction of those to receive it.

According to almost all Charismatic teachers, the anointing is accompanied by physical manifestations. Benny Hinn says that sometimes when the anointing is on him, his legs are so weak he thinks he will fall. His body tingles. His hands burn like fire. Hinn recently has suggested that when he is anointed, his face feels like it is on fire, so much so that people are not even able to touch his face. Those who attempt to do so are knocked backward, often onto the floor.

In researching beliefs on the anointing, remember that our authority is always the Bible. Ask yourself if the teaching is sustained by what the Bible says. Does it go beyond what the Bible says? It is obvious that Hagin uses his vision of Jesus as his authority. He received his anointing in a vision from Jesus. He cites his vision as his authority. Let's continue to explore this topic and push the *unction function* key again.

## Searching

The culmination principle is very important in studying the anointing. Though we begin our study in the Old Testament, we must follow the subject to the New Testament. Context is very important. We must study carefully the context of the passages that relate to the anointing. The use of figures of speech in the Bible must be recognized. This will help us understand a great deal of what the Bible says about the anointing.

Let's log on to our Bible Net. Now click your mouse on the links that are used. In the Old Testament, the Hebrew word is *mashach*, which means "to rub with oil" or "to consecrate." In the New Testament the primary word is *anoint*, or *chrio*, which means "to smear with oil." *Anointing* is the noun form *chrisma*, which means anything smeared on. These two words convey the idea of anointing for sacred purposes. There is another word, *aleipho*, which means to anoint for cosmetic and medicinal purposes. Oil was a kind of antibiotic in the ancient world. So that's why my parents insisted on giving me castor oil when I was a boy! Whatever had me "ailing" was no match for the castor oil. The Good Samaritan poured oil and wine in the wounds of the man who was mugged and beaten by thieves.

But our primary interest is in the words *chrio (anoint)* and *chrisma (anointing)*. These words convey a beautiful image of the Holy Spirit. Oil and anointing with oil are Bible emblems for the person of the Holy Spirit and his work. The Holy Spirit is not oil. But oil represents the Holy Spirit. Picture a flash card with oil on one side and the Holy Spirit on the other.

The anointing oil was made of specially prepared spices (Exod. 30:24ff), and each of these spices represents the Lord Jesus. This is just what we are told the Holy Spirit is to do. So the anointing oil is a beautiful symbol of the person of the Holy Spirit and his empowering to point to the Lord Jesus Christ.

In the Old Testament, places could be anointed. Think of the tabernacle. Moses was instructed that all of the offerings and every article of furniture were to be anointed with the holy oil (Exod. 40:9ff). The anointing oil was used to consecrate, to set apart, or to make holy the wilderness worship center for the Jews.

People were also anointed in the Old Testament. When lepers were cleansed, they were anointed with oil (Lev. 14:10ff). Actually, three liquids were applied in the cleansing ceremony. Look at this figuratively, and you see that each of these liquids teaches spiritual truth. The blood is applied, picturing salvation by the blood of Christ. Water is used to wash the leper, picturing the need for new believers to be sanctified by the Word of God. Then oil is applied, pointing toward empowering for service. The priest pours the oil in the palm of his left hand. With his right hand he smears oil on the right ear. We are to hear for God. It is smeared on the right thumb. We are to work for God. It is smeared on the big toe of the right foot. We are to go for God. Then the rest is poured over the leper's head. We are to be all for God!

In the Old Testament, people in special offices were also anointed. God anointed prophets to speak to the people, and priests were anointed to speak to God for the people. Kings were anointed to lead the people for God. For example, David, Israel's great king, was anointed to be king three times. On the first occasion, when he was anointed, "the Spirit of the LORD came upon David from that day forward" (1 Sam. 16:13 KJV). In the New Testament these three offices are beautifully merged in the Lord Jesus who is the Christ, *Christos*, the Anointed One.

The anointing of the priest (Exod. 40) should be examined further. The priest was sprinkled with the blood, washed with the water, and clad in holy garments. Then he was anointed with oil. The purpose of this anointing was to set the priest apart to minister. The anointing sets apart the priest for the purpose of service. In the Old Testament, anointing has two primary purposes: setting apart and empowering to service. The anointing of the Holy Spirit gave power to each person to minister or serve in that office.

We're talking about the anointing; and in the Old Testament several passages mention this. Charismatic teachers make a great deal of Isaiah 10:27,

"The yoke shall be destroyed because of the anointing" (KJV). This passage is often taken out of context. A careful study of the passage indicates a reference to the Assyrians. After devastating the land of Judah, they attacked Jerusalem. The passage promises such great blessings from God that His people will grow fat and thus break off the yoke of the Assyrians. The NIV renders the verse,

> The yoke will be broken
> because you have grown so fat.

Some writers translate, "Because of the ointment." Think about the context here before applying the verse today.

Now let's click on the New Testament. Actually, there are very few references to the anointing in the New Testament. Why is that? There are only seven of them that apply to this. The other references have to do with the burial of Jesus and people being anointed for cosmetic purposes, etc.

There are four specific references to the anointing of the Lord Jesus (Luke 4:18; Acts 4:27; Acts 10:38; Heb. 1:9). Let's look at two of them. Acts 10:38 states that Jesus was anointed and, as a result, he was anointed with the Holy Spirit and with power.

Jesus then "went about doing good, and healing all that were oppressed of the devil; for God was with him" (Acts 10:38 KJV). I remember the first time I went back to preach at my home church in Georgia. Family and friends were there, all checking out the local boy who made a preacher. In Luke 4:18–19 Jesus visits his home church. The Scripture reading that day was from Isaiah 61:1–2. He found the Scripture and then read,

> "The Spirit of the Lord is on me,
>     because he has anointed me
>     to preach good news to the poor.
> He has sent me to proclaim freedom for the prisoners
>     and recovery of sight for the blind,
> to release the oppressed,
>     to proclaim the year of the Lord's favor."
> Then he closed the book and said to the people, "Today this
> scripture is fulfilled in your hearing" (Luke 4:18–21).

Look at the big picture. Luke 3:22 records the baptism of Jesus. After he was baptized, the Holy Spirit descended in a bodily shape like a dove upon him. My belief is that this is when he was anointed by the Holy Spirit. Luke 4:1 indicates that he returned from his baptism experience "full of the Holy Spirit." So Jesus had experienced a special anointing.

In quoting Isaiah 61:1–2, Jesus identified himself as the "Anointed One." How does this work? His anointing is related to preaching and to ministering to the needs of people. This anointing equipped Jesus to preach the Word with precision. Jesus did not read the entire Isaiah text. He stopped after "to proclaim the year of the Lord's favor." Yet, the passage in Isaiah continues, "and the day of vengeance of our God." You've probably heard Paul Harvey on radio tell "the rest of the story." Jesus did not tell "the rest of the story" because it would not be fulfilled until a later time.

So the anointing enabled Jesus to use Scripture precisely. The anointing also enabled Jesus to preach with pathos. Jesus met many needs in his preaching. When he finished, Luke 4:22 says that the people "all spoke well of him and were amazed at the gracious words that came from his lips."

Regarding believers, the anointing is used three times (2 Cor. 1:21; 1 John 2:20, 27). Look at 2 Corinthians 1:21, "Now it is God who makes both us and you stand firm in Christ. He anointed us." The verb for "anoint" here is an aorist participle, indicating something which occurred in the past. The next verse says he has "set his seal of ownership on us, and put his Spirit in our hearts as a deposit, guaranteeing what is to come" (v. 22). The verbs in this verse also indicate past action. First John 2:20 says, "But you have an anointing from the Holy One, and all of you know the truth." Verse 27 says, "As for you, the anointing you received from him remains in you, and you do not need anyone to teach you. But as his anointing teaches you about all things and as that anointing is real, not counterfeit—just as it has taught you, remain in him." The verb "received" in verse 27 is also aorist, pointing to something which occurred at a definite point in the past.

These verses also describe further understanding of the Word of God and being able to discern the truth of Scripture when it is taught. All references seem to point to a place of service (in Paul's instance, preaching) and power for service. Position of service and power to fulfill the position are indicated. Being anointed to preach (indicated by Paul in 2 Cor. 1) is one clear example of this.

Some people in the Charismatic movement distinguish between an inside anointing and an outside anointing. They may take the position that the anointing mentioned in 1 John 2 is the inside anointing. But the reference to the Holy Spirit being "on" believers indicates an additional outside anointing. What does this mean? Hagin says that they even feel different.[7] Look at the use of the preposition "on" or "upon." It is used in reference to Jesus (John 1:32–33; Luke 3:22; 4:18). Jesus was anointed in a manner we can never be. As it relates to believers, the word *on* occurs in several significant places (Luke 24:49; Acts 1:8; 2:17; 8:16; 10:44–45; 11:15; 19:6).

Consider again that "on" in these passages is used as a figure of speech. The Holy Spirit comes on Jesus like a dove lighting on (John 1:32); the Holy Spirit is sent on (Luke 24:49); the Holy Spirit comes on (Acts 1:8); the Holy Spirit is poured out on (Acts 2:17); and the Holy Spirit falls on (Acts 10:44). In connection with believers, such terminology occurs only in Luke and Acts, dealing with Spirit baptism and the coming of the Holy Spirit upon him.

"On" or "upon" is used in a similar fashion once more in the New Testament. First Peter 4:14 says that if a believer is reproached for the name of Christ he is to be happy, "for the Spirit of glory and of God rests on you." The "on" references indicate the same experience as Spirit baptism. The terms refer to the same experience.

Frederick Bruner, in his classic work on the Holy Spirit, indicated that the use of the preposition *epi* (translated *on* or *upon)* is not so much a space usage as a source usage. It is not that the Holy Spirit moves from point A to point B. It is a source usage—the point being that the power of the Holy Spirit does not originate from the emotional life or the spiritual life of the recipient but rather that the power originates from God. The Holy Spirit comes not from within the person but from "on high" (see Luke 24:49).[8]

Let's hit the *unction function* key again.

## Explanation

Some of the terminology and the experiences used by Charismatics to describe the anointing are not found in the Bible. There is no indication that the anointing is an experience which comes after salvation or beyond Spirit baptism. The anointing cannot be transferred from one person to another, and there is no evidence that the Holy Spirit feels like electricity or fire. No one ever described such sensations in the New Testament. Finally, nothing in

Scripture reveals that certain physical manifestations occur when one receives an experience that might be described as the anointing.

Second Corinthians 1:21 and 1 John 2:20 and 27 make it apparent that all believers have the anointing. It is not an experience for elite Christians. All have the anointing. At the moment of salvation, the anointing of the Holy Spirit is received. A person does not have to have a vision of Jesus to be anointed. Nor does one need for another to pass it on. It never says anyone laid hands on a New Testament Christian and he or she received an anointing. It is nowhere said that people were touched and had certain physical feelings as a result of an anointing. When were you anointed? It happened when you were saved.

It is clear from the New Testament that each Christian has a special place of service. Preachers need the anointing to preach sermons. I never walk into a pulpit to preach without claiming the anointing of the Holy Spirit. My place of service is the ministry of the Word. If you are a Christian, you have also been given a job to do. The presence of the Holy Spirit in your life means that you have been set apart, or sanctified, to serve Jesus in some capacity.

Here's the good news. Click on this: As you serve, the Holy Spirit will provide the power. The Holy Spirit provides the anointing necessary to do the job. The anointing is available for whatever service you give in Jesus' name. When you teach, the Holy Spirit will provide the power to teach effectively and with blessing. As a Christian wife and mother, you can have the blessings of and be empowered by the Holy Spirit. Christian businesswoman or Christian doctor, the Holy Spirit will provide the power to serve Jesus in your place of opportunity.

Because of the presence of the Holy Spirit in your life, you have great potential to do what God wants you to do. Power is available. Paul says in 1 Timothy 1:12, "I thank Christ Jesus our Lord, who has given me strength, that he considered me faithful, appointing me to his service." It is the Lord who puts us in a ministry or place of service, and it is the Lord who enables us to carry out his purposes. This enabling from God is the anointing.

Remember, you can claim Holy Spirit anointing for every instance of service. Because the Holy Spirit is in your life, the anointing is available twenty-four hours a day, seven days a week. But you must appropriate what is already yours in Christ. The Bible commands us to be filled with the Spirit. So we must seek the filling of the Holy Spirit by yielding our life to the control of the Holy Spirit. Then we must claim the anointing for whatever service we give.

What a truth! We can claim Holy Spirit anointing as we work and witness for Jesus.

Do you want fulfillment and joy in life? Serve in the anointing of the Holy Spirit, and it will do something for you. You will feel the power and bless those around you. Remember what Jesus said about his own ministry anointed by the Holy Spirit? The gospel will be preached to the poor. People who are broken-hearted will be healed. Captives will be delivered. Those who are spiritually blind will see.

## Testing, Testing . . .

1. The Bible Test. What does the Bible say about the manifestation? Is it clearly taught in the Bible?

2. The Jesus Test. Does it honor and glorify Jesus? Is Jesus, the Holy Spirit, or the Christian the focus?

3. The Character Test. Does it contribute to a more Christlike life?

4. The Decency and Order Test. Is this within the guidelines of decency and order?

5. The Evangelism Test. Does it place the focus on winning people to Christ?

   Does it pass?
   YES _____
   NO _____

## CHAPTER 8

# IS THIS
# A GOD THING?

Have you noticed any TV commercials lately? Or the promos on the radio? They are very slick! If a product or a TV show isn't advertised within about an eight-second sound bite, good-bye audience!

This shows that our culture today is entertainment driven. We want a show. We seek experiences that feed our emotions and our senses. Look at pro football. What is the appeal? The violence, the physical action, and the high-powered emotion. It's a live entertainment experience!

This quest for experience and entertainment has seeped into our churches. Pastor Jerry Spencer says, "This is the day of the tabloid with an emphasis on the wild and the weird, the odd and the outlandish, the freaks and the fakes."[1] There is almost a freak-show mentality to our church services today—Jerry Springer at the altar! If the parishioners can't be thrilled and entertained, they won't come back to church.

In some churches today you'll hear about strange experiences like being "under the power," or "soaked in the Spirit," or "resting in the Spirit." A phenomenon, known as being "slain in the Spirit," is sweeping through many pentecostal-Charismatic churches today. Have you heard of it? When "slain," some people are knocked to the floor unconscious. Others shake. Some laugh.

Others lie paralyzed, unable to move. Many Charismatic leaders teach that believers need to experience this "slaying" or "soaking" with the power often.

The "slain in the Spirit" phenomenon is consistent with the Charismatic emphasis. Virtually every experience one has with God is accompanied by physical manifestations. This fits our entertainment-driven culture. Yet the focus has shifted from proclamation of the Word of God to manifestations of the Spirit of God. In some settings the emphasis on physical phenomena overrides and obscures the preaching and teaching of the Bible.

Supporters of the "slain" movement point out that these experiences have historical context and were part of revivals in America's past. At the Cane Ridge camp meetings in Kentucky, for example, many unusual physical manifestations occurred. There were many converts, and it seemed that great good was done in the lives of people. Yet there were some harmful extremes. While "slain," some unconsciously stripped and exhibited lewd behavior.[2] Special patrols checked the grounds because of a great deal of sexual immorality.[3]

Is this "slain" movement a God thing? What's up with the bizarre and extreme behavior? Christians need to be careful in evaluating all phenomena which occur under the umbrella of Christianity. This chapter will help you in this way.

Let's find out if this is a God thing.

## Observing

Being "slain in the Spirit" is not new. Pentecostalism has always had experiences fitting into the "slain" category. This was true at the Azusa meeting (see preface) early in the twentieth century. It was also true when I was a boy. My father sang in a quartet, and I attended many Pentecostal churches with him. I often saw people fall on the floor, exhibiting strange behaviors. Because of this, some call Pentecostals "Holy Rollers."

People still fall to the floor and lie for a period of time. In some places there is laughing, even making animal sounds. Some even lose consciousness for hours, and some report they are unable to walk. Others say such experiences leave them feeling drunk. This modern phenomenon needs to be examined.

What about this "slain" experience? Is it transferred from one place to another? I have mentioned that people traveling to the Toronto Blessing or to the Pensacola Revival have received this experience. By visiting churches where the "slain" experience is occurring or by an influential leader's visit, the experience seems to be transferred from location to location.

The "slain" experience may also be transferred from one person to another. Richard Roberts, president of Oral Roberts University, says that his experience of being "slain" in a Howard Rodney-Browne laughing service changed his life. Returning to Oral Roberts University, he canceled classes for two days so students might have the opportunity to receive the gift of holy laughter.[4]

Howard Rodney-Browne's experience is interesting. In 1979, he was praying for a deeper experience with God. In his words, he told God, "You come down here and touch me or I will come up there and touch you." This sounds more like "my will be done" than our Lord's "thy will be done." In the midst of that prayer, Rodney-Brown says that "his whole body felt like it was on fire." He began to laugh uncontrollably. Then he wept and began to speak in tongues.[5]

The "slain" manifestation has different aspects. Normally it occurs publicly, but some "slain" experiences take place privately. In addition, it seems that the power of this experience can be passed on. By laying on of hands, such as touching the forehead or chest, the experience happens. Some leaders even blow upon people or strike them with their coats.

Have you heard about catchers? No, not the baseball guys. These are people who catch the other people as they fall to keep them from hurting themselves. And there are also those who move quickly to cover women with coats or blankets when they fall prostrate on the floor.

Teaching varies about the meaning of the "slain" experience. It is not easy to determine one uniform belief. Some say it is an evidence of receiving the baptism. Others say it is receiving the anointing. Some even say that the direction one falls is significant. If one falls backward, he or she is a follower. If one falls forward, he or she is a leader.[6]

The reviews are mixed—some thumbs up, others thumbs down. Some churches report that the "slain" manifestation has brought great blessing and revival. For others, disruption and confusion have been the aftermath. A young man from the church where I am pastor served as youth director in a church. His pastor went to a place where the "slain" experience was occurring. The pastor was "slain." He returned to the church and passed it on to many in the congregation. The church split over the matter. The pastor left, and great harm was done.

What can we say about the "slain" phenomenon? To some people, even questioning the reality of the movement causes hostility. Some discourage any examination of the manifestation by the teachings of the Bible. Surely manifestations may occur which are not of God, and this fact should cause all Christians to be not only willing but also eager to examine any manifestation by the teachings of Scripture. Is this a God thing?

## Searching

Let's get real about this "slain" manifestation. It definitely has worldwide, interdenominational appeal. But truthfulness isn't determined by mass appeal. When some unusual or out-of-the ordinary phenomenon occurs (like an episode of the TV show *The X-Files*), we must investigate it carefully by the teachings of the Bible. First John 4:1 tells us we are to "test the spirits to see whether they are from God." We must be like the Berean Christians in this matter by searching the Scriptures to find whether these things are true (Acts 17:11).

Many Scriptures are used to support the Bible teaching of the "slain" experience. I have studied every passage I have encountered as Bible precedent for the "slain" phenomenon. I can't possibly deal with all of them. So I'll look at a few representative passages.

As we look at these passages, we should ask questions like these: Who is involved? Where do the manifestations happen? Did people fall? How? Why? Is the Holy Spirit mentioned in the passage? What is the purpose of the experience? Is God teaching some new truth here? Is this intended to be a normal experience for Christians today? Is this something all believers should seek?

Look at a few Old Testament passages. First, consider Abraham's experience in Genesis 15:1–21. God came to Abraham in a time when Abraham was evidently alone. God instructed him to cut several animals in two. As you read, you will discover that God was initiating a covenant with Abraham. Verse 12 says, "As the sun was setting, Abram fell into a deep sleep, and a thick and dreadful darkness came over him." It does not say that Abraham fell. But a deep sleep and a horror of darkness fell upon him. Abraham was not touched by any person. Only the Lord was there. The Holy Spirit is not mentioned in the passage. There was a very special purpose for Abraham's experience with God. God revealed to Abraham the future of his people and that he had entered into a covenant with Abraham that his people would be given the land.

Look at 2 Chronicles 5:14. It's about the dedication of Solomon's magnificent, beautiful temple. The priests were involved. As they ministered before the Lord with sacrifices, singing, and great praise, the glory cloud of God filled the place. The glory cloud (in the Old Testament) is always an indication of the presence of God. The presence of God in the cloud was so awesome that verse 14 says, "The priests could not stand to minister by reason of the cloud: for the glory of the LORD had filled the house of God" (KJV).

God had moved into the temple. There was a new phase of God's relationship with His people, the Jews. There was a sense of awe and an overwhelming consciousness of God's presence. No one touched the priests. This certainly does not indicate something that is to be considered normal today.

Remember Daniel? He was the great prophet-statesman of the Old Testament. God revealed to Daniel the whole history of Gentile world rule and the truth concerning the return of Jesus Christ at the end of the age.

Daniel 4:19 is about Nebuchadnezzar's dream. God had given Nebuchadnezzar this dream as judgment. The verse says that Daniel was "greatly perplexed for a time, and his thoughts alarmed him." Here he was, standing before Nebuchadnezzar. There is no record that he fell. No one touched him. There's no mention here of the Holy Spirit. Basically, this passage shows how "blown away" Daniel was at the magnitude of this dream which pronounced judgment on a pagan king.

In Daniel 8:16–18 Daniel was visited by the angel Gabriel. When Gabriel came near to him, Daniel said, "I was terrified and fell prostrate" (v. 17). We don't know whether Gabriel touched him. In verse 18 Daniel says, "I was in a deep sleep, with my face to the ground." He was physically overwhelmed and awed by the angel's appearance. Did the angel touch him? Yes. Verse 18 continues, "he touched me and raised me to my feet." Rather than knocking Daniel down, the angel touched him and put him back on his feet. Remember the context here. It's about the end times. There is no indication that this experience of Daniel is to be a normal, expected experience for believers today.

Look at a few New Testament passages. In John 18:1–6 Judas brought a group of soldiers to the Garden of Gethsemane to arrest the Lord Jesus. As they approached, Jesus said, "Who is it you want?" They replied, "Jesus of Nazareth." Jesus responded, "I am he." Literally he said, "I AM," using the Old Testament name for God.

At this the soldiers "drew back and fell to the ground" (v. 6). No one touched them; they fell because of fear. But they evidently got off the ground quickly and arrested Jesus. They were not believers, and the Holy Spirit is not mentioned. They fell as ungodly, fearful men in response to the presence of the great I AM himself, the Lord Jesus. This has nothing to do with salvation or experiences with the Holy Spirit.

Remember Saul's conversion experience (Acts 9:3–9)? Saul and others with him were on the way to Damascus to arrest Christians. A light from heaven suddenly shined upon him. He fell to the earth and heard a voice asking, "Saul, Saul, why do you persecute me?" (9:4). He was told to arise and go into the city. Saul got up, after this encounter with a resurrected Lord Jesus, blinded. For three days he couldn't see. There is no indication that anyone touched him. Evidently he was not unconscious. The Holy Spirit is not mentioned in the passage until verse 17 when Ananias laid hands on Saul.

At this time, Saul was filled with the Holy Spirit and received his sight again and was baptized. See, Saul was a chosen vessel of the Lord. He was unique. Saul was one of the apostles, and he would be used to write Scripture. Is what happened to Saul on the Damascus road normative for today? Not really, because there is no indication that it is. In many other places in Acts, people who have no such experience are saved. What about your own experience? Were you struck blind for three days? We have no evidence that Christians are to seek this experience.

Acts 10:9–10 is often used to teach a "slain in the Spirit" experience. Simon Peter was alone on the rooftop of Simon the tanner in Joppa. It was prayer time. He was hungry. Verse 10 says, "He fell into a trance" and received a significant vision from heaven. Actually, after reading the Greek text, one realizes it does not say that Peter fell. I have checked many translations and have found only one that translates the text correctly. Moffatt translates the statement, "A trance came over him." The Greek text says, "An ecstasy fell upon him." The Greek word *ekstasis* indicates a state in which a person stands outside himself. By some sudden emotion he is transported out of his usual realm. This carries the idea of being amazed, astonished, or being thrown into a state of wonder. It often indicates the reaction of people to a manifestation of God's presence.

So did Peter fall into a trance? No, an ecstasy fell upon him. Why? Peter was going to receive a world-changing revelation. The Gentiles as well as the Jews would be part of the church. No believers were to be considered common or unclean any more. All could come to Christ equally for salvation. One did not have to become a Jew in order to become a Christian. Receiving such a revelation had to be awesome. But we have no evidence that what happened to Simon Peter in any way portrays what we can expect as Christians today.

Look at one other New Testament example. The apostle John was exiled on the island of Patmos. Revelation 1:10 says that he was "in the Spirit" "on the Lord's Day." On that lonely island of Patmos, John received a vision of the risen Christ. He was given a revelation that would lay out the entire future of the world and the final triumph of the Lamb of God, the Lord Jesus Christ. John's response to this vision is given in verse 17, "When I saw him, I fell at his feet as though dead." Was John "slain"? No, John was afraid. This is why verse 17 continues, "Then he [Jesus] placed his right hand on me and said: 'Do not be afraid.'" The Lord laid his hand on John after he fell, not before. This is certainly not the model for Christians today. John was going to receive revelation that would become a part of your Bible. This cannot be compared to the "slain in the Spirit" experience today.

Looking at these Bible passages, we can summarize that most of the time when people fell it was out of fear or as a worshipful and reverent response to a holy God. Every fall was caused by the presence of God or angels. There is no indication in any of these instances that the person or persons expected such an experience or sought it. There is also no evidence that there were "catchers." None of the people we have examined lost their self-control.

In every Bible example I have found, a significant purpose was intended by the manifestation. Comparing what is happening today to these Bible instances is questionable.

There is not one instance in the New Testament where Jesus or his apostles laid hands on people and they were "slain." In Matthew 17:5–7, when Jesus was transfigured before them and they saw and heard what was taking place on that mountain, "They fell facedown to the ground, terrified." Then and only then did Jesus come and touch them, telling them to "get up; . . . don't be afraid" (v. 7). This is far different from today's experiences.

*The Dictionary of Pentecostal and Charismatic Movements* was written by and for Pentecostal and Charismatic scholars. The book's statement on the "slain" phenomena is informative: "An entire battalion of Scripture proof texts is enlisted to support the legitimacy of the phenomenon, although Scripture plainly offers no support for the phenomenon as something to be expected in the normal Christian's life."[7] My own examination of Scripture leads me to the same conclusion.

## Evaluating

Is this a God thing? Certainly, God is a God of all power, and it is an awesome experience to be in his presence. I would never deny or minimize his power. But I am bound to discover what Scripture says and to follow wherever it may lead. My own study of the Bible as it relates to the "slain in the Spirit" phenomenon leads me to believe that what we see today has no counterpart in the Bible. Nothing in the Old Testament or New Testament even comes close to the mass falling out, laughter, or "glued to the floor" experiences reported today. There is no shouting "more," "fill," or "sic 'em" experiences anywhere to be found. The experiences in the Bible are revelations God gave to people like Abraham, Daniel, Peter, Paul, and John. Today's experiences just don't compare.

Acts gives no clear record that anything like a "slain" phenomenon happened in the early church services. The believers of the day did not go somewhere to get this experience. Their leaders didn't bring the experience with them. There are no clear-cut statements in the epistles of the New Testament to support it. No verse mentions such an experience or encourages people to seek such an experience. Any attempt to tie today's phenomenon to Bible passages is a real stretch.

If this manifestation is something of God, why are "catchers" needed? The power of the Holy Spirit is quite able to let a person down safely. If the practice is continued, however, I would encourage continued use of "catchers." Some caution should be exercised because there are reports of physical harm being done. One woman fell, hit her head on the concrete floor, and spent a week in the hospital.[8] Does the Holy Spirit come on people with lethal force through touch, slapping, or shouting by a third party?

Are there other explanations? It may be satanic. I do not say it is. I say we must recognize the possibility that it may be. We have examples in the Bible of demonic activity causing these kinds of things. A man with an unclean spirit was thrown down (Luke 4:35). A young child was also thrown down and torn by a demon in Luke 9:42. We do know whether similar phenomena occur today in other religions. Oriental Ramakvishna Samadhi trances involve similar experiences like involuntary falling down, rapturous states of superconscious bliss, beautiful visions, and astral projection. The Samadhi could send others into this state with a single touch to the head or chest.[9]

New Age Kundalini Energy reports similar experiences. Those involved in this process find it difficult to control their behavior. They exhibit unnatural laughter, talking in tongues, and animal sounds and movements.[10] More than twenty years ago Watchman Nee, a widely read Christian writer, issued a warning to the church. He pointed out that man's soul power is often Satan's working instrument. His view was that man's soul power would be used in the last days as a substitute for God's gospel and power. He predicted that many Christians in the last days would be deceived by Satan's use of counterfeit power.[11]

Crowd manipulation may also be an explanation. I'm not saying it is. I am saying we need to look at the possibilities. We know that through the strong suggestions, touching, or motions of a powerful teacher, unusual phenomena can occur. The repetition of certain musical rhythms can produce altered states of consciousness. Anyone who has ever attended a rock concert knows this. Under the influence of a driving beat and repetitive rhythm, people can do unbelievable things. People have disrobed, shouted profanities, and thrown undergarments on the stage. The simplest gestures and motions can have powerful effects on people conditioned for an experience. Thoughtful Christians should consider other explanations.

Why was the "slain" experience not common to great saints of Christian history? Why don't all spiritual Christians have it? Does this mean they are less spiritual? Are they missing out on something big? Why doesn't this happen when Jesus comes into a person's life? Is Holy Spirit power greater than that of the Father and of the Son? If the Holy Spirit comes in at salvation, does God hold back this kind of power until some time later?

Here are some final observations. God is real. He is all-powerful. He does manifest himself. He manifests himself preeminently in the Son of God, the Lord Jesus Christ; the Word of God; the Bible; and the Spirit of God, the Holy Spirit. Simply put, to have a relationship with such a God is an overwhelming experience.

When the Holy Spirit is at work in our lives, there will be a profound sense of God's holiness and our sinfulness. Like Isaiah, when we see the Lord lifted up in all of his majesty, holiness, and power, our response can only be, "I'm in trouble big time!" Yet we do not have to fear the Holy Spirit. You can safely place your life, mind, emotions, and will in the hands of the Holy Spirit. Keep in mind, however, that our emotions are the shallowest part of our personality. God does not do his deepest work in the shallowest part of our lives. We need to recapture a sense of reverence and humility in the awesome presence of God. My view is that when the Holy Spirit works in our lives we will not be "slain" but we will "come alive" in the Spirit.

Also remember discernment. It is always right for Christians to search the Scriptures and to ask the Holy Spirit for discernment. Just accepting what comes because many are involved is not evidence of the presence and power of God.

I have talked with many people who got caught up in certain physical manifestations and became disillusioned. They have experienced great anxiety, depression, and even doubt about God. I believe even more will "crash" in the future. We need to be there for them, informed with the truth of God's Word.

Many people who seek physical manifestations have a real hunger for God. We should deal with the deadness and the lack of reality existing in our churches. But we must never accept a substitute for the real thing. Don't be fooled by those who say that if the church services are not some kind of wild frenzy, then the church is dead. Our hunger for God shouldn't cause us to seek the sensational. Instead, seek the substantial power of God and pray for genuine Spirit-led revival. Phil Roberts says, "The marks of great revival are worship, evangelism, and reformation of society through Christian service."[12]

We must seek what God says—his enabling, enduring, empowering presence. Remember that true spirituality will not cause you to be out of control but will give you a Spirit-aided self-control. Don't seek a party; seek a Person and know what is and what isn't a God thing.

## My Commitment to the Holy Spirit

I daily surrender my life to your majestic might, O Holy Spirit. For many years now I have known your special presence and have been awed by your power. I am too far down the road with you to get caught up in the passing trends of emotion and religious thrill seeking. I continue to long for your true manifestations. I will not get sidetracked by the glamour and the glitter of the supersensational. Take control of me, O Spirit of God. Make me alive by your quickening, energizing, witnessing, life-changing, Jesus-exalting power. You are Holy, O Spirit. You are in me. I will never have to be ashamed or fear what you cause me to do. You will never cause me to focus on you but will always point me to the Lord Jesus. You will give me a burning desire to tell others about the Lord Jesus.

## Testing, Testing . . .

1. The Bible Test. What does the Bible say about this manifestation? Is it clearly taught in the Bible?
2. The Jesus Test. Does it honor and glorify Jesus? Is Jesus, the Holy Spirit, or the Christian the focus?
3. The Character Test. Does it contribute to a more Christlike life?
4. The Decency and Order Test. Is this within the guidelines of decency and order?
5. The Evangelism Test. Does it place the focus on winning people to Christ?

   Does it pass?
   YES _____
   NO _____

# CHAPTER 9

# GET ON THE BUS!

Have you ever been on a bus ride? What about a bus tour? Sometimes I see a big name performer like Garth Brooks, and I think about his life on the road. While on tour, he must stop in lots of small and big towns and perform. I'm sure he meets many fans. This must be some life.

Think about this chapter as a bus tour—a power tour—a journey to find out about signs and wonders and the power or lack of power behind them today. So get on the bus and come along for the power tour.

Recently I was interviewed on radio at a Midwestern station. During the call-in segment of the show, a man suggested that I needed his experience of receiving Spirit baptism to win more people to Christ. He explained that he began to have visions after his baptism in the Holy Spirit and that these visions helped him win multitudes to Christ. One time, he said, he went into a convenience store and talked with the clerk. It was revealed to him, apparently, that her name was Kim and that she had almost been in a car crash. She immediately began to weep, and she wondered how he knew her name and about the near-death experience. The man won Kim to Christ, and he said it was because of these visions he had been given.

This is called "power evangelism" in the Charismatic movement. The idea is that the power of the gospel lies not only in the message itself but also in supernatural demonstrations of Holy Spirit power.

John Wimber, one of the originators of the power evangelism concept, defined it as "a spontaneous, Spirit-inspired, empowered presentation of the Gospel . . . preceded and undergirded by supernatural demonstrations of God's presence."[1] What a concept! The gospel is to be accompanied by healings, exorcisms, visions, and special words of knowledge. In the New Testament, it is pointed out, early Christians did signs and wonders and miracles resulting in the salvation of the lost. Proponents of power evangelism say we should expect the same supernatural occurrences today.

Proponents of power evangelism contrast it with proclamation or programmatic evangelism. In this kind of evangelism, the message of the gospel is presented, people make decisions, but they do not encounter God's power. Their salvation experience, then, is somewhat inadequate. If they do not experience signs and wonders, they miss out somewhat on what God is doing.

Power evangelism, as it is called, is especially appealing to people in Third World countries who are keenly aware of the spiritual realm. So to see many kinds of miracles, such as healings, visions, etc., opens the door for effective evangelism. Power evangelism also is appealing in American culture. Americans love power. We like power football. We have power lunches. We are impressed by demonstrations of power in every realm. An entire movement is developing in America, as well as in other countries, around the idea of power evangelism.

The two men most associated with power evangelism are John Wimber (deceased) and Peter Wagner. As mentioned previously, Wimber was the founder of the Vineyard Fellowship movement. As a result of his study of the Gospel of Luke, he became convinced that healings, tongues, and other manifestations are necessary to produce dramatic evangelistic results. By implementing these concepts in his own church, his church experienced phenomenal growth. It moved rapidly from just seventeen people to more than six thousand. Wagner is a former missionary and a professor at Fuller Seminary. He became impressed by the phenomenal growth of Pentecostal-Charismatic churches worldwide. He too became convinced that power evangelism is the method to reach multitudes for Christ. It is said of Wagner that he has "done a remarkable job of marketing various Pentecostal themes in a way that appeals to Evangelicals."[2]

Power evangelism is also a part of a latter-day rain revival concept, tying into the belief that before Christ returns a great final harvest will occur. There will be an unprecedented ingathering of lost people. One belief integral to power evangelism is that signs and wonders must be practiced to prepare for the preaching of the Word. These miracles provide powerful evidence for the message of the gospel and bolster the credibility of the Word as it is preached. Multitudes can then be saved. The idea is that the church is weak today because it hasn't taken advantage of these sign gifts. These signs and wonders provide a blending of fervor to reach the lost with Holy Spirit manifestations such as healing, being slain in the Spirit, speaking in tongues, prophecy, and visions. All of this is appealing today.

Do you have passion to reach the lost? Then you'll be interested in power evangelism. The church I serve as pastor has had a great history of reaching lost people for Christ. I am part of a denomination (Southern Baptist) which has been in the forefront of reaching people for Christ in America and throughout the world. Are we missing out on something? Is there a power available to us that could help us reach multitudes for Christ?

Let's begin our power tour.

## Observing

Power evangelism takes place in what's called a "power encounter." This is especially effective in Third World countries where the kingdom of God and the kingdom of Satan often clash. Signs and wonders provide a visible, dramatic demonstration that Jesus Christ is more powerful than the gods and spirits of the people. Wimber suggests that these power encounters were similar to the one between Elijah and the prophets of Baal on Mount Carmel. Elijah prayed down fire out of heaven. The prophets of Baal could not. The people were convinced that the God of Israel was the true God. Wouldn't you be?

Many accounts illustrate the idea of the power encounter. Peter Wagner tells about a witch doctor in India. A flyer with a picture of Jesus announced a gospel preaching service. The witch doctor put the picture on a shelf in his hut with pictures of his other gods. He needed a test. He placed tiny balls of cow dung fuel in front of each picture. A flame ignited in front of the picture of Jesus. This convinced him. According to Wagner, he is now a fervent evangelist for Jesus.[3]

What's up with power in the Third World? It's all about the nature of the Eastern worldview which involves three levels of reality. The first is the natural world. The middle level is the world inhabited by spirits, ghosts, demons, and ancestors. The third is the level of heaven and hell, God or gods. Some say supernatural demonstrations are necessary in a culture like this to convince the people of the reality of the gospel.

Think about American culture. America was once dominated philosophically by three "isms." First, *secularism* left no room for divine intervention. Second, *materialism* taught that matter is all there is and that there is no supernatural reality in existence. Third, *mechanism* taught that the universe is simply made up of physical causes and effects. Some say Christians have been affected by these "isms." This is not, of course, correct of all Christians. All Bible-believing Christians have faith in the supernatural. Most do not believe in the supernaturalism prevalent in Third World countries.

But the failure of science and technology are painfully obvious today. The basic problems of life defy scientific or technological solutions. Technology can bring the world to our computer screens, but it can't bring peace to our hearts. A recent study indicated higher rates of depression among Internet users. Americans are now willing to accept the supernatural—to accept the reality of a world beyond the one they can see and touch. So America is now ripe for "signs and wonders" evangelism. Too many churches in America have been influenced by the "isms" and are not growing like the churches in Third World countries, according to advocates of power evangelism. If a church will just seek New Testament demonstrations of signs and wonders, so they say, great revival and ingathering of the lost in America will happen.

So what's the deal here? What is the purpose of power encounters? Power encounters using signs and wonders overcome resistance to the gospel. Advocates say gospel preaching and teaching alone will never reach the masses for Christ. Signs and wonders must be a part of our evangelism, they say, to produce strong evidences of the truth and power of the gospel. Otherwise, today's culture will not be reached.

How is a sincere Christian who believes the Bible and has a burning desire to reach unsaved people for Christ to respond? We must always ask, What does the Bible say? If there is something available to help us win the lost and it is clearly taught in the Bible, we would be terribly wrong to miss out on it.

## Searching

Let's tour the Old and New Testaments looking for signs and wonders. Throughout the Old Testament supernatural acts of God occur. Many of the miracles in the Bible, a category of signs and wonders, happen in heavy doses at particular periods of time. When Moses led the people of God out of Egypt, for example, manifestations of signs and wonders occurred. Moses himself, by means of a leprous hand made clean, did signs and wonders. He also had a miraculous rod capable of doing signs (Exod. 4:9, 17, 31). The people of Israel believed Moses' signs and wonders (Exod. 4:32; 7:3, 5). They found God to be real.

Next stop on the bus tour are the times of Elijah and Elisha when many miracles occurred. They both performed miracles on Mt. Carmel. Elijah prayed down fire from heaven. Elisha raised a young man from the dead.

The confrontation between Elijah and the prophets of Baal on Mt. Carmel is notable. We must remember that Elijah was an Old Testament prophet, not a New Testament saint. His encounter with the prophets of Baal cannot be a model for encounters today. The power encounter did not accomplish its intended result. Though the people did acknowledge the reality of God, they did not truly repent. The heathen religion of Baalism was not rooted out of the Northern Kingdom.

During the time of Daniel, Israel's exile years, signs and wonders were everywhere. In Daniel 4:2–3, Nebuchadnezzar acknowledged the signs and wonders of the true God. Darius said in 6:27 that

> he performs signs and wonders
> in the heavens and on the earth.

Several miracles are recorded in Daniel, including the interpretation of the dreams by Daniel, the supernatural deliverance in the fiery furnace, and Daniel's rescue from the den of lions.

The prophecy in Joel 2:28–32 also confirms a time when signs and wonders would be done. In other words, prophecies, dreams, and visions would occur with wonders in the heavens and on the earth. Simon Peter quoted this passage on the day of Pentecost and applied it to what was taking place on that occasion (Acts 2).

What was the purpose of these Old Testament signs and wonders? A common thread can be seen throughout all of them. Signs and wonders happened in the Old Testament with new revelation. The signs and wonders were intended to authenticate these revelations. Keep in mind the culmination principle. Using Old Testament passages to establish practices for the church today demands caution. In other words, the bus is approaching a yellow traffic light.

The bus is now rolling into the New Testament. In examining signs and wonders, we see three specific words used. The word *miracles* describes the power of God miraculously manifested to people. It is often translated *power*. The word emphasizes the inherent power of God that produces the miracle. What is a miracle? A miracle is a supernatural intervention of God into the natural course of things. I like to say a miracle is God doing what he chooses to do with his own creation.

The second word is *wonder*. This word refers to the reaction which the miracle causes. New Testament people were filled with wonder when a miracle occurred.

The third word is *sign*, meaning that which indicates authenticity. In other words, the miracle causes wonder among the people, and it points the people to something else in order to authenticate it. The miracle made credible the message that was delivered and the person who delivered it.

Didn't the miracles of Jesus do this when he was on the earth? For instance, the miracles of John's Gospel are called "signs." John 20:30–31 says, "Jesus did many other miraculous signs in the presence of his disciples, which are not recorded in this book. But these are written that you may believe that Jesus is the Christ, the Son of God, and that by believing you may have life in his name." Why was John so selective? His purpose was to convince people that Jesus was the Son of God. As a result, people might believe on Jesus and be saved.

Acts 2:22 talks about the purpose of our Lord's miracles: "Men of Israel, listen to this: Jesus of Nazareth was a man accredited by God to you by miracles, wonders and signs, which God did among you through him, as you yourselves know."

When Jesus did miracles, some people believed, but others did not (see John 2:23–24; 3:2). Further, there were actually times when Jesus preached and no mention of signs and wonders is given (see Matt. 13:1–52; 18:1–35; John 7:14–44). Yet Mark 1:29–34 is interesting. Jesus was performing many miracles and healings in Galilee. Early one morning, Simon Peter and the other disciples went looking for Jesus. He was in a quiet place in prayer. When they found Jesus, they said, "Everyone is looking for you!" (v. 37). Jesus responded, "Let us go somewhere else—to the nearby villages—so I can preach there also. That is why I have come" (v. 38). Jesus placed emphasis on his purpose to preach, not upon his miracles.

Let's survey the teachings of Jesus on signs and wonders. Sometimes he chastised those who were seeking signs (Matt. 16:4; John 4:48). He then pointed to two primary signs. The first was his resurrection (Matt. 16:4; John 2:18–22). The second was his return (Matt. 24:29–30; Luke 21:11, 25). His resurrection marked the beginning of the church age, and his return indicates the end of the church age.

Jesus gave warnings about end-time signs and wonders. He said, "For false Christs and false prophets will appear and perform great signs and miracles to deceive even the elect—if that were possible" (Matt. 24:24). In the parallel passage he said, "For false Christs and false prophets will appear and perform signs and miracles to deceive the elect—if that were possible. So be on your guard; I have told you everything ahead of time" (Mark 13:22–23).

Jesus knew about our tendency to feed on the sensational—our tabloid mentality. He refused, however, to place strong emphasis on the sensational aspects of his ministry. One time his disciples returned to him, pumped up about casting out demons. But Jesus said to them, "Do not rejoice that the spirits submit to you, but rejoice that your names are written in heaven" (Luke 10:20). Jesus told them to derive their joy from the miracle of salvation, the miracle of miracles, not from the miracle of casting out demons.

Jesus gave his disciples, the apostles, a clear commission. Mark 16:15–20 is one version of this commission: "Go into all the world and preach the good news to all creation" (v. 15). He indicated in verse 17, "These signs will accompany those who believe." Who believes? The context of verse 14 points to those who believed in his resurrection. Belief in his resurrection was imperative.

Jesus then named the kinds of signs that will accompany their preaching. He said, "In my name they will drive out demons; they will speak in new tongues; they will pick up snakes with their hands; and when they drink deadly poison, it will not hurt them at all; they will place their hands on sick people, and they will get well" (v. 18). Add verse 20 to this: "Then the disciples went out and preached everywhere, and the Lord worked with them and confirmed his word by the signs that accompanied it." Could it be clearer? The apostles' signs were to accompany their verbal proclamation of the Word.

Read the Book of Acts, and you find out that is exactly what the apostles did. You might want to read Acts 2:43; 4:30; 5:12. They point to signs and wonders done by the apostles. Stephen and Philip also did signs and wonders (Acts 6:8; 8:6). Paul, who was also an apostle, did signs and wonders (Acts 14:3; 15:12; 19:11). So signs and wonders were done by apostles and by those closely associated with them.

The apostles were doing groundwork. They were laying the foundation for the church of our Lord (see Eph. 2:20–22). Why were signs and wonders necessary? The people of that day had no New Testament. It was being revealed. The signs and wonders helped the people believe these New Testament messengers and their messages.

In the epistles of the New Testament, references are made to some signs and wonders as spiritual gifts (1 Cor. 12:12, 29–30). Keep in mind that these are sign gifts. When the purpose for the sign is removed, there is no longer a need for the sign. The connection between the apostles and signs and wonders cannot be missed (Rom. 15:19; 2 Cor. 12:12; Gal. 3:5; Heb. 2:4). Their time was one of new revelation. God used them as human messengers to bring New Testament revelation to its completion. When the New Testament canon was completed, there was no further need for these signs and wonders.

Before the bus leaves the exposition stop, one other facet should be noted. Just as Jesus warned of signs and wonders done by false christs and false prophets, Paul warned about end-time signs as well. In 2 Thessalonians 2:9, Paul discussed the career of the Antichrist. The Antichrist will be the ruler of a one-world government, combining political, economic, and religious entities. Part of his end-time deception will be "all power and signs and lying wonders" (KJV). Further reference is made to these false signs and wonders in Revelation 13:13–14; 16:14; 19:20.

These passages are warnings. More is said in the New Testament about false signs and wonders in the end time than about true signs and wonders. In other words, no verse in the New Testament indicates that signs and wonders will be a prominent part of church activity in the end times.

## Evaluating

It pays to evaluate. Evaluating signs and wonders in the Bible can be very helpful. In the New Testament, signs and wonders had a specific purpose. Their purpose was to authenticate the message of those who preached in the apostolic era. The Bible was in the process of being written. Therefore, the signs and wonders were temporary in nature. The sign gifts ceased when the written Word was completed. This is a logical deduction, but is there more? Is there any direct Bible evidence that would indicate this? You bet!

In Jesus' account of the rich man in hell, the rich man requests that Lazarus be sent to his brothers so they can be warned about hell. He is told by father Abraham, "They have Moses and the Prophets; let them listen to them" (Luke 16:29). At this point, the reference to Moses and the prophets is a reference to the written Word of God available to the people at that time. Then the rich man says, "No, father Abraham, . . . if someone from the dead goes to them, they will repent" (v. 30). This guy is asking for a miracle! To raise someone from the dead should certainly be worthy of a prime-time slot on TV!

But the reply is given, "If they do not listen to Moses and the Prophets, they will not be convinced even if someone rises from the dead" (v. 31). This is heaven's perspective on the preeminence of Scripture. When the written Word is available, signs and wonders don't confirm belief. Moses and the prophets (the Old Testament) were available. Even the miracle of raising a person from the dead would not be convincing without the written Word.

Remember, Jesus and the disciples were in the process of bringing new revelation, and it would have confirming signs. But when Scripture is completed, it is enough. Raising the dead will do no more than the written Word of God will do in bringing people to faith in Christ. Romans 10:17 is very clear: "Faith comes from hearing the message, and the message is heard through the word of Christ."

Signs and wonders are not necessary to convince people of the Bible's salvation message. The Holy Spirit does the convicting and the convincing work. This work causes a person to believe the gospel of Jesus Christ and to cry out to God for mercy and for forgiveness of sins (John 16:8–11). Romans 1:16 says, "I am not ashamed of the gospel, because *it* [author's italics] is the power of God for the salvation of everyone who believes: first for the Jew, then for the Gentile." Salvation involves the reception of the truth of the Gospel as revealed in written form in the Bible.

I have observed that often when there is an emphasis on signs and wonders there is no clear presentation of the gospel. Listen carefully to sermons on television where signs and wonders are taught. Does the preacher give an understandable, simple presentation of the way of salvation?

A few years ago I attended a church growth conference. The speaker was advocating signs and wonders as a necessary part of effective evangelism. He told about a great crusade in a Third World country where people were healed and miracles took place. Then he said, "People started being saved before a gospel message was presented." Think about that. Saved before they heard the gospel? Romans 10:13–14 says, "How, then, can they call on the one they have not believed in? And how can they believe in the one of whom they have not heard? And how can they hear without someone preaching to them?" How can anyone be saved before he or she hears the gospel? This kind of emphasis on signs and wonders actually undermines the gospel. It minimizes the preaching of the Word of God.

What about the signs and wonders of the modern movement? Are they like those of the New Testament? A survey of the kinds of miracles occurring today is interesting. Have you heard of teeth being filled? Or people being healed of back pain and headaches? Or relieved from their inner emotional pain? I am not minimizing these. But I am a bit skeptical about teeth being filled. There are reports of limbs being restored and of the dead being raised. Documentation is, however, hard to come by. Often there is only hearsay. The people involved sometimes quote one another as their sources.

What about miracles? Can we experience them today as people in the New Testament did? Go to Mark 16. The language in this commission to the apostles is clear. Jesus did not say they "should" do these things. He said specifically they "shall" (no failures) do these things. If signs and wonders are to convince people today, they must include all the things Jesus mentioned.

An article in the local newspaper told about a man whose six-year-old daughter died. He packed her body in a picnic cooler and drove 350 miles to a signs and wonders center. The ministers at his church tried to talk him out of it. When he arrived, they prayed over the body two hours before giving up.[4] That church has had people say that people would be raised from the dead. They believe that the miracles and signs and wonders of the New Testament are occurring today. I can only imagine the hurt in the heart of the man who desperately wanted to see his little girl raised from the dead. My point in mentioning this: if New Testament signs and wonders are occurring today, then raising people from the dead must be a normal, expected activity.

Some people even take up serpents in response to this commission. At least they are being consistent! If signs and wonders are to convince people today, there must be a 100 percent success rate. If there is any failure, the failed attempt would discredit the gospel rather than authenticate it.

Signs and wonders are not necessarily a sign that God is at work. They are mentioned prominently in relation to satanic counterfeits in the end time. We know the movement has been plagued with a number of fakes. However, this does not mean there are not some sincere people in the movement. But realize that some charlatans are at work.

On the *Tonight Show* years ago, a balding man with white hair and a beard performed surgery. The "surgeon" began to knead the "patient's" abdomen with his hands and thumb. Blood began to flow and there was a sickening, squishing sound. Clumps of bloody tissue were pulled out and displayed for the camera. When it was over, the white-haired man wiped away the blood, revealing uncut skin. The bloody tissue had been taken from animals, even though the TV coverage made it look like it belonged to the patient. The viewers of the "Tonight Show" had witnessed James "The Amazing" Randi exposing the sleight of hand used by "psychic" surgeons in the Philippines. People routinely spend their money in the Philippines for these fakes, then go home to die.[5]

Do you wonder about the possibility of miracles today? Do they occur now? Yes. God is sovereign. He may perform any miracles he wishes when the gospel is being proclaimed. Never limit the power of God.

Perhaps a missionary may find himself on a foreign field in a "Book of Acts" situation. The people may not have the Word of God and may be in a totally demonic atmosphere. If God chooses to give that missionary the ability to speak the native languages, so be it. If God heals people in Third World countries or here in North America, what do I think? Praise God! This does not mean that the sign gifts have been restored. God does heal. He heals through medical science and in answer to believing prayer (see James 5).

My own study of the Bible indicates that we will have an end-time apostasy (a rejection of the Christian faith), not an end-time revival. But I do believe we can experience revival in some measure. We should pray for national revival and church revival. But the evidence of Scripture seems to indicate that the end time will be characterized not by revival but by widespread unbelief. Paul, talking about the coming of our Lord Jesus, says, "That day will not come until the rebellion occurs and the man of lawlessness is revealed, the man doomed to destruction" (2 Thess. 2:3).

We can still see many people saved. We can still see churches grow. But let's not get caught up in the "numbers game." Successful church growth is more than building buildings, breaking records in Sunday school, and adding more names to a church membership roll. There are more authentic gauges. The inward, spiritual growth of the people of God must be a part of successful church growth.

What is success? It's about being faithful to God and staying obedient to his command to witness to the lost. In the last days, people may not beat down the doors of churches. Am I defeatist? No, I'm an optimist. We have the Great Commission. Our job is to obey it and to make disciples. Sometimes obedience is hard. Work, study, and prayer are involved in the salvation of the lost. People are not easily won to Jesus.

So where is the power? The last stop on this power tour is the gospel. It's the death, burial, and resurrection of Jesus Christ. According to the Scriptures, those who will receive this message into their hearts by faith will be saved (1 Cor. 15:1–2). The gospel has power in and of itself to make maximum impact on the human soul. There's the true power!

Always consider the gospel messenger. The gospel is communicated by preachers who stand in pulpits and by Christians who faithfully share it as a lifestyle. A changed life shouts a gospel message. God will save a lost sinner, use him or her to tell other people about Jesus, and then save these people. This is a miracle. This is "the bomb," as the teenagers say.

Remember John the Baptist? We are told that "though John never performed a miraculous sign . . . many believed in Jesus" (John 10:41–42). John the Baptist sounds so ordinary. No signs and wonders. No healings. He didn't raise anyone from the dead. He just preached the simple message of Jesus. He told the truth about the Lord. And God used this messenger so that "many believed in Jesus." There's the power!

The final stop on our tour is the gospel miracle. Jesus said in John 14:12, "I tell you the truth, anyone who has faith in me will do what I have been doing. He will do even greater things than these, because I am going to the Father." What are the "greater things" mentioned in this passage? Jesus did works of creation. He created bread out of thin air. He healed blind eyes and lame limbs. He cast out demons. He did miraculous works in nature. He walked on the water. He withered a fig tree. He raised the dead. What can be greater than this? Jesus lived in one land, ministered for three and one-half years, and reached a few thousand people. Millions of believers today can reach millions of unsaved people. The totality of believers proclaiming the gospel to a lost world makes it possible to win far more people than Jesus ever did. There's the power.

Are we to believe there is something inadequate about a person who is saved by the simple message of Jesus? Are we to believe that the evangelistic work of great men like D. L. Moody, Billy Sunday, and Billy Graham was somehow lacking because they did not perform miracles? Any time a soul is saved, it is the miracle of miracles!

## Testing, Testing . . .

1. The Bible Test. What does the Bible say about this manifestation? Is it clearly taught in the Bible?

2. The Jesus Test. Does it honor and glorify Jesus? Is Jesus, the Holy Spirit, or the Christian the focus?

3. The Character Test. Does it contribute to a more Christlike life?

4. The Decency and Order Test. Is this within the guidelines of decency and order?

5. The Evangelism Test. Does it place the focus on winning people to Christ?

   Does it pass?

   YES _____

   NO _____

# CHAPTER 10

# A VISIT TO
# THE DARK SIDE

I remember when the movie *Star Wars* was released—1978. People knew all about it. Luke Skywalker, C3PO, and Han Solo. I knew American culture was interested in alien worlds at that time, but I didn't know that one motion picture could become or remain that popular.

Remember Darth Vader, the man in black? As I read more about the movie and its creators, I learned that Darth Vader ruled "the dark side." He was the villain whose objective was domination of the universe.

There are some parallels between this story and the eternal struggle between good and evil, God and Satan. There is a battle going on for power over the universe. The forces of light and darkness fight for control of our world.

In fact, today's Charismatic movement has had a great interest in the study of demonic influences from its inception. Many Charismatics have a strong consciousness of the reality of the dark side. Christians can be thankful that our Charismatic brothers have made us aware of the world of Satan and his demons. There seem to be two tendencies when it comes to this area of study. Some make too little of demons. Liberal theologians tend to deny the existence of demons and attribute all unusual behavior to psychological rather than demonic causes. To ignore the reality of demons is to create a false security. Christians ignore demons at their peril. The other tendency is to make too much of demons. Some people tend to see a demon behind every tree.

Darth Vader's dark side may have seemed real on the big screen, but it was fiction. Satan's dark side is, however, true and real, constantly causing problems for believers all over the world.

Let's talk about the true dark side and how it is impacting Christians and their work for the Lord today. Let's take a visit to the dark side.

## Observing

The books by Frank Peretti, *This Present Darkness*, published in 1986, and *Piercing the Darkness*, published in 1989, were big sellers. Highly imaginative and entertaining, they made enjoyable reads for Christians. There was no profanity, no promiscuous sex, nothing to offend. Interestingly enough, the books crossed over and sold quite well in the secular market. Both books provided a fictitious treatment of the cosmic struggle between the forces of God and Satan. Peretti introduced his readers to the dark work of the demonic.

Some Charismatics believe that most people's problems are influenced by demons. The solution to these problems is deliverance from demonic influence.

If a person has a problem with depression, a spirit of depression must be cast out in Jesus' name. Is someone poor? The spirit of poverty must be rebuked. If someone becomes sexually promiscuous, he or she is surely afflicted with a demon of lust that needs to be driven away.

Many Charismatics teach that Christians and non-Christians can be demon possessed. If they are, they must get deliverance from demons that have invaded their lives.

Many Charismatics believe that to deal with demons, one must discover the demons' names, speak those names, and confront them directly. Remember Jesus' encounter with Legion (Mark 5:9)? When Jesus encountered the man possessed with demons, he asked his name. The man replied, "My name is Legion . . . for we are many." Then Jesus sent them out of the man and into a nearby herd of swine.

The example of Paul's rebuking the spirit of Python in the slave girl in Philippi is used (Acts 16:18). Paul, unwilling to accept demonic publicity, spoke to the fortune-telling spirit in the slave girl, and commanded the spirit in the name of Jesus to come out of her. Charismatics also say the demons must be rebuked in Jesus' name and commanded to leave those who are possessed.

Some Charismatics teach that nations, cities, and entire neighborhoods are under demonic control. In other words, there are "territorial" demons and spirits, according to some Charismatics. Ephesians 6:12 and its reference to powers, rulers of darkness of this world, authorities, and spiritual wickedness in high places is used as support for this belief. Peter Wagner, a teacher in the Charismatic movement, says, "Satan does indeed assign a demon or a corps of demons to every geopolitical unit in the world and they are among the principalities and powers against whom we wrestle."[1]

Programs to free geographical areas of the demons controlling them have been undertaken. Knowledge of what kind of demon is in control is sought. Much effort has been exercised in California. For instance, some say that San Francisco is ruled by the spirit of perversion. Oakland is ruled by the spirit of murder. San Jose is ruled by the spirit of greed. Marion County, California, is ruled by the spirit of the New Age.

Peter Wagner mentions a former occultist who said that Satan gave him control of twelve spirits, each controlling six hundred demons (totaling 7,200). Every town in Nigeria was controlled by one of these spirits. Wagner supposed this to be true around the world.[2]

Some even give names to the territorial demons. Rita Cabezas of Latin America says she has received "revelatory words of knowledge," giving her the names of the demons. There are six worldwide principalities under Satan, she says: Damian, Asmodeo, Manquelesh, Arias, Beelzebub, and Nosferasteus. She also knows the names of demons lower on the demonic hierarchy. Each is given a name and assigned a certain area of evil.[3]

Charismatics have gone even farther into territorial spirit warfare. Have you heard of spiritual mapping? This effort seeks to see a nation or city as it is spiritually. Teams are sent in to investigate the most active and powerful demons. This sounds like an episode of X-Files. The "10/40 window" refers to countries located between latitudes 10 and 40 degrees north. Actually, these nations are spiritually barren. Some Charismatics say they comprise the last final remnants of demonic possession.

There are several levels of spiritual warfare, according to Charismatic teachers. First, there is ground level, which is casting demons out of people. Then there is the occult level, including witches, satanic priests, and other demonic leaders. Finally, there is the strategic level where territorial spirits are encountered.[4]

Some Charismatics also believe that a list of demons and their categories should be made known. One Charismatic teacher has listed as many as 53 "common demon groupings" and at least 220 types of demons such as bitterness, rebellion, jealousy, and sexual impurity.[5] Enough on the darker side? Let's look on the brighter side!

## Searching

As always, we ask, "What does the Bible say?" Go to what the Bible teaches, not what people say they have heard or experienced. The Bible isn't all warm and fuzzy. It does deal with the dark, fallen world of the demonic.

The Bible clearly teaches the reality of the devil. He is presented as the devil, literally meaning "the accuser." He is also called "Satan" or "the adversary." He is referred to as "the evil one," "the god of this age," "the tempter," "the serpent," "the prince of the power of the air," and "Beelzebub," the prince of the demons. Isaiah 14 and Ezekiel 28 show us that the devil is a fallen spirit being. As an anointed cherub, he fell from heaven because of pride. He now operates primarily on the earth, striving to hinder the purposes and the people of God (1 Pet. 5:8).

Yet Satan's doom is sealed. Isaiah 14:15 predicts he will be

> brought down to the grave,
> to the depths of the pit.

Revelation 20:10 says he will be "thrown into the lake of burning sulfur." Matthew 25:41 says that he will go to a place "prepared for the devil and his angels." "Angels" is a reference to demons.

Demons are the devil's angels. When the devil fell, some angels fell with him (Rev. 12:4, 7–9). The King James Version of the Bible uses the word *devils*. One could say "demons" as a better translation. Some demons are kept in prison (2 Pet. 2:4). Evidently, these demons will be unleashed on the earth during the Great Tribulation (Rev. 9). However, there are other demons who roam over the earth. They are extremely wicked and vicious. They are described as evil (Judg. 9:23), lying (1 Kings 22:22–23), foul (Mark 9:17), and unclean (Mark 5:2).

What about this demonic hierarchy? The King James Version of Ephesians 6:12 mentions "principalities," which may refer to Satan's closest helpers. "Powers" are evidently spiritual authorities. Drawing references to the prince of Persia and to the prince of Greece in Daniel 10:13–20, these powers may reside over entire nations. Many people believe Hitler was a member of the Thule Group, a satanist society which practiced black magic and communed with demons. "Rulers of the darkness" or "demons" may be the sinister influences in politics, entertainment, and educational and religious structures of our society. "Spiritual wickedness in high places" may refer to demons who create evil on the earth.

The New Testament indicates that demons work primarily in relation to people. Evidence suggests that they can possess unbelievers. Matthew 4:24 says, "News about him [Jesus] spread all over Syria, and people brought to him all who were ill with various diseases, those suffering severe pain, the demon-possessed, the epileptics and the paralytics, and he healed them."

The Greek word for *demons* used in this verse is *daimonizomai*. It is used thirteen times in the New Testament. The King James translates it "possessed with devils." The NKJV and the NIV render it "demon-possessed." The New American Standard Bible translates it "demoniacs." According to most Greek dictionaries, the word means "to be under the power of a demon" or "to be possessed by a demon." Whether one renders it "demonized" or "demon-possessed," the resulting meaning seems to be the same.

Ephesians 2:2 talks about the "spirit who is now at work in those who are disobedient." This indicates possession. Another Greek term used sometimes is "having demons" (Luke 8:27). Thayer indicates this phrase means "to be possessed by a demon." The simple truth is that people can be under total control of the demonic. Think of Judas. John 13:2 indicates that Satan placed thoughts of betrayal in his mind. Verse 27 specifically says that Satan entered Judas.

What about sicknesses? Not all illnesses are demonic. Yet the New Testament indicates that demons can cause many sicknesses. Sometimes people were blind because of demonic activity (Matt. 12:22). Emotional sicknesses were traced to demonic spirits. An example of this is the woman with the spirit of infirmity (Luke 13:11). There are just too many reliable reports today which confirm that it is indeed possible for people to be possessed by demons.

Demons can oppress believers. Look at the specifics in Acts 10:38. The word *oppress* expresses the idea of using one's power against. You'll see it only one other time in the New Testament. James 2:6 asks, "Is it not the rich who are exploiting you?" This verse uses the same word. The New King James translates it "oppressed by the devil." The New International Version renders it "under the power of the devil." The NASB translates it "oppressed by the devil." I do not believe that Christians can be possessed by demons. The Bible teaches that the Holy Spirit indwells the believer. The believer's body then becomes the temple of the Holy Spirit. No unholy spirit can live in the temple of the Holy Spirit. We have been rescued "from the dominion of darkness" (Col. 1:13).

But Christians can be attacked by demons. We are warned in Ephesians 4:27 not to "give the devil a foothold." Christians can let the devil gain ground in their lives. Demons can assault us externally by suggestion, temptation, or influence. They try to influence Christians to think demonic thoughts, feel demonic emotions, and do demonic actions. When Christians break under these temptations, they give demons a "stronghold" in their lives (2 Cor. 10:4).

Now for a quick review. When Jesus came, demonic activity on the earth seemed to intensify because the demons knew who he was and that he would ultimately destroy them (Matt. 8:29; Luke 4:34). There is no hint of a struggle between Jesus and the demons. In the wilderness temptation, three times Satan leveled heavy artillery against Jesus. He responded with the powerful Word of God. He won total victory over Satan.

Once the temptation experience was over, Jesus never again argued with the world of the demonic. Jesus simply ordered demons out of people. He rebuked them (Luke 4:41) and cast them out (Matt. 8:16), sometimes not allowing them to speak (Mark 1:34). He also commanded them to come out of people by his Word (Matt. 8:32), by the finger of God (Luke 11:20), and by the Spirit of God (Matt. 12:28). Jesus asked for the name of a demon only once, in the case of Legion in Mark 5. Casting out demons was a vital part of his ministry.

In Jesus' day, some physical ailments were clearly demonic, but Jesus did not view all sickness as demonic. He never called or addressed a demon by name. He did not attribute all sinful behavior like anger, lust, murder, or greed to demonic forces. He even indicated it is possible to cast out demons and not be saved (Matt. 7:22–23)! As we shall see, Jesus commissioned his apostles to cast out demons (Matt. 10:8; Mark 3:14–15; 16:17). Jesus said that the power to cast out demons is not to be the greatest source of joy. The ultimate source of joy is the fact that our names are written in heaven (see Luke 10:17–20).

Why are demons so prominent in the Gospels? In the life, death, and resurrection of Jesus, the battle between God and Satan and good and evil is played out. I have good news for you: Jesus won the battle! Colossians 2:15 says, "And having disarmed the powers and authorities, he made a public spectacle of them, triumphing over them by the cross."

Consider the apostles in relationship to the world of the demonic. Acts describes the apostles casting out demons. Peter evidently did this in Acts 5:16. Philip cast them out in Acts 8:7. Paul cast out demons on two occasions. I have mentioned the girl who had a demon cast out by Paul. Paul said to the spirit, "In the name of Jesus Christ I command you to come out of her!" (Acts 16:18). The demon came out at that very moment. The second occasion is in Acts 19:11–12. We are told that Paul did special miracles. These were so special that handkerchiefs and aprons from his body were carried to people. Diseases and evil spirits left them.

The New Testament letters don't mention the devil and demons very much. In 1 Corinthians 10:20–21, Paul talked about sacrificing to demons, fellowshipping with demons, and the table of demons. In 1 Timothy 4:1, he warned that in the last days "some will abandon the faith and follow deceiving spirits and things taught by demons." Then in the extensive passage in Ephesians 6, Paul seemed to lay out the believer's strategy in dealing with the devil and all things demonic.

Does all this mean that Paul regarded every human relationship problem as demonic? No. The Corinthian church was over the top with problems. Strong factions split the church. Yet Jesus did not tell them to rebuke the spirit of factions. One man committed incest. But Paul never urged them to cast out a spirit of incest. Some believers were suing one another. Paul did not rebuke a demon of lawsuits.

There is no clear, specific teaching about a local church ministry of casting out demons. So where do Charismatics derive their teaching on deliverance ministries? Usually these teachings come from the example of Jesus and the example of Paul, not from any specific instruction.

Matthew 12:24–29 is sometimes used by Charismatics to establish a method of dealing with the demonic. This passage is interesting. Jesus was accused by the Pharisees of casting out demons by the power of Beelzebub, the prince of demons. Their accusation was demolished by Jesus' logic. His point was that if he were casting out Satan by Satan, then Satan was dividing his own kingdom. That would be preposterous.

Jesus closed his argument with a simple parable of one entering a strong man's house. He said, "How can anyone enter a strong man's house and carry off his possessions unless he first ties up the strong man?" The parable is beautiful in its simplicity. Charismatic teachers may make more of it than what Jesus intended. If Satan controls a house, so goes their reasoning, doesn't he also control cities and nations? A house then is a territory controlled by Satan or his spirit delegates. Satan or his delegates can't be removed unless the demon is bound. Once bound, the kingdom of God can move into the territory and "plunder the strong man's goods."[6]

But this is a parable. The strong man is the devil. His goods are lost sinners. How is the devil's house robbed? He is tied up. The one stronger than the devil is Jesus, the One who can bind the devil. We don't bind the devil; Jesus does!

The New Testament offers little information about territorial spirits. There is no indication that Jesus or Paul bound local demonic rulers in Nazareth, Jerusalem, Athens, or Corinth. Territorial warfare is not mentioned in any version of Jesus' Great Commission.

## Evaluating

The Charismatic emphasis on the world of the demonic has positive aspects. Christians are made aware of the reality of the demon world and of the importance of prayer in our spiritual struggles. Another benefit is the heightened concern for world missions. We can be grateful for all of this. Yet some observations about Charismatic teachings on the demonic need to be made.

Little evidence exists in the Bible for such elaborate presentations as these found in Charismatic teachings on territorial spirits. There is no indication in the New Testament that believers today are to seek or find information about territorial spirits, such as determining their names. Nothing in the Bible teaches that we are to break strongholds over cities. Geography is not the main concern of demons. They want souls! They are after body count. They are slave traders.[7] Demons are looking for people to enslave, not territories.

There is also no indication that we are to cast out spirits to allow the gospel to gain influence through territorial praying. Do you know about "prayer walks"? The idea of prayer walks is to drive evil spirits from particular territories. If this gets people praying, fine. The exercise certainly won't hurt! But to make "prayer walks" a requirement in casting out spirits before the gospel can be more effective is not taught in Scripture. Actually, there isn't much evidence that these walks have done cities any recognizable good. Perhaps we should pray for boldness to preach and to witness in our cities and that God would draw people to himself.

Our imaginations can run wild about the demonic. While Peretti's books can make us aware of the reality of the demon world, we must be careful not to let them and other books like them cause us to speculate into the fantastic. For example, one teacher suggests that the serpent is still in Eden and has "established a global command and control center atop the oily residue of the garden's once flourishing vegetative and animal life."[8] That's a pretty big leap, wouldn't you say?

It is possible for us to give more power to demons than they have. They are not all-knowing, and they are not everywhere, and they do not have all power. Jesus and the apostles never focused on looking for demons. Demonic activity was viewed as a distraction more than anything else. Jesus and Paul didn't go to cities "mapping" them out, looking for evil, and praying down strongholds. That's not how they spent their valuable time. Further, nothing is said in Scripture about finding out the names of demons or rebuking them. Second Peter 2:10–11 and Jude 9 caution us against these activities. Jesus rebuked the devil. For the believer, the Bible says more about resisting the devil (1 Pet. 5:8–9).

Preoccupation with demonic activity can take away responsibility for one's personal behavior and sin. We have three enemies, not one—the devil, the world, and the flesh, according to Ephesians 2:1–3. This is why to blame human sins such as bitterness, rebellion, jealousy, and sexual impurity on the demonic can be harmful. These human struggles fall into the area of "works of the flesh" (Gal. 5:19–21). To develop elaborate categories of specific demonic influences borders on the absurd. Some sins of the flesh can be blamed on demons, making it possible for a person to commit adultery, blame it on demons, get them cast out, and go one's merry way. We cannot shift blame for our behavior to demons by claiming, "The devil made me do it."

There is no specific command for us to bind or rebuke the devil. Jesus bound the devil in that he won the victory over him at the cross (Col. 2:15). He defeated the devil and his demons and will ultimately bind them forever. The strong man, Satan, has already met his match in the One who is stronger.

There is growing disillusionment with the result of territorial warfare activity. Groups have gone to San Francisco and other places to rebuke the demons. Yet, if demonic powers of evil in San Francisco have been broken and bound, why is it still a leading center of homosexuality and pornography? In his excellent book, *Fresh Wind, Fresh Fire*, Jim Cymbala tells of a seminar he attended on spiritual warfare against territorial spirits. He says, "I could find no evidence that these speakers were implementing their concepts at the local church level. Their books and tapes were selling well, but I wondered why they hadn't come to Brooklyn or other dark places and put their teachings into practice."[9] Although some people give glowing reports of great success, there are few reports of the many failures.

It is possible to get so focused on the dark side that one diminishes the person and power of the Lord Jesus Christ. Let's not elevate demons so that Jesus and Satan are seemingly corulers competing for control of the universe. Our focus must be on Jesus. Isaiah 26:3 says, "You will keep in perfect peace him whose mind is steadfast, because he trusts in you."

Much of our culture today seems to be reverting to pagan thinking. In this atmosphere, demonic influences become even more prominent in the culture's thinking. Christians must stay separate. Our view must be biblical, not pagan. Sometimes it's hard to do this. Just remember not to neglect personal soul winning or fail to look to Jesus for victory in the battle for souls.

The Bible shows us the way of victory over demons. James 4:6–7 teaches us first to submit our lives totally to God. We claim the victory of the cross, the shed blood of Jesus, and the power of the Holy Spirit. Then we are to resist the devil, and we are told he will flee from us. How exactly does this work?

Ephesians 6:10–18 shows us how to resist the devil. Each day we are to put on the armor of God. The first articles of the armor are more defensive in nature, truth, righteousness, etc. Then we have an offensive weapon, the sword of the Spirit, which is the Word of God. Jesus used this spiritual sword to overcome the wilderness temptation of Satan. We should fill our minds and hearts daily with the Word of God. Then when temptations come, we can attack the dark side with the sword of the Spirit!

Finally, verse 18 explains the great weapon of prayer. Prayer is not some magical formula exposing demonic powers. Prayer is the way we communicate with God. We don't pray to the devil. The Bible doesn't command us to address prayer to the devil or demons. We pray to the Father, by the Spirit, in the name of Jesus.

During the Civil War, General George McClellan, commander of the northern forces, greatly frustrated President Lincoln because he never attacked the enemy. He always seemed fearful of superior forces. Approaching Richmond, McClellan sent a spy named Pinkerton to assess the strength of the Confederate forces. Pinkerton assumed there were more Confederate soldiers than he could see, so he inflated the figures. McClellan believed Pinkerton and did not attack.

Christians can get caught up in similar fears when it comes to the world of demons. Don't be afraid of demons. We don't have to be. First John 4:4 says, "You, dear children, are from God and have overcome them, because the one who is in you is greater than the one who is in the world."

Are you a Christian? If not, come to Christ. First John 3:8 says that Jesus was manifested "to destroy the devil's work." Do you want to know the very best way to get the demons out? Get Jesus in!

## Testing, Testing . . .

1. The Bible Test. What does the Bible say about this manifestation? Is it clearly taught in the Bible?

2. The Jesus Test. Does it honor and glorify Jesus? Is Jesus, the Holy Spirit, or the Christian the focus?

3. The Character Test. Does it contribute to a more Christlike life?

4. The Decency and Order Test. Is this within the guidelines of decency and order?

5. The Evangelism Test. Does it place the focus on winning people to Christ?

   Does it pass?
   YES _____
   NO _____

## CHAPTER 11

# LORD OF
# THE DANCE

We have come to one of the most interesting aspects of the entire Charismatic movement—dancing. If there is anything obvious about our Charismatic friends, it is that they believe in worship. They know how to do it! Charismatics teach us that worship is a very special time when we come before the Lord privately or in public service. And talk about enthusiasm! One cannot sit bored at a Charismatic service. Charismatics also teach us the importance of congregational participation in worship. In too many churches, the congregation watches rather than participates.

And the music! Some of our most meaningful, moving music has been written by our Charismatic friends. We love to sing Andre Crouch's "The Blood Will Never Lose Its Power." We are exalted at the stanzas of Jack Hayford's "Majesty, Worship His Majesty." We love the exciting gospel rhythm of Nancy Harmon's "The Blood-Bought Church." We are moved by Dottie Rambo's "We Shall Behold Him."

Worship in and of itself is deeply personal. Christians should never belittle or make fun of how other people worship the Lord. This is the lesson we learn from Michal's disgust at David's exuberant worship before the Lord in 2 Samuel 6. The Lord takes criticism of worship very seriously. There are many different styles of worship among Christian people. Visit ten evangelical churches around the country and you might find ten different worship styles. Some evangelical services are formal. Others offer loose worship. Evangelicals worship differently. So do other Christian groups.

If you visit a Charismatic service, you might find similarities or differences in the way they worship. Worship style usually is very relaxed and informal. Praise choruses are used. There may be a small musical combo, with prominence given to the guitar. Often tambourines are used, even by people in the congregation. The worship is very expressive and open. These features may cause Charismatic worship to be very attractive to modern churchgoers. Casual dress is appealing today. So is informality in the order of service. The high energy, participation-oriented, spontaneous style is very attractive to the modern churchgoer. You might even see some worshipers dancing.

Dancing in Charismatic services may take several forms. Some of it may be formally choreographed. You might see trained dancers robed in special attire formally dancing. Or you might see what Charismatics term "dancing in the Spirit." This is a more spontaneous, individual kind of worship style, including tap dancing or just leaping up and down.

Actually, dancing is not a new innovation in Charismatic or Pentecostal circles. It has been a part of pentecostal worship since the inception of the movement. Pentecostals have always accepted different kinds of manifestations in worship. Recently, however, some manifestations of dancing in worship have caused older Pentecostals to raise their eyebrows, according to the *Dictionary of Pentecostal and Charismatic Movements*. The dictionary goes on to say that while older Pentecostals would not eliminate dancing, they do have doubts whether some of the current forms of dancing are "Spirit-filled."[1] Certain aspects of recent worship dancing have become controversial. What does the Lord think? Is our Lord the Lord of the dance? Let's see.

## Observing

Not all Charismatic churches worship in the same way any more than other Evangelical churches do. So it is not easy to present a typical Charismatic worship service. But in many Charismatic services, there seem to be four basic phases. First, the chorus singing—praise and worship time led by a worship team. Occasionally you'll hear a hymn, but the main menu consists of praise choruses, accompanied by many physical manifestations. There is generally shouting, lifting of hands, and dancing.

Testimony time is next. Individuals in the congregation share what God is doing in their lives. Some share salvation testimonies. Others talk of being healed. Some rejoice about financial miracles. Then it's preaching time—the third phase. There are many capable, wonderful Charismatic preachers. Through the years I have enjoyed the preaching of many Charismatics. Assembly of God preacher C. M. Ward was one of my favorites. Church of God preacher Ray Hughes is another. Another Church of God pastor, Paul Walker, has always blessed me. Thank God for all Charismatic preachers who faithfully proclaim the Word of God.

Finally, there is ministry time. Other Christians might call it the invitation time. But in Charismatic churches it's when people come forward to receive a "hands-on" time of ministry. Pastors and other spiritual leaders may lay hands on the people for a variety of reasons. Some are "slain in the Spirit." Others are "anointed with oil" for healing. Some come to be saved. Very often people dance at this time.

In Charismatic worship dancing, several things are involved. There is a cultural component. Jewish and African cultures commonly use dance in their worship. Jewish dancing is often round dancing with lots of leaping and clapping of hands. Though not as common in our American culture, many cultures have a strong need for physical movements such as dancing in their worship. Remember, what might seem to be chaos to some cultures is considered spontaneous order to others.

Charismatic dancing also has a biblical component. Many believe what they do is consistent with the examples and exhortations in the Bible. The *Dictionary of Pentecostal and Charismatic Movements* says, "The rise of singing psalms and spiritual songs as well as the rebirth of dance in worship in the Charismatic Movement is directly attributed to Old Testament examples."[2]

Charismatic dancing also has a physical component. Charismatics have a very positive attitude toward bodily movements in worship. Hand raising, clapping, laying on of hands, kneeling and prostrating oneself, and dancing are all viewed positively.

There is a definite doctrinal component in Charismatic dancing. Underlying the renewed emphasis on praise and dance in worship is a teaching on the restoration of praise worship, including dancing, as a fulfillment of Old Testament prophecy. Citing 2 Samuel 6 where David danced before the Lord as the ark was brought to Jerusalem, some Charismatics believe that Amos 9:11 predicts a restoration of this Davidic worship in the time just before Jesus comes back. They also refer to Acts 15:16 as the New Testament indication that this prophecy will be fulfilled. They believe there will be a great end-time revival before the return of Jesus.

Paul Wohlgemoth says, "Some theologians see the 20th Century Charismatic renewal movement as the spiritual restoration of Davidic worship around the Ark of the Covenant, especially through praise singing."[3] Vocal, instrumental, and physical manifestations in praise and worship are considered by some to be part of the several restorations which will help start this end-time revival.

From this perspective, worship is viewed in distinct stages. Other groups may view worship as a total package, but Charismatics break it down into a series of stages approaching deep intimacy with God. The preparation begins in the outer court, as in Old Testament worship. At this stage the worshiper expresses his thanksgiving to God. Such physical acts as clapping hands, singing, shouting, and dancing before the Lord bring the worshipers into a state of abandoned humility before the Lord. This prepares them to go further in worship. People are encouraged to "abandon themselves to the Spirit."[4] The tempo of the music picks up. The sound increases. The people are on their feet clapping, singing, dancing, jumping, and whistling (even blowing whistles).

This reminds me of those marching bands and the drum major with his whistle.

The next stage brings the worshiper into the "holy place." In this stage choruses of the Spirit are used repetitively to proclaim the attributes of God and his names. From thanksgiving they proceed to praise, based on Psalm 100:4. Finally a hush or silence comes in the service. At this point, the worshipers enter into the very presence of God in the holy of holies. Here worship takes place—singing in tongues, praying in tongues, and giving of prophecies.

Terry Law, an internationally known Charismatic worship leader, is quoted by Don Hustad: "First we will praise God, then we sanctify our minds through the power of the Spirit, then our emotions take over and bring us into the veil, into the presence of God in worship."[5]

Certain Charismatic teachers are emphatic about this kind of worship experience. Some even say that if churches don't get in on this "move of God," they will miss out on the great end-time revival and, like Michal, will become spiritually barren, winning few souls to Christ. Basically this viewpoint adds a seriousness to the whole matter of praise worship and dancing which cannot be ignored by sincere Christians. In other words, Christians who are vitally interested in winning people to Christ and who want to be a part of what God is doing today cannot ignore such a teaching. What do we do? To the law and to the testimony! Let's pick up our Bibles again and find out more about the Lord of the dance.

## Searching

Praise and worship are such big topics that we won't be able to give a comprehensive study of the subject. Entire volumes have been written about praise and worship. We're studying what the Bible says about dancing in worship and evaluating the teaching that the restoration of Davidic worship is a key ingredient of an end-time revival. What does the Bible say about dancing in worship?

There are many references in the Old Testament to bodily movements in worship. Movements such as raising of hands, standing to worship, kneeling or prostrating oneself to worship, and clapping are described. Speaking of clapping, in the Bible it seems to be very different from what commonly occurs in worship today. Often the clapping today is a spontaneous response of enjoyment for music presented or an acknowledgment of what the preacher has said. We'll deal with this more in a later chapter. What about dancing? Actually, about eleven different terms are used in the Old Testament to describe the act of dancing. It is described as whirling, leaping, and even skipping.

A few of these references will give us some idea of the role of dancing in Old Testament worship. At the miraculous crossing of the Red Sea, Miriam led the women in rejoicing and praising with timbrels and dancing (Exod. 15:20). David, as we have mentioned, danced before the ark (2 Sam. 6; 1 Chron. 15–16). Psalm 30:11 says, "You turned my wailing into dancing." Psalm 149:3 urges to praise him with tambourine and dancing.

Some Bible teachers take the view that many of the references to dancing in the Psalms point toward a future fulfillment in the millennium. John Phillips says, "God's people will sing and dance in a coming millennial morn when dancing is cleansed of its present impurities and is restored to spiritual men and women as a legitimate way of expressing the overflow of their love for the Lord."[6]

In the Old Testament, dancing happened on many occasions. They danced in processional marches and on feast days. Military victories and weddings were celebrated with joyful dances. They also danced in their religious celebrations. The Jewish dance of the Old Testament seems to be similar to folk dances. Men and women never intermingled in their dances, except where pagan influences crept in (cf. Exod. 32:19). Usually the dances were done by women, with one leading as in the example of Miriam. Most of the time the dances took place outdoors.[7]

Isn't it interesting that there are so few references to dancing in the New Testament? Of course, there is the reference to the daughter of Herodias dancing before Herod at a drunken banquet in Matthew 14:6. But I don't think this one applies to our study. In the marvelous parable of the prodigal son, Jesus told about the elder brother who heard the sound of music and dancing in his father's house upon the prodigal's return (Luke 15:25).

There are also references to praise and worship in the New Testament. Hebrews 13:15 says, "Through Jesus, therefore, let us continually offer to God a sacrifice of praise—the fruit of lips that confess his name." At the triumphal entry of our Lord into Jerusalem, the disciples of Jesus began to rejoice and praise. When they were rebuked, Jesus said if they didn't praise him, the stones would cry out in praise (Luke 19:37–40). It's easy to imagine the leaping and dancing for joy on this occasion even though the text does not specifically mention this.

Acts 2:47 indicates that the disciples were "praising God and enjoying the favor of all the people." Remember when the lame man was healed? He went "walking and jumping, and praising God" (Acts 3:8). This might be considered a form of dancing before the Lord. I would have been leaping, too.

In the familiar midnight experience of Paul and Silas in the Philippian jail, they were "praying and singing hymns to God" (Acts 16:25). Did they dance at midnight? The Bible doesn't say so, but they may have danced after the Lord shook the place with an earthquake.

There is no evidence in the New Testament that dancing was a prominent part of the worship of the early church. However, *Zondervan Pictorial Bible Dictionary* says that church history indicates there was some dancing in the early church. It also says that primitive Christian churches did permit the dance, but because of the degeneracy, it was banned.[8]

So what about the teaching that praise, worship, and dancing are part of an end-time restoration of Davidic worship? To examine this, let's turn to 2 Samuel 6. This passage is rich and fascinating. It is helpful to me to read the parallel passage in 1 Chronicles 15–16. The ark of the covenant is being returned to Jerusalem. From this passage we also learn the importance of following the teachings of Scripture. David's first attempt at returning the ark to Jerusalem was aborted. He made the same mistake we do today. He tried to carry the ark on a cart as the Philistines did. Does this tell us something about our mistake of wrapping worship in modern, worldly forms? After David searched the Scriptures carefully, he understood that the ark was to be carried on the shoulders of the Levites.

David led the procession of worshipers returning the ark. Verse 14 in the King James Version says, "And David danced before the Lord with all his might." Picture this—a joyful, blessed time. Sacrifice had been made (v. 13). Today we worship around the sacrifice of Jesus on the cross. You know what? This should cause spontaneous joy and worship in us. Realize, however, that there is no command for us to follow David's actions in this passage. Upon arriving at Jerusalem, verse 17 says that David set the ark "in its place inside the tent that David had pitched for it." The word for *tabernacle* here is *'ohel*, which is the most frequently used word in the Old Testament for tent or temporary shelter. It seems that David erected a tent in Jerusalem to house the ark.

First Chronicles 15–16 gives more interesting details about the worship that took place around this ark. First Chronicles 15:23 tells us that there were doorkeepers for this ark, indicating some kind of entrance for use by the priests.

Move to Amos 9:11–12 and following. Amos predicted,

> "In that day I will restore
>      David's fallen tent.
> I will repair its broken places,
>      restore its ruins,
>      and build it as it used to be,
> so that they may possess the remnant of Edom
> and all the nations that bear my name," declares the LORD,
> who will do these things (Amos 9:11–12).

Some people say this is a reference to the same tent David erected for the ark in Jerusalem.

But now let us move to Acts 15:16, where the prophecy of Amos is quoted. It is vitally important to understand the context of this quotation. From this quotation at the first church council in Jerusalem comes the belief of some Charismatic teachers that a part of the end-time restoration will be seen in Davidic worship and the result will be a great salvation harvest of the Gentiles. Look at the complete context beginning with the first verse of Acts 15. It mentions that a controversy had developed concerning how people are saved. Some teachers in the Jerusalem church were saying everyone had to be circumcised and become a Jew in order to be saved. This caused great dissension and argument among the early believers.

Acts 15:2–5 tells us that Paul and Barnabas declared the conversion of the Gentiles, and they were being saved without being circumcised and becoming Jews. So a church council was called by the apostles and elders of the Jerusalem church. In this meeting, Peter declared that the Gentiles were being saved as a result of his preaching as well. He specifically said, "We believe it is through the grace of our Lord Jesus that we are saved, just as they [the Gentiles] are" (Acts 15:11).

So Gentiles were being saved in the ministry of Peter without being circumcised and becoming Jews. Again, Barnabas and Paul declared what miracles and wonders God was working among the Gentiles through them (v. 12). Finally, James addressed the group. He pointed out that Simon Peter had told them how God was visiting the Gentiles to remove from them a people for his name (v. 14). In this context, he continued in verse 15 by saying, "The words of the prophets are in agreement with this, as it is written." Then he quoted Amos 9:11–12. There is only one point to his quotation of Amos 9:11: Gentiles can be saved without becoming Jews. The reference to building the tabernacle of David is incidental.

Go back to Amos 9. Note that there is an intermingling of truth which applies to Israel and which applies to the church in the Acts passage. Don't misapply truth intended for Israel to the church. It is a common error. Not all of the Amos passage was fulfilled on the day of Pentecost. In fact, it will not all be fulfilled during the time of the Gentile harvest which began at Pentecost and will continue until the end of the age. Amos 9:13 talks about a time when those who plow will overtake the reapers, and those who tread the grapes will overtake those who sow the seed, and the mountains will drop like sweet wine, and all the hills will melt. These are references to events occurring during the future one-thousand-year reign of Christ on the earth.

What does Amos mean when he talks about the fallen tabernacle of David being built again? This refers to the restoration of the dynasty or royal family line of David. In Amos's time, David's dynasty was not in power. But Amos predicted it will be in power again "as it used to be." This points back to 2 Samuel 7, where God promises David he will build him a "house." God was not talking about a literal house. He was referring to a dynasty, a royal line for David.

By the time of Amos, though, David's house or dynasty had degenerated into a tent or hut. Keil and Delitzsch observed, "The raising up of the fallen hut of David commenced with the coming of Christ . . . it will continue through all the ages of the Christian church and be completed when the fullness of the Gentiles enter the kingdom of God."[9] This is a generally accepted view.

*The Spirit-Filled Bible*, edited by Charismatic pastor Jack W. Hayford, says about this reference, "The Tabernacle of David is literally a 'booth' or 'hut,' usually made of branches. Here it stands for the dynasty of David, and its descendants, which is most often termed a 'house.'"[10] It is clear that a description of the fallen condition of the Davidic monarchy is the point of the passage. Remember, Amos predicted that the Davidic house would be repaired and restored through David's son, the Lord Jesus. Through the Savior, the dilapidated house of David will be raised up and God will fulfill his promise that a king will sit forever on his throne. This King is the Lord Jesus, who will rule over Israel during the reign of Christ on earth.

Further indication of all of this is found in the word that Amos uses. He uses a different word for tabernacle. Remember, in 2 Samuel 6 (and also in 1 Chron. 15–16) the word *'ohel* is used. But Amos uses another word, *sukkah*. *The New Brown, Driver, Briggs, Gesenius Hebrew and English Lexicon* says that this word is "used poetically of the fallen house (dynasty) of David." Also, the use of the word translated "fallen" indicates that the complete ruin of the royal family of David is intended. David's descendants no longer dwelt in a palace (figuratively), but in a miserable, fallen hut (figuratively).[11] Amos predicted that the hut will be raised up by God. Amos's prediction provides no evidence that a restoration of the tent that housed the ark in Jerusalem is predicted. Let's continue learning more about the Lord of the dance.

## Observing

There are differences in what Christians consider to be proper worship forms. A Charismatic visiting a Baptist service might feel it is dull. A Presbyterian attending the same service might feel it is too out of the box. We must not establish forms of worship which are comfortable and preferred by our church as standard for all others. To say "If you don't worship the way I do, you are not spiritual" is wrong. If you dance in your services, I don't condemn you. If we don't dance in ours, don't condemn us.

We should never get to the point where we are unwilling to offer the Lord Jesus our heartfelt, expressive worship. God does enthrone the praises of his people (Ps. 22:3). We are encouraged to offer to the Lord verbal expressions of praise (Heb. 13:15; Ps. 145:21). When we think of all the Lord has done for us, how wonderful he is and how worthy he is, our worship should definitely be filled with great exaltation and joy.

It is best to look more to the New Testament than to the Old Testament for guidelines about our worship (more on this in a later chapter). To me, New Testament worship revolves around the proclamation of the Word of God. If Davidic worship is intended to be a part of the New Testament church in the end times, why is there no clear teaching about it in the New Testament, especially in the epistles?

I also feel that we should not allow our emotions to be the dominant factor in worship. Emotions can be so easily manipulated. I agree with Don Hustad: "In my judgment, thirty minutes of singing songs in one musical style, with much repetition of a few words of 'pure praise' is an excessive invitation to emotional manipulation."[12] I also agree that we must not make more of our praise than the Bible allows. He quotes some Charismatic leaders, "With human praise, God is able to do things He could not do otherwise." God is not more God with our praise or less God without it.

One cause for concern is the current teaching concerning the restoration of Davidic worship as part of a "latter rain/kingdom now" doctrine. This teaching arose from William Branham, a Charismatic teacher, and a group from Saskatchewan called the "Sharon Brethren." They taught that the prophecies relating to the restoration of Israel were to be fulfilled in an end-time restoration of the church. Calling themselves "Manifest Sons of God," they believed in a perfecting process, empowering saints of God to take dominion over the earth and establish the kingdom of God.

This doctrine has several features. First, the return of Jesus will be preceded by an outpouring of the Holy Spirit which coincides with the former and latter rain of Joel 2:28. The former rain, they say, was fulfilled on the day of Pentecost. The latter rain, according to them, will occur just before the return of Jesus. This will be a time of great bringing of souls to Christ. As part of this, gifts of the Spirit will be restored. The offices of apostles and prophets will be restored. There will also be a restoration of praise and worship. According to them, this includes singing and exuberant praise in tongues and dancing. So, this makes Davidic worship a required part of the end-time revival. Through all of this, God will be brought into the presence of worshiping believers and God's people will be moved into his presence.

This doctrine was disputed by mainline pentecostal denominations. Their view was that the teachings did not stand up in the light of the Word of God. The result is that many independent pentecostal churches which hold these teachings sprang up around the country.[13] This teaching is one of the basic premises of the Word of Faith movement and is also a large part of the "signs and wonders" movement today. This is a cause for concern.

Having said this, let's not react harshly when dealing with praise in our worship. Ephesians 5:19 clearly presents the role of "psalms, hymns, and spiritual songs." But there is more to praise than just music or dancing. It is inclusive of many spiritual activities. In one sense, prayer is praise. Proclamation of the Word of God is also a form of praise. What about submission of a person's total life to God? This is also praise. Praise and worship need to be tied to prayer and to the proclamation of the Word of God and not allowed to become ends in themselves. To focus only on praise and worship is to remove the purposes of evangelism and Bible teaching. This emphasis also gives the impression that the initiative to worship lies within human beings. But Scripture is clear that we can only know God in reality through God's self-revelation of himself in the Bible, the written Word, and in Jesus, the Living Word.

Christians today are hungry for engagement in genuine, heartfelt, spiritual worship. Many of our churches are dull and lifeless. Too often people leave church services with starving hearts. Our Charismatic friends should be thanked for reminding us of the importance of worship and the vital place it fills in the life of the believer. Let's be sure that those who come to our worship services don't just sit there like knots on a log. They should actively participate in the worship of our great God and Savior.

Finally, remember that nothing we do brings us into the presence of God— not even our worship and praise. Though we are to

> enter his gates with thanksgiving
> and his courts with praise (Ps. 100:4),

we "enter the Most Holy Place by the blood of Jesus" (Heb. 10:19).

## TESTING, TESTING . . .

1. The Bible Test. What does the Bible say about this manifestation? Is it clearly taught in the Bible?

2. The Jesus Test. Does it honor and glorify Jesus? Is Jesus, the Holy Spirit, or the Christian the focus?

3. The Character Test. Does it contribute to a more Christlike life?

4. The Decency and Order Test. Is this within the guidelines of decency and order?

5. The Evangelism Test. Does it place the focus on winning people to Christ?

   Does it pass?
   YES ____
   NO ____

## CHAPTER 12

# NAME IT AND CLAIM IT?

My wife Janet and I were young; we had four small children, and we didn't have much money. I admit the radio preacher who spoke about his miracle pocketbook got my attention. He said he needed money, but he had only a few one-dollar bills in his pocketbook. By some miracle, his one-dollar bills became twenty-dollar bills. Apparently, the pocketbook held the miracle and for just a small donation, he would send me one.

I didn't know it then, but I was listening to an early version of the "name it and claim it" philosophy. That preacher was one of an endless stream of teachers proclaiming that it's easy to have financial blessings. All you have to do is name them and claim them. They're not timid about their view. Here it is: God "wants his children to eat the best, he wants them to drive the best cars, and he wants them to have the best of everything."[1]

The prosperity gospel is big business. Some estimate it is the fastest-growing segment of the Charismatic movement. It's sold on TV and radio. Tapes and books on the subject sell in the millions. It has great appeal. For those strapped for cash and driving an old car about to collapse, it is especially tempting. What about you? An '89 Plymouth or a '99 Lexus? Living from paycheck to paycheck or having one hundred thousand dollars in the bank?

It's called by many names: "Name it and claim it," "health and wealth," "prosperity gospel," "positive confession," "word of faith." The leading proponents are Ken Hagin, Oral Roberts, Ken Copeland, Marilyn Hickey, John Avanzini, and Joyce Meyers. It's controversial even in the Charismatic movement. Many Pentecostals and Charismatics raise serious questions about it. In fact, some of the sharpest critics of prosperity teaching are those within the Charismatic movement.

In my previous book *SpiritLife*, I discuss the matter of healing. Healing has always been a part of the Charismatic movement. The prosperity teaching is a relatively new wrinkle. For older Charismatics becoming wealthy was not a part of their doctrine.

The basic premise of the prosperity gospel is that God wants believers to have the best of everything. This means no financial difficulties. The Christian can have whatever he or she wants, spiritual or material. Check out these book titles. They are startling: *God's Key to Success and Prosperity*; *God Doesn't Want You Poor*; *Redeemed from Poverty*. Many sincere believers log onto this prosperity gospel.

## Observing

Where did all this come from? The prosperity teaching seems to have originated in the teachings of E. W. Kenyon, a Bible teacher and author, whose writings greatly influenced the Charismatic movement. The leading teacher today is Ken Hagin. He has spoken and written much on the subject. The main idea of the teaching is that every Christian should have plenty of money and an abundance of material things. They teach that prosperity is the right of every Christian who claims it by faith. Not to prosper is to be out of God's will. The universe is governed by certain spiritual laws and physical laws. By faith, one can maximize these laws and become prosperous. Also, if a person is God's child, then he or she can always go first-class through life.

This prosperity is viewed as a divine right. Using Galatians 3:13–14, proponents teach that Christ has redeemed us from the curse of the law so the blessing of Abraham will come upon us through Jesus. From this, they go to Deuteronomy 28. Many curses are pronounced upon the Israelites for their disobedience to the law. Obeying God's principles will bring removal of the curse. Their view is that Christ has redeemed us from all the curses. Abraham was a wealthy man, they say, so you can be also, through Christ.

The prosperity gospel teaches that certain principles in the spiritual realm control material prosperity. If you find them, use them in the right way, and speak them audibly, then God has to do what you say. The teaching is certainly compelling. You have the power to command God! Prosperity teachers also speak in terms of "success formulas." Financial success comes to those who have faith to believe it and use the formulas. Any surplus gained is to be used to bless and benefit others.

Mark 10:29–30 is also commonly used in the prosperity movement. In this passage Jesus promised his followers a hundredfold blessing. Does it sound like guaranteed prosperity? One teacher summarized it this way: "If I'm not prospering, it is not God's fault, nor the fault of the Word of God—it is my fault."[2]

Another element tied to the prosperity gospel is *positive confession*. To get what you want, you need a positive confession. You've got to say audibly what you want from God. Here's a good definition of positive confession: "A statement, made in faith, that lays claim to God's provisions and promises."[3] Do you see it? Your words determine reality. If your words are negative, you bring into existence negative elements. You had better not use negative words like "tickled to death" carelessly, because this is inviting death. If your words are positive, life's a party. You bring positive elements into existence. While doubt sets the devil at work, faith releases the ability of God. The positive confession aspect also teaches the inherent power of God.

Words determining reality? Here's how it works. All Christians are to be prosperous. If they have a financial need or desire, they just find a verse that promises prosperity. Then they audibly quote that verse, no matter what. By believing it in the heart and speaking it with the mouth, the financial provision will be manifested, according to the believer's faith. He or she will experience a positive result.[4] This is why the movement is sometimes called "name it and claim it." Supposedly what is named with words can be claimed by faith.

There is another element to the prosperity gospel. It's the Rhema doctrine. Prosperity gospel teaches that the Greek word for the "word" in Romans 10:8 is *rhema*. The reference is to a spoken word. Therefore, whatever is spoken by faith is inspired and takes on the creative power of God.

There is yet another element in the teaching. Some people say they are given revelations that God will prosper certain people. A leading prosperity gospel teacher was in my city recently. He assisted in taking an offering for the church where he was speaking. He told the audience that God had given him a revelation. There were twenty in the audience whom God would make millionaires if they would give to this special offering. Probably two hundred people in the audience said, *I'm one of them!*

There is another new twist. Some say Jesus was wealthy. Because he had a treasurer, this means he had a great deal of wealth. He lived in a big house in Jerusalem and wore designer clothes.[5]

### Searching

What does the Bible say about believers and prosperity? Prosperity teachers have assembled carefully selected Bible verses to prove their point. There is no way to look at all of them here. So let's look at some of the main ones.

Third John 2 says, "Dear friend, I pray that you may enjoy good health and that all may go well with you, even as your soul is getting along well." Latching on to the word *prosper*, some teach that God's will for all believers is for them to be financially prosperous. What does the verse really say? The word *prosper* literally means "to get along well." The word was used as a common greeting and desire expressed in the letters of New Testament times.[6] This verse is not a blanket guarantee that Christians will be healthy and prosperous. To teach that it is God's will for all Christians of all ages in all places to be prosperous is foreign to the verse's true meaning.

Look at Galatians 3:13–14. Those verses say, "Christ redeemed us from the curse of the law by becoming a curse for us, for it is written: 'Cursed is everyone who is hung on a tree.' He redeemed us in order that the blessing given to Abraham might come to the Gentiles through Christ Jesus, so that by faith we might receive the promise of the Spirit." Verse 29 adds, "If you belong to Christ, then you are Abraham's seed, and heirs according to the promise." Prosperity teachers say the Christians' right to claim material blessings has its origin in the Abrahamic covenant. What was the blessing of Abraham? They say it was material prosperity. It is true he was very rich. They also add that in the Old Testament material prosperity was one of the blessings promised.

Referencing Deuteronomy 28, prosperity teachers say that every part of life—spiritual, physical, and financial—can be released from the curse of the law. Well, what is the curse of the law referred to in Galatians 3:13? Go just three verses before verse 13 to verse 10. It says, "All who rely on observing the law are under a curse, for it is written: 'Cursed is everyone who does not continue to do everything written in the Book of the Law.'" So the curse of the law is the curse of trying to do the works of the law in order to be saved. This is not a material curse but a moral curse. Christ has redeemed us from that. He became a curse for us. We are saved not by what we do but by what Jesus did for us on the cross.

So what is the blessing of Abraham? Salvation by faith. We are saved by faith like Abraham was. Verses 27–28, leading to verse 29, point out that to be "in Christ" deals with salvation benefits. Material benefits are not discussed. Remember many Old Testament promises were specifically made to the nation of Israel, not to the church. All God's promises are not given to all God's people. For instance, God specifically promised the land of Palestine to his chosen people Israel. That promise is not intended for Christian believers today.

Also consider Romans 10:8–10. To teach that a person may speak a *rhema* word and bring prosperity into existence is to take this passage totally out of context. Verses 9–11 make clear that Paul was talking about the message of salvation, not some magic formula. Verse 10 says, "For it is with your heart that you believe and are justified, and it is with your mouth that you confess and are saved."

Consider Mark 10:30. Remember, Jesus promises the hundredfold blessing. This is certainly no promise that if a person gives ten dollars to someone's ministry, he will receive a thousand dollars in return. This takes the promise completely out of context. Jesus is talking about spiritual blessings, not material.

Another troubling doctrine connected with the prosperity gospel and with the Word of Faith teaching is the idea that we are all little gods. Using Psalm 82:6, "You are 'gods'; you are all sons of the Most High," they teach this doctrine. The verse must be read in context. These words were spoken in judgment to ungodly men. Jesus quoted this verse with the same idea of judgment in John 10:34. In his quotation, Jesus declared his deity. The Pharisees knew the context very well. He was hurling the passage of Scripture in their faces with sarcasm and irony.

Was Jesus rich? Those who teach he was give a strained interpretation of Luke 9:57–58. In this passage, Jesus said he had no place to lay his head. But the prosperity teachers say he meant, "I don't have a place to stay in Samaria." So he had to go back to his luxury home in Jerusalem.[7] No respectable Bible teacher I have ever heard or read holds to this view. Jesus came to the world and made himself poor for us. Second Corinthians 8:9 says, "For you know the grace of our Lord Jesus Christ, that though he was rich, yet for your sakes he became poor, so that you through his poverty might become rich."

What about the Rhema teaching? There are two Greek terms for the word. One is *logos*, which refers to the written word. The other is *rhema*, referring to the spoken word. To make such a distinction between the two words, as the positive confession teachers do, cannot be justified. A survey of the two words in the New Testament points out that they are used interchangeably. For instance, 1 Peter 1:23 refers to "the living and enduring word of God." It is the word *logos*. Verse 25 continues by saying, "The word of the Lord stands forever." It is the word *rhema*. The two words are used interchangeably. In Ephesians 5:26, "cleansing her by the washing with water through the word" uses the Greek word *rhema*. A similar passage in John 15:3 says, "You are already clean because of the word I have spoken to you." The word here is *logos*.[8]

Does God bless us only when we use positive words? Scripture does not sustain this view. In the Old Testament, King Jehoshaphat confessed his lack of strength against his enemies. This was a negative statement. Yet God gave Jehoshaphat a big win (see 2 Chr. 20). In the New Testament, Paul speaks of his weakness. But he said he was strong because God's strength was made perfect in his weakness (see 2 Cor. 12:9–10).

Prosperity teachers conveniently ignore hundreds of verses which stand in clear opposition to their teachings. Many verses could be named here, especially the ones that warn about the dangers of wealth. One will serve our purpose. Paul warned young Timothy, "People who want to get rich fall into temptation and a trap and into many foolish and harmful desires that plunge men into ruin and destruction. For the love of money is a root of all kinds of evil. Some people, eager for money, have wandered from the faith and pierced themselves with many griefs" (1 Tim. 6:9–10).

## Evaluating

Okay, let's evaluate the prosperity teaching in light of Bible teaching. There are pieces of truth found in the prosperity teaching. God *is* concerned about our need for material things. He knows we need food to eat and promises to give us our daily bread. He knows we need dresses and jeans, and he promises to provide them. God *does* meet our needs. God gives us the ability to acquire cars, houses, and boats. And if you give, God will bless you. But placing one's sole focus on material prosperity obscures the central point of the gospel. The great promise of the gospel is eternal life and spiritual well-being. Other than that, there's no guarantee of freedom from trouble in this life.

In prosperity teaching, the Christian uses God. The Holy Spirit becomes a power we can use for our own desires instead of a Person with whom we can have a relationship.

If you have ever been to a nice hotel and called for room service, you felt pampered. But God is not some bellboy on call for us day and night. God is sovereign. He doesn't serve us; we serve him. Prosperity teaching puts you in charge instead of God. God's will becomes dependent upon our will. Man, not God, becomes the center of all things.

What about the spiritual laws in the Bible? They are there, but they don't run the universe. God runs his universe. Psalm 24:1 says,

> The earth is the Lord's, and everything in it,
> the world, and all who live in it.

The prosperity doctrine teaches us to believe that God will go along with whatever lifestyle we pick. *When you start telling God what to do, sirens should sound in your ear.*

All New Testament Christians were not prosperous. Some were, but most were not. Many faced the loss of material things when they came to Christ. Does this mean they were out of the will of God? Did they fail to discover and utilize the keys to material prosperity? I don't think so. What about Paul? His words in Philippians 3:7–8 are moving: "But whatever was to my profit I now consider loss for the sake of Christ. What is more, I consider everything a loss compared to the surpassing greatness of knowing Christ Jesus my Lord, for whose sake I have lost all things. I consider them rubbish, that I may gain Christ." Jesus was not rich. He died alone, naked, and penniless on the cross.

It's easy for Christians to read contemporary culture back into the Bible. That's one draw of the Charismatic movement today. It sets Christianity in a materialistic lifestyle. America's God today is materialism. We're in the business of acquiring and assembling toys. Did you see the bumper sticker, "When we die, the one with the most toys wins"? But even the person with the most toys still dies. What then?

Success is a deeply rooted idea in American culture. If we are not careful, we will reshape Christianity into our own contemporary American image. God does promise to supply our need but not our greed (see Phil. 4:19). Material prosperity is not always a blessing. I have been a pastor for more than forty years. I know from my own ministry that to have new cars, big houses, and memberships in country clubs may not be a sign of God's blessings. It may instead be a sign that one has sold out to materialism. The prosperity teaching is basically carnal teaching. I have known many Christians who turned from the Lord when they prospered. Remember Demas? He left Paul and went back home because "he loved this world" (2 Tim. 4:10).

Jim Bakker taught and lived prosperity. The glitzy, glamorous lifestyle of PTL certainly got America's attention. Now, looking back on a 1989 conviction for twenty-four counts of fraud and five years in prison, Jim Bakker calls the prosperity gospel a deception of Satan. He says, "I was proof-texting all the time. Just looking up Scriptures to prove my belief."[9]

Several aspects of the prosperity teaching are serious. One of these aspects is that positive confession teaches a denial of reality. Proponents of positive confession say there are two kinds of truth—truth based on our senses and truth based on the Word of God. You are to deny what your senses tell you. If you are sick, you are not sick in reality; you just see and feel the symptoms. A pastor friend told me about a man in his city who was going blind, but he refused insulin. He said he was not going blind; he just had symptoms from the devil. But he did go blind.

The prosperity gospel also teaches a futile view of faith. It is actually exercising faith in faith. Faith becomes a kind of magic lever. The lever turns on God's spiritual laws. The key is not our faith but the *object* of our faith. A.T. Robertson was probably the greatest Greek scholar of our time. He pointed out that the faith mentioned here is the faith of which God is the object.[10]

You don't create your own reality by your faith. Your words don't bring anything into existence. Faith is not a way to get things from God but the way we put our trust in God. Actually, faith is not the primary ingredient of the Christian life. Love is. Paul specifically said, "The greatest of these is love," in contrast to faith and hope (1 Cor. 13:13).

An even greater concern with prosperity teaching is the problem of claiming new revelation. Some prosperity teachers say that new secrets of prosperity have been revealed to them. For instance, Ken Hagin claims that an angel gave him keys to prosperity in a vision.[11] Hagin's view on prosperity is not original. While he says he got the message by "revelation knowledge," that does not seem to be the case. Dr. D. L. McConnell, a professor at Oral Roberts University, has documented extensively that Hagin took his teachings directly from E. W. Kenyon.[12]

Even more serious is the faulty view of Jesus Christ and man taught by prosperity teachers. Jesus had to be born again to make it possible for us to be prosperous, according to some. As I have noted previously, some also teach we can become little gods. One teacher put it this way, "Until we comprehend that we are little gods and we begin to act like little gods, we cannot manifest the kingdom of God."[13] They say, "You don't have a god in you; you are a god!" Therefore, if we are gods, we can expect to have the best. Listen to this: "He's [God] given us power to create wealth. . . . I believe in those days the believer is not going to be at the back of the bus taking a back seat any longer!"[14] Of course, this is exactly what the devil teaches. The devil promised Adam and Eve that they would be "like God" (Gen. 3:5). God is God. We are not God. We are God's children.

The connection between prosperity teachings and cultic teachings has been clearly shown by several writers. H. Terris Neuman, professor at the Southeastern College of Assemblies of God in Lakeland, Florida, has proven that the sources for many of E. W. Kenyon's ideas are the New Thought Philosophy Movement and Christian Science. The major tenets of these movements are health, prosperity, and happiness.[15] Neuman says that positive confession originated in the nineteenth century from the mind-healing cults such as New Thought, Christian Science, and the Unity School of Christianity. Christians should be concerned about the underground Christian origins of the prosperity gospel.[16]

McConnell believes the Charismatic movement is at a major crisis. Will it remain true to the faith or become cultic? He says, "Nothing less than the doctrinal orthodoxy of our movement is at stake."[17]

Here's one more observation about the "name it and claim it" teaching. It doesn't work. Check out the parking lots at places where it is taught. What kinds of cars do you see? There will be Plymouths and Cadillacs, Toyotas and Lincolns, just like at your church. But check the reserved spaces. Are the big cars there? Chances are, these are reserved for the teachers. The only people the prosperity gospel seemingly works for are those teaching it. Notice they always teach that God will prosper you if you give to *their* ministry. Why don't they get a blessing by giving to *your* ministry?

I've thought a lot about that miracle pocketbook the radio preacher talked about all those years ago. I've wondered: Why didn't he use it himself? If he had such a pocketbook, why couldn't he let it produce twenty-dollar bills out of one-dollar bills and provide for his ministry? What a concept!

I'm sure there are prosperity teachers who are sincere in their teaching. But for those who are insincere, God's judgment is promised. Those who take advantage of God's people for their own selfish ends are severely condemned in Scripture. Jude 11 says they "have rushed for profit into Balaam's error." Second Peter 2:3 says, "In their greed these teachers will exploit you with stories they have made up." These teachers have a platform other believers don't—TV, radio, books, and tapes. Their platform makes it possible for them to receive large amounts of money.

Many people buy into this prosperity teaching and discover that it doesn't work for them. Maybe they didn't believe hard enough? Is there some secret sin in their lives? They may just drop out. Then they figure they tried Christianity, but it didn't work.

The true gospel can be preached anywhere. Here is a good test for the message you preach—will it work in Nigeria? Will it work in Bosnia? Will it work in the ghetto? Will it work at college?

There's more to life than material possessions. Jesus taught that we should "not store up for yourselves treasures on earth" (Matt. 6:19). In Luke 12:15, he declared, "Watch out! Be on your guard against all kinds of greed; a man's life does not consist in the abundance of his possessions." Think about the parable of the rich fool in Luke 12.

The will of God should be our ultimate desire. It is not wrong, as the prosperity gospel teachers suggest, to pray "if God wills." First John 5:14 says specifically, "If we ask anything *according to his will*, he hears us." James 4:15 says, "*If it is the Lord's will*, we will live and do this or that."

Jesus was facing the cross. He would die poor, in pain and shame. What were His words the night before the cross? "Not my will, but yours be done" (Luke 22:42).

Sometimes unpleasant things may be in God's will for your life. God may make you rich. He may not. God prospers some people but not others. He knows what we can handle and what we cannot. You may *want* a Rolex watch. You may *need* a good Timex. So what should our attitude be? Paul said, "I have learned to be content whatever the circumstances" (Phil. 4:11). God will not give us everything we want. But he will supply our needs. Remember Philippians 4:19. While we must have "things" to exist, we must look at life from a heavenly, eternal perspective, not just an earthly, material point of view. Examine Philippians 3:19–20 for more on this.

Proverbs 30:8–9 is a good prayer:

> Keep falsehood and lies far from me;
> give me neither poverty nor riches,
> but give me only my daily bread.
> Otherwise, I may have too much and disown you
> and say, 'Who is the LORD?'
> Or I may become poor and steal,
> and so dishonor the name of my God.

What's in a name? The abundant, Spirit-filled life is in the name of Jesus.

## Testing, Testing . . .

1. The Bible test. What does the Bible say about this manifestation? Is it clearly taught in the Bible?

2. The Jesus Test. Does it honor and glorify Jesus? Is Jesus, the Holy Spirit, or the Christian the focus?

3. The Character Test. Does it contribute to a more Christlike life?

4. The Decency and Order Test. Is this within the guidelines of decency and order?

5. The Evangelism Test. Does it place the focus on winning people to Christ?

   Does it pass?
   YES _____
   NO _____

# CHAPTER 13

# A GRAVE
# IN INDIANA

Through the foggy beam of the car lights we see it. A strange, foreboding stone structure shaped like a pyramid. Each side has a different inscription. What is it and where am I?

It's 1:00 in the morning, and I'm in a graveyard in Indiana with Al Mohler, president of Southern Baptist Theological Seminary in Louisville, Kentucky. A preacher and a president in a graveyard. What's going on?

We're at the grave of William Branham, a healing evangelist during the 1940s to 1960s. According to him, an angel appeared to him early in his ministry saying, "As John the Baptist was sent for the forerunner of the first coming of Christ, you have a message that will bring forth the forerunning of the second coming of Christ." This angel, he said, stayed with him throughout his life. He also said he was able to detect diseases in people by vibrations in his right hand.

I see a large pyramid monument over William Branham's grave, with an eagle on top of the pyramid. Branham was considered the founder of the "latter rain" movement (mentioned in the chapter on Davidic worship). Among other things, he taught there would be a great end-time revival preparing for the second coming of Christ. A series of restorations would be part of this. A restoration of signs and wonders. A restoration of Davidic worship. And a restoration of the offices of apostles and prophets. Dr. Mohler and I, through the beam of the car lights, read the inscriptions on the pyramid. The name *Branham* is on one side. Underneath, I read, "as John the Baptist was sent to forerun the first coming of Christ, you will forerun His second coming!" June 1933. Under that, "Jesus Christ, the same yesterday, today and forever. Hebrews 13:8" What does it all mean?

On the back side of Branham's grave the seven churches of Revelation are listed, beginning with Ephesus on the bottom, moving up to Laodicea on the top. Branham taught that these represent the seven successive church ages, each with its own specific messenger.

Now Dr. Mohler and I move to the third side of the tombstone. Names are listed beginning with Paul, including Irenaeus, Martin Luther, and John Wesley. Right by Ephesus from side two, Branham's name appears. Branham proclaimed himself the angel of Revelation 3:14 for the church of Ephesus.

Branham was strongly antidenominational. In 1977, he prophesied that all denominations would be consumed by the World Council of Churches, under the control of Roman Catholicism. The rapture would then take place, and the world would be destroyed.[1] I'll tell you about side four of the pyramid later.

The latter rain movement was rejected in the late 1940s by mainline established Pentecostal denominations. In a position paper issued April 20, 1949, the Assemblies of God officially repudiated the teachings.

The most questionable aspect of the entire Charismatic movement is the restoration of the offices of apostles and prophets, who will speak new revelation. What is this about? Is God speaking new revelation today? Are there fresh messages beyond what we find in our Bible? Is the Bible enough, or do we need more? We will come back to Branham's grave later.

## Observing

All over the place in books, on radio, on TV, and on the Internet, people calling themselves apostles or prophets are speaking messages given to them by God. Some talk about the Lord's return, and others discuss winners and losers of football games. One prophet, according to his so-called "God-given dream," said that the Beatles had a special anointing from God to bring in a music revival, but they wasted it.[2] "Prophets" are saying "God told me" in conferences and seminars. Oral Roberts said in 1987 that he had a vision of a huge Christ who told him that God would call him home if he didn't raise eight million dollars for his now-closed City of Faith Medical Center.

Recently a family from our church came to visit me. The daughter is involved in a religious group with "prophets." One of the "prophets" told her to marry a certain boy and when she should marry him. This is not unusual. Some people believe and teach that all Christians can receive messages from God through visions and dreams. I recently got an anonymous letter from a lady who said, "God told me there would be a drought. I should have let you know." Her letter delivered the bad news, but she did not tell me what to do about it.

Years ago, just before the morning service at my church, a man came in telling me God had told him to preach for me. Using an old Spurgeon idea, I told him God had given me a later revelation that I was to preach that morning. He left, telling me judgment was coming to me. That was about forty years ago.

What about these prophecies? Does the information being broadcast today match up with what is in your Bible? Many people involved in the new revelation and prophecy movement say it doesn't. They say the prophecies are just reminders and information about Bible truths and future events. God is giving us the "411" for today.

Remember William Branham's angel? He claimed this one stayed with him throughout his ministry. This angel also told him he would be able to know the details of people's lives through special words of knowledge. Those who make such prophecies admit that they are not always right. They admit to being right about two-thirds of the time. This means they miss one prophecy out of three.

What about the restoration of apostles? Currently these restoration groups teach that this is the final piece in the puzzle. They claim these end-time apostles will go way beyond anything the New Testament apostles did. Their belief is based on Ephesians 4:11 which talks about the gift of apostle and then it says in 4:13, "Until we all reach unity in the faith and in the knowledge of the Son of God and become mature, attaining to the whole measure of the fullness of Christ." This means to them that we must have apostles until the end of the age.

I recently read David Cannistraci's book on the subject. His ideas couldn't be clearer. In the end time, according to his teachings, there will be several restorations—gifts, praise/worship, office of apostles. He says the apostle/prophet link is the missing one in the chain of restoration. Cannistraci affirms, "We still need the office of the prophet to manifest in its fullness."[3] He also states that he does not mean these apostles will be on the level of New Testament apostles. Even though he distinguishes between modern apostleship and the unique New Testament apostleship, he assigns authority and New Testament powers to these modern apostles and gives them even more significance than the New Testament apostles.

Networks of apostle-led churches are growing worldwide. Many Charismatic churches are independent. Some of their pastors feel the need for direction, supervision, and encouragement. So "apostles" all over the world are creating churches and providing this direction and supervision. Some of these "apostles" are self-appointed. Others are ordained by church networks. Check them out in Peter Wagner's recent book *The New Apostolic Churches* where he lists several churches which he considers to be apostolic in nature.[4]

What about the restoration of the office of "prophets"? "Prophets" and "prophetesses" are making prophecies about end-time events today. They often say, "Thus says the Lord," or "This is the word of the Lord." These prophets teach that the Lord speaks to the church today through prophecies. The message of these prophecies is very important. One church says, "Any and all prophecy that goes forth will be audio-taped for the person receiving the prophetic word. They will be asked to take it home, write it out and wait. Receive the 'Word' (and it is your choice or will if you yield to the word) and God will provide the 'way.' Second Chronicles 20:20 says, 'Believe his prophets; so shall you prosper.' To accept and appreciate the ministry of the prophet is to accept and appreciate Jesus, The Prophet."[5]

What does all this mean? Most Charismatics affirm that this is not adding to the Bible. But some say that these current revelations are modern expressions of God's voice. The Christian faith has always clearly believed and communicated that God's full and final revelation is in the Bible and that the Bible, the Holy Scripture, is the Word of God. So if God is now giving additional truth, the Bible is only a partial revealing of God's truth. If this is true, we must be open to what current so-called "prophets" are saying. If it's true, then the Word of God includes more than just sixty-six books. It also includes dreams, visions, words of knowledge, and special messages given by prophets.

William Branham has his followers to this day. Although he died a few days after an automobile accident in 1965, his followers, called Branhamites, persist to this day. His sermons are called "The Message." His message, according to Branhamites, is the word of God.[6]

### Searching

As always, look to the Bible. What does it say? Let's search the Scriptures.

Think about the idea of new revelation and our Bible. We believe the sixty-six books in our Bible compose the Word of God. When the Bible was completed, I believe Scripture revelation stopped. The Bible is God's final, complete revelation of saving truth. Revelation 22:18–19 specifically forbids adding to this revelation. Jude 3 says, "Contend for the faith that was once for all entrusted to the saints." The word *entrusted* is an aorist passive participle in the Greek language, meaning an act completed in the past with no future orientation.

Second Corinthians 3:16 says that all Scripture is God-breathed. The Bible is God speaking to us. The Bible's words are God's words. Many passages make this clear. For instance, Jeremiah 1:9 says, "Now, I have put my words in your mouth." The phrase "thus saith the Lord" occurs more than three thousand times in the King James Version of the Bible.

But some people say there is other revelation mentioned in the Bible. The Bible does talk about the revelation of God's judgment (Rom. 1:18; 2:5). Also, the return of Christ is called revelation (1 Pet. 1:13). When a person is saved, Jesus Christ is revealed in that experience (Matt. 11:27; Gal. 1:15–16). But revelation as it relates to Scripture is different.

Basically, to teach that God is still giving new revelation is to undermine the authority of the Bible. Liberals teach that revelation is still open and ongoing. Certain hymns, they say, are the same as the psalms. You are treading in treacherous water when you take the view that God is giving new revelations today. If it's true, let's write these revelations down, put them in books, and study them.

Think about the office of apostles. What does the Bible teach? The word *apostle* means "one sent." It was an ordinary word used for messengers. As best I can determine, it is used three different ways in the New Testament. First, Jesus is referred to as *the* apostle (Heb. 3:1). He was sent from heaven to earth. Secondly, the word is sometimes used in the common, wider sense. For instance, Andronicus and Junia are called apostles (Rom. 16:7). We would use the word *missionary* today. In this wider sense, anyone who preaches Christ where Christ is not known is a messenger. It amazes me that Cannistraci places Paul in this category. He uses the term *secondary apostle* and says Paul was a secondary apostle. What do you say about that, Brother Paul? "But I do not think I am in the least inferior to those 'super-apostles'" (2 Cor. 11:5).

Thirdly, the word *apostle* is used in the New Testament in a very limited, technical sense, referring to those who were in the office of apostle. The Twelve chosen by Christ were apostles (see Matt. 10:2; Acts 1:2–3). The word also refers to the apostle Paul (see Rom. 1:1; 11:13; 1 Cor. 9:2). Although he staunchly affirmed that he was an apostle, he also considered himself to be the least of them (1 Cor. 15:9).

How did these men get their jobs? What were the requirements? One clear requirement was that an apostle had to be an eyewitness to the resurrection of Jesus (Acts 1:22; 1:2–3). Paul saw Jesus alive, so he qualified (1 Cor. 9:1). To authenticate their witness to the resurrection, they were given power to do signs and wonders (Acts 2:43). These signs and wonders are specifically called signs or marks of an apostle (1 Cor. 12:12).

New Testament apostles had authority. They could give commands (2 Pet. 3:2). They taught doctrine which came to be known as "the apostles' teaching" (Acts 2:42). They also made decisions about doctrine (Acts 15:6). The apostles are called "holy" (Eph. 3:5). The word means they were set apart for a special task. They were to write down Scripture. This was foundational to the life and growth of the church.

The New Testament also warns us about false apostles. Second Corinthians 11:13 and Revelation 2:2 make clear that some will claim to be apostles when they are not. When anyone claims to be an apostle, this question was to be asked: Was he an eyewitness to the resurrection of Jesus Christ?

What does the New Testament teach about the office of prophet? The office of the prophet is often tied to that of the apostle (see Rev. 18:20; 2 Pet. 3:2; Eph. 3:5). Sometimes the same individual is both an apostle and a prophet. According to the King James Version, this was true of John, the apostle who also gave the prophecy of the Revelation (Rev. 1:1–3).

There were prophets and prophetesses in the Old Testament and the New Testament. The word *prophet* simply means primarily to "forth tell" rather than to foretell. Although at times they foretold future events, this was not their primary function. A prophet was one who spoke for God.

The New Testament uses the idea of the prophet in two senses. There is the wider or more general sense we could call the gift of prophecy. One who proclaims the Word of God is one who has the gift of prophecy. First Corinthians 12–14 evidently refers to this wider gift of prophecy. A prophet is neither a fortune-teller nor one who predicts the future. He is one called to preach the Word. It has to do with proclamation, not revelation (see 1 Cor. 14:3; 1 Thess. 5:20). I believe God has given me the gift of prophecy. I seek, with the anointing of the Holy Spirit, to proclaim the written Word.

The terminology is also used in a more restricted and specific sense, referring to the office of prophet. In the Old Testament, men like Moses, Elijah, and Isaiah had the gift of the prophet. God used them to speak and to write Scripture. Once the Old Testament books were completed, the office of the prophet ceased. There was no more office of the prophet until John the Baptist began to speak, announcing the coming of Christ.

In the New Testament, some people had the office of prophet: John the Baptist, Paul, etc. Before the New Testament was completed, they spoke messages unique to the era of the apostles. This office of the prophet is referred to in Ephesians 4:11. These prophets were involved in the foundational work for the church along with the apostles, and they verbally declared the Word of God before it was written down. New Testament apostles were given the ability to write Scripture. The New Testament apostles were given the ability to declare Scripture. Those of us who preach today are declarers of Scripture. Back then they were bearers of Scripture.

Does the New Testament teach that the apostles and prophets will be needed in the end time? First of all, in Ephesians 4:13 the word *until* does not refer to a continuation of the offices of apostles and prophets in verse 11 but rather to the process of the building up of the church to full maturity. What role did the apostles and prophets play in that? Ephesians 2:2 makes it clear. Their role was to build a foundation. The foundation of the church of the Lord Jesus Christ is the person and work of Jesus himself (1 Cor. 3:11). The oral and written witness of the apostles and prophets to the work of Christ is how they laid the foundation of the church.

The church in Ephesians 2:20–22 is referred to as a building. I don't know much about building. But I do know that once the foundation is laid, then comes the superstructure, and finally the roof. The foundation is laid only once. It comes at the beginning of the project, not at the end. The apostles and prophets did foundational work. They gave us our New Testament. When that work was completed, their part in the process ended.

It should also be noted that there are specific warnings about false prophets. These false prophets will appear in the end times. Jesus indicated this in Matthew 24:11, 24. So did Peter (2 Pet. 2:1). The apostle John declared, "Dear friends, do not believe every spirit, but test the spirits to see whether they are from God, because many false prophets have gone out into the world" (1 John 4:1).

## Evaluating

It is clear to me that the offices of apostles and prophets have ceased. Apostles were special men for a special purpose in a special age. They were chosen by Jesus Christ. They were eyewitnesses of his resurrection, and they had unique authority to teach doctrine and to write Scripture. This was foundational to the church. When the last apostle laid down his pen, the New Testament was complete, and the office of apostle ceased. They had and will have no successors.

The office of prophet also ceased. This is why 1 Corinthians 13:8 says, "Where there are prophecies, they will cease; . . . where there is knowledge, it will pass away." This doesn't mean there won't be people who preach. Nor does it mean a time will come when we will have no more knowledge. But

1 Corinthians 13:9 describes the foundation of Scripture being put together piece by piece.

At the time Paul was writing, only James, Matthew, Galatians, 1 and 2 Corinthians and a few other books of the New Testament had been completed. More books were on their way. Then, as 1 Corinthians 13:10 indicates, "When perfection comes, the imperfect disappears." The office of prophet, vital to the giving of Scripture, would end. The gift of the knowledge to write Scripture would end. There was no more need for the New Testament offices of apostles and prophets. The Word of God is complete and sufficient, and we have no need for more.

Secondly, there is no need for new revelation. By the second century A.D., the books of the Bible were recognized as God's complete revelation to man. Remember that the Holy Spirit speaks through the Scripture. I don't know who said it, but I agree: "If it's true, it ain't new; if it's new, it ain't true." That may be poor grammar, but it's correct theology.

Here is the question: Does the Bible have everything Christians need for faith and godly living, or do we need further revelation? If the Word of God is sufficient, why do we need any additional prophecies or revelations? This suggests that God hasn't said enough in the Bible. Some say that some prophecies and revelations today are just rehashing truths already found in the Bible. If it is already in the Bible, why not go to the Bible?

I admit there is something tantalizing and exciting about the idea of receiving a fresh, current message instead of studying an ancient book. Why spend time reading and searching Scripture when you could have a vision or dream in contemporary language? But 2 Timothy 3:16–17 makes clear that the Word of God provides all we need for guidance and growth.

Just about everyone who talks about prophecies being given today says the prophecies are not on the level of Scripture. But if they are from God, why are they not equal to Scripture? How can any word from God be on a lower level than any other word from God?

Some suggest that the "prophet" may not distinguish clearly between what God is saying and his own thoughts. Some say these prophets may inaccurately report what God has said. But the Bible gives a very simple test. Deuteronomy 18:21–22 says, "You may say to yourselves, 'How can we know when a message has not been spoken by the LORD?' If what a prophet proclaims in the name of the LORD does not take place or come true, that is a message the LORD has not spoken. That prophet has spoken presumptuously. Do not be afraid of him."

How do you determine if a prophecy is of God? It must be 100 percent accurate. What about your pastor who preaches the Bible on Sunday? There is a simple way to evaluate his message. Check it out by using the Bible. By the way, verse 20 of Deuteronomy 18 gives the Old Testament judgment for those who make incorrect prophecy: "But a prophet who presumes to speak in my name anything I have not commanded him to say, or a prophet who speaks in the name of other gods, must be put to death."

I'm back at the grave of William Branham. He predicted the world would end in 1977. It did not. His followers emphasize it was only a prediction, not a prophecy. What's the difference between the two terms? I don't think there is any.

We should be alert to false apostles and prophets. Remember that the Bible says more about the prevalence of false prophets in the end-time than at any other time. Anyone can claim to have a message from God. The idea of prophecies and revelations being given today is really a formula for chaos in the church. One person in a group claiming to speak for God can exercise tremendous control. I fear that some people use prophecy to control people and put them under bondage. Jeremiah 23:16–32 should be read and contemplated very carefully in dealing with this.

There is also the danger that people will rely on and make life-changing decisions based on what people think is a prophecy from God. People tied to a strong leader tend to do what the leader says God told them to do. Let's be very careful about such terminology as "God told me" or "I have a word from God for you." You're dealing with the big time if you claim to speak the very word of God.

Neil Babcox is a former Charismatic pastor who left the movement. In his fascinating and devastating book on the Charismatic movement, he says the matter of prophecy finally convinced him he should no longer be a Charismatic. He says the four words "Thus saith the Lord" were what caused his realization. He saw people's lives wrecked because of so-called prophecies. He concluded that prophecy in the New Testament sense was a vehicle of the verbal revelation of Scripture. Talking about Ephesians 3:5, where the mystery of Christ had been fully revealed to the apostles, he concluded that prophetic revelations could add nothing to that. So, he says, if prophecies today are only repetitions of Scripture, they are unnecessary. He also states that unlike New

Testament Christians, we have the completed Scripture. So there is no need for prophecy to supplement that which we already have.[7]

The matter of God's guidance of people today is involved in our subject of prophecy and new revelation. There is a difference between being led or guided by the Holy Spirit and being moved by the Holy Spirit in order to write Scripture. The Romans 8:14 experience, "those who are led by the Spirit of God," is not the 2 Peter 1:21 experience, "Men spoke from God as they were carried along by the Holy Spirit." All Christians are led by the Holy Spirit, but only the New Testament writers were "moved" by the Holy Spirit.

We may receive illumination or explanation to help us understand Scripture, but not revelation to enable us to speak or write Scripture. Check out your impressions by the Scripture. God may impress us in certain ways. But there is a difference between impressions and revelations.

Let's talk about Paul's statement in Ephesians 1:17. This verse causes some Charismatics to teach that God gives new revelation today. Paul prayed, "I keep asking that the God of our Lord Jesus Christ, the glorious Father, may give you the Spirit of wisdom and revelation, so that you may know him better." But, also read verse 17 in light of verse 18 which says, "That the eyes of your heart may be enlightened."

Paul was not saying that we might have new revelation beyond what is taught in the Bible. The work of the Holy Spirit in the life of the believer today is to contribute to our understanding of it and to empower us to live it and to proclaim it to others. Probably Paul was praying that God would give them insight into the letter (Ephesians) they were reading. By extension, we apply this emphasis to Spirit-assisted understanding of God's entire revelation in Scripture.

Now my concerns become very heavy. Virtually every cult and false religion started when a leader claimed some new revelation. Joseph Smith claimed an angel appeared to him and gave him tablets of gold with new Scripture. He started the Mormon church.

Back at Branham's grave, I now view the fourth side of the pyramid. On the bottom it gives the name, place of birth, and death of William Branham and his wife Marie. Above that it says, "Behold I will send you Elijah the prophet before the coming of the great and dreadful day of the Lord; but in the days of the voice of the seventh angel, when he shall begin to sound, the mystery of God shall be finished, as he hath declared to his servant the prophet." As you recall, Branham said this is what the angel told him. The words of Paul were ringing in my ears at Branham's grave: "But even if we or an angel from heaven should preach a gospel other than the one we preached to you, let him be eternally condemned!" (Gal. 1:8).

When the door is opened to further revelation, words of knowledge, or prophecies through the restoration of apostles and prophets who supposedly speak for God, the authority of Scripture is undermined. This gives me real concern about the idea of the restoration of apostles and prophets and new revelation. Remember the "latter rain" teaching of Branham? This is part of it. The other doctrines of Branham are serious, too. He denied eternal hell. He taught if you belonged to a denomination, salvation was blocked for you. He denied the Trinity. He also taught the controversial serpent seed doctrine—that Eve had sex with the serpent, thus causing the Fall of man. And he taught the restoration of apostles and prophets.

In my opinion, Charismatic groups are faced with a serious decision. They must ask themselves where all of this will end. The decision of the Assemblies of God in 1949 to reject "latter rain" doctrines was a wise one. In their position paper on the matter, they say, "The true test of any movement is whether or not it will stand up under the light of the Word of God."[8]

Great extremes in doctrine usually start with slight deviations. I live not far from Cape Kennedy in Florida. When spaceships are launched, they must be on target to the finest degree. Just a slight deviation at the beginning can lead to great disaster. The same is true in matters of Bible doctrine.

Second Peter 1:19 says, "We have the word of the prophets made more certain." Peter was referring to the Word of God. The next time someone wants to give you a prophecy, just say, "We have a more certain word." If you read a book that tells you to expect messages from God through visions and predictions, say, "We have a more certain word of prophecy."

Pastor Monty and his two prophetesses, Prissie and Maxine, were involved in a movement that was sweeping the country. Monty had been a former priest in a mystery religion. He was receiving "new prophecy." These special messages would come when he was asleep and through ecstatic trances. So did the prophetesses. He claimed they spoke for God himself because the office of prophet had been revived to bring in the second coming of Christ. The movement became so popular that Dr. Tully, the famous theologian, joined it. Its wildly popular teaching and phenomenal growth was pointed to as proof that the end-time revival had come and the return of Christ was near.

This happened in Phrygia, Asia Minor, A.D. 150. I changed the names just a little. The man was Montanus. The prophetesses were Prisca and Maximilla.

The theologian was Tertullian. Their restoration movement brought great division in the church. It was condemned by the church council at Constantinople as heresy.[9]

Want another true story from church history? A pastor and a woman walked into a meeting. A denominational committee was talking with the pastor about some of the doctrines and practices of his church that were not in keeping with the position of the group. The pastor then announced to the committee that he was an apostle. When asked, "Who told you that you were an apostle?" he pointed to the woman, telling them she was a prophetess.

"Are you a prophetess?" a member of the committee asked.

"Yes," she said, "I can walk in a room and tell what people's spiritual gifts are. And that man [pointing to the pastor] is without a doubt an apostle."

"What if your words contradict what the Bible says? Which do you take?" she was asked.

"Oh, my words, of course," she said.

Where did this happen? It happened in Florida in 1995.

So there I stood at Branham's grave. I had read all four sides of the pyramid. The story doesn't end there. Dr. Mohler told me that each Easter Sunday morning Branham's followers gather at his grave, expecting his resurrection, which will signal the second coming of Christ. The next time you think someone is an apostle or a prophet or that new revelation is being given, come visit a grave in Indiana.

### Testing, Testing . . .

1.  The Bible Test. What does the Bible say about this manifestation? Is it clearly taught in the Bible?

2.  The Jesus Test. Does it honor and glorify Jesus? Is Jesus, the Holy Spirit, or the Christian the focus?

3.  The Character Test. Does it contribute to a more Christlike life?

4.  The Decency and Order Test. Is this within the guidelines of decency and order?

5.  The Evangelism Test. Does it place the focus on winning people to Christ?

    Does it pass?

    YES _____

    NO _____

# PART 3

# EXHORTATIONS

This section includes three practical chapters about the Holy Spirit's work in the matters of our emotions, public worship, and witnessing. These chapters can be wrapped up in three words: Enjoy, Worship, Go.

## CHAPTER 14

# YOU, ENJOY!

When I woke up that morning, I had the distinct feeling that my father had died. It was overwhelming. I couldn't shake it. All those emotions.

As I left my dorm room for dinner, I walked by the hall telephone. I dreaded that it would ring. It did! My heart skipped several beats as I walked over to answer it.

"Long distance call for Jerry Vines," the operator said. My heart stopped.

"This is he," I replied.

"Jerry, this is Stewart Martin." Mr. Martin was the director of the local funeral home in my hometown. I just knew that my father was dead.

But he wasn't. I was pastor of a church in my home county. A member of the church had died, and Mr. Martin had called to tell me.

In the span of one day, I had been through the emotional ringer. I had experienced all types of emotions. But none was based on truth. Emotions can be extremely unreliable.

We humans are capable of many emotions: love, hate, joy, sorrow, hope, fear, etc. Do you want a genuine, authentic relationship with the Holy Spirit? Then you're going to be emotional. This isn't too difficult because we humans are emotional beings.

The Holy Spirit can be in our lives. As humans, we have a mind to think, a will to act, and a heart to feel. The King James Version of Romans 6:17 talks about these facets of personality working in spiritual matters. "That form of doctrine which was delivered to you" points to the intellectual element. The mind is where we receive the truth of God. It is understood and accepted. "From the heart" speaks of the emotional aspect. With our hearts (the emotions), we embrace the truth, and the Holy Spirit stirs our hearts with it. "But ye have obeyed" is the volitional aspect. Once we hear and receive the truth and feel stirred in our emotions by it, we exercise our will by obeying the truth presented to us.

Where do emotions come from? They result from our temperament, physical surroundings, and relationships with people. We can't change our temperament. We can learn to control it. We may not be able to change our surroundings or the behavior of others, but we can determine what our response to them will be. We can act, not react. Our emotions are the shallowest part of our personality. And as I have said previously, the Holy Spirit does not do his deepest work in the shallowest part of our personality.

Having said that, we must admit that emotion is valid in the Christian life. I believe in "heartfelt religion." Christians are told to "keep your spiritual fervor, serving the Lord" (Rom. 12:11). Jesus said we are to love God with all our heart and soul (Mark 12:30). You can't observe the early Christians in the New Testament without seeing emotions involved. These Spirit-filled believers experienced the love, peace, and joy of the Holy Spirit in their emotions.

I think most Christians are too unemotional in their Christian faith. I used to hear the beloved evangelist Vance Havner say that we have gone all the way from hallelujah to ho-hum; from amen to so what. What about you and your relationship with the Holy Spirit? Fire or ice? I heard a story of an old deacon who, in the midst of a stirring revival prayed, "Oh, Lord, if there is a spark of fire among us, water that spark!"

Nothing is worse than dead, dry-eyed, heartless, cold religion. The average Christian in church today feels very little genuine emotion. I think this is why extreme emotional experiences are popular today. We have enough hotheads. We need some "hothearts." I'm not talking about cheap or questionable emotionalism where people foam at the mouth and roll on the floor. I'm talking about genuine emotion produced by the Holy Spirit.

Humans have a tendency toward extremes. For some, it's all heart. J. I. Packer says, "Only a fine line divides healthy emotion from unhealthy emotionalism, and any appealing to or playing on emotion crosses that line every time."[1] The Christian world has many emotional thrill seekers looking for the biggest show in town.

Vance Havner was asked about a particularly emotional denomination. "Dr. Havner, do you think those folks are going to heaven?"

Havner replied, "I think they will, if they don't run past it."

The opposite extreme is all head, no heart. For these Christians, their faith is merely an intellectual matter. They know doctrine, and they stand for the faith. But there is also a blockage somewhere between the head and the heart. They haven't let the truth of God grip their heart. These aren't the people you go to for sympathy when you have a problem. Reaction to Charismatic excesses shouldn't cause us to lose the emotional side of the work of the Holy Spirit. Emotion is an essential result of a real experience with God.

Jim Cymbala, pastor of the Brooklyn Tabernacle, says, "We have become proud of what we know. We are so impressed with our doctrinal orderliness that we have become intellectually arrogant . . . such an attitude takes the heart out of the very word we preach."[2] Balance is the key. I have heard Warren Wiersbe say many times, "Blessed are the balanced."

Let's talk about the work of the Holy Spirit and our emotions. Look at Romans 6:17 again. It is clear that the mind and the will must be involved in emotion that is genuinely of the Holy Spirit. Genuine emotion, which is the product of the Holy Spirit in your life, is initiated by the truth of the Word of God and culminates by obedience to the Word of God.

When I think about the Holy Spirit and our emotions, several words come to my mind.

## Communion

Think of that word *communion*. It may not be familiar to you. Look at the King James Version of 2 Corinthians 13:14 where the phrase, "communion of Holy Spirit, be with you" occurs. This is all about fellowship. Maybe the word *relationship* makes it clearer—the relationship of the Holy Spirit. The Holy Spirit is a person. He loves us. Romans 15:30 talks about "the love of the Spirit." Colossians 1:8 speaks of "your love in the Spirit." Romans 5:5 says that "God has poured out his love into our hearts by the Holy Spirit, whom he has given us."

Salvation brings us into a relationship with the Holy Spirit. What's life all about? Life is relationships. Parents with children and children with parents. Husband and wives. Friends. Social relationships. Relationships on the job. Christianity is a relationship, not a set of rules or a mere philosophy. It's about love between us and God the Father, God the Son, and God the Holy Spirit. This experience certainly touches our emotions.

Galatians 4:6 says, "God sent the Spirit of his Son into our hearts, the Spirit who calls out, 'Abba, Father.'" How can this not be emotional? I know we don't all have the same emotional responses. I'll bet your children respond to you differently. One may be bubbly and excited. The other may be calm and quiet. Do they express their love to you in different ways? This doesn't mean one child loves you more than the other. It's dangerous to place too much emphasis on emotional response in salvation. We are never told we are saved by our feelings or that we should experience a certain feeling to be saved. We are saved by repenting of our sin and believing on the Lord Jesus Christ.

While we are not saved because we feel good, it sure feels good to be saved! I agree with one of my country preacher buddies who says about salvation, "If you can get it and not feel it, you can lose it and not miss it!" People express their emotions in different ways. Some may weep at their salvation experience. Others may shout. Some may even laugh. Some may show no outward emotion at all.

Relationships with people keep us from feeling lonely. But sin can really create a sense of loneliness. It separates us from others and from God. With the Holy Spirit in your life, you can have communion, fellowship, and relationship. We can sense the Holy Spirit's presence. Second Corinthians 13:14 talks about how the Holy Spirit can "be with you." He is with you. Wherever you are, he is there, because he dwells in our hearts. He is in us, and we are in him. Romans 8:16 says, "The Spirit himself testifies with our spirit that we are God's children." So we can have a sense of the presence of the Holy Spirit and not feel lonely.

This relationship with the Holy Spirit should be cultivated. Second Timothy 1:6 talks about stirring up the gift of God that is in us. Have you ever sat before a warm fire on a really cold day? It's so comforting. But if you don't tend the fire, it can burn low and lose its warmth. The same is true in any love relationship. A marriage relationship must be maintained constantly. This confirms the importance of a personal devotional life, meaning a daily time of Bible reading and prayer. How did Paul keep the flame burning through all the hard knocks he experienced? Remember when he was in prison? Death was right ahead of him. He told young Timothy to bring "the parchments" (2 Tim. 4:13). I take this to mean the Scriptures. The Word of God kept Paul's heart on fire.

Bible reading does stir the heart. You may not get goose bumps every morning as you read your Bible. Some mornings are better than others. But the fact is that the truths of the Bible warm the heart. Who can read the great truths of the Bible and not be awed? Who can read of the cross and not be stirred with the emotion of gratitude for Christ's sacrifice for us? Can we read about God's grace, his undeserved favor to us, and not be overwhelmed? We need to recover the heart, the heat, and the hallelujah of some basic Bible truths.

Read of the lostness of people. Get compassion. Read of the awfulness of hell. Get charged up to tell people about Jesus. Read of the price Jesus paid on the cross. Get motivated. After the disciples had walked with the living Jesus on the Emmaus road, they exclaimed, "Were not our hearts burning within us while he talked with us on the road and opened the Scriptures to us?" (Luke 24:32). Their hearts were glowing like pieces of burning wood. Think about Jeremiah, the prophet, who said,

His word is in my heart like a fire,
a fire shut up in my bones (Jer. 20:9).

Prayer is also a part of our daily devotional time. It's when we talk with the Lord. "Praying in the Holy Spirit" (Jude 20 NKJV) and asking for his help is an especially moving experience. I have known in my life what I call some old-time "pray-ers." These people were dear, simple saints of God who really knew how to pray. Some had a prayer rock in the woods near their home. Others had a prayer rug in their bedrooms. These people knew how to grab hold of the horns of the altar and get through to God. In our culture we are often too busy and too noisy. We need to learn how to pray with fervor and with great power again. Nothing moves the heart of a believer more than that special time when he or she has communion with the Lord through prayer.

I think about my own personal prayer time. Sometimes when I come to pray, I am cold and unconcerned, with burdens that have numbed my heart. Like the Black spiritual, I begin, "Nobody knows the trouble I've seen." But as I begin to pray and have communion with my Lord, something happens. I often conclude my devotional time like the Black spiritual, "Glory, hallelujah."

How does communion with the Holy Spirit make you feel? It makes me feel warm, accepted, loved, and secure.

## Consolation

When I think about the work of the Holy Spirit and my emotions, the second word I think of is *consolation*. You may not be familiar with this word. The King James Version of Acts 9:31 uses the phrase "the comfort of the Holy Spirit." The word *comfort* here is a synonym for the word I'm using—*consolation*. Both words actually tie together one of the titles for the Holy Spirit—*Comforter*. I prefer to translate this word "Friend," meaning one who is called beside us to encourage us. The Holy Spirit is the one who consoles us. Of all the titles of the Holy Spirit, this one brings the most warmth to my heart.

Remember losing your job? The phone rang. You heard the kind, reassuring words of a friend. That was consolation. Remember when your mom died? The doorbell rang. You opened the door. There stood a friend. She didn't say anything; she just hugged you and wept with you. Consolation again. Think of the night before the crucifixion. Everything was coming down on the disciples.

They were hopeless. Demons of fear were attacking them. Panic was overwhelming them. In the midst of it all Jesus said, "I will ask the Father, and he will give you another Counselor to be with you forever" (John 14:16). "I will not leave you as orphans; I will come to you" (John 14:18). This is true consolation.

Do you want some sweet consolations the Holy Spirit may use to assure our hearts in times of need? You are God's child. Romans 8:16 says, "The Spirit himself testifies with our spirit that we are God's children." A little girl falls and skins her knee. She runs weeping to her father. He takes her in his arms, holds her, and kisses her. That's consolation. God has a plan for us. We usually ask, "Why?" when things go wrong. But the Holy Spirit reminds us of the meaning and purpose to life. The Holy Spirit is working out a divine plan in our lives.

A while ago I visited the DreamWorks studio in Hollywood. They were producing the animated movie *The Prince of Egypt*. I was really interested in the storyboard. It basically mapped out the plot of the animation. Each scene was placed on the storyboard. God has a storyboard for our lives. He assures us that each piece fits the overall picture. That's consolation.

The Holy Spirit assures us that he is with us every step of the way, whatever the circumstance. Perhaps you are experiencing pain. You visit the doctor for a checkup, and he explains what's going on and what he's going to do about it. His treatment may bring more pain to you, but it will help you get well. It's easier to stand the pain if you know it will help you get well. One reason the Holy Spirit allows us burdens and heartaches is to help us learn about his consolation. Why did Jesus send his disciples into a storm? Because they learned some things about Jesus they could not know in any other way.

I have seen many Christian people lose loved ones. Of course, all the normal loss emotions are present: sorrow, pain, loneliness. But so many of them talk about experiencing an indescribably sweet sense of consolation. Many testify that Philippians 4:7, which promises the peace of God to stand guard in our hearts and minds, was their experience.

How does the consolation of the Holy Spirit make us feel? It makes us feel confident. We sense his peace. We feel that we are important to the Lord, that he is with us in what we're going through, and that he has a purpose and plan for it all.

## Conviction

When I think about the work of the Holy Spirit and how that affects our emotions, an unusual word comes to my mind—*conviction*. Normally, we think the Holy Spirit produces good feelings in our hearts. But the Holy Spirit can also cause bad feelings. On the day of Pentecost, when Peter preached the gospel, listeners were "cut to the heart"(Acts 2:37). The word actually indicates they were stabbed in their hearts. I'm sure that didn't feel good. The idea that the Holy Spirit might make us feel uncomfortable is not popular. We live in a "feel good" society. People want to come to church to feel good. But sometimes you have to feel bad before you can feel good.

Did you hear about the man who was hitting himself on the head with a hammer?

Someone asked him, "Why are you doing that?"

He replied, "Because it feels so good when I quit!"

In my previous book *SpiritLife*, I devoted a chapter to the Holy Spirit's work of convicting the lost. This is one of the works of the Holy Spirit—to convict people of their sin and their need of Christ. Jesus clearly indicates this by his statement in John 16:8, "When he comes, he will convict the world of guilt in regard to sin and righteousness and judgment." This is his initial work in the life of a lost person. A person can't be convicted of sin by the Holy Spirit and not have strong feelings. These feelings may consist of sorrow, guilt over sin, or even fear or shock. The lost person responds to these emotions produced by the truth of God in his heart. The bad emotions are replaced by the good emotions of joy, peace, and love.

It is also true that the Holy Spirit does convicting work in the life of a Christian. Just because we are saved doesn't mean he stops convicting us of our sin. I have repented more after being saved than I ever did before I was saved. Revelation 3:19 fits here. Jesus was writing to the church of Laodicea. He closed each of these letters by saying, "He who has an ear, let him hear what the Spirit says to the churches" (v. 21). He said, "Those whom I love I rebuke and discipline." He is writing to saved people, to lukewarm Christians at Laodicea. He is rebuking them. It is the same word used in John 16:8, referring to the Holy Spirit convicting lost people.

This rebuke is tied to discipline, or chastening. Chastening has to do with a parent disciplining a child. Hebrews 12:11 says that discipline is "not pleasant at the time, but painful." Remember your last spanking? You felt painful, not pleasant. But if discipline was done correctly and in the right spirit, you probably felt that you were part of a family that valued you. You had a father who cared enough about you to keep you from doing things that would be harmful to you. The conviction and discipline of the Holy Spirit are also designed to produce positive emotions in the long term. Hebrews 12:11 continues, "Later on, however, it produces a harvest of righteousness and peace for those who have been trained by it."

What about conviction? How does it make you feel? It makes me feel uncomfortable, miserable, and unhappy. But it makes me run to my heavenly Father for forgiveness and restoration, making me feel the Lord loves me enough to rebuke me and to discipline me. I feel valued as a member of the family. I have a sense of peace and belonging.

## Celebration

When I think about the work of the Holy Spirit and our emotions, the word *celebration* also comes to mind. Several verses talk about this aspect of the Holy Spirit's work in our hearts. First Thessalonians 1:6 mentions "the joy given by the Holy Spirit." Romans 14:17 talks about "joy in the Holy Spirit." Immediately after the command of Ephesians 5:18 to be "filled with the Spirit," verse 19 says, "Speak to one another with psalms, hymns and spiritual songs. Sing and make music in your heart to the Lord."

How do we express joy? People are different. Some shout, others weep, many sing. Others have warm, tender feelings and a sense of well-being and commitment. It would be wrong for any of us to try to impose our emotional responses on others. But no matter how we express it, the Holy Spirit can produce a great sense of joy in our hearts.

A saved person who has the Holy Spirit living in his or her life has the capacity to enjoy experiences that are peculiar to the spiritual world. This involves experiences like sensing forgiveness for past sins or failures and a sense of celebration. The believer is future oriented because he or she knows of the promise of heaven. The behavior is peaceful about the present because he or she has a purpose and blessings and reasons for existence. Jesus put it this way in John 4:14: "But whoever drinks the water I give him will never thirst. Indeed, the water I give him will become in him a spring of water welling up to eternal life." There is a difference between Spirit-worked rejoicing and feeling happy. Happiness comes from what happens. Joy comes from our relationship with God.

What's the natural result of the joy of the Holy Spirit? A desire to tell others about it. The primary purpose is not just to make you feel warm and fuzzy. It is to stimulate you to tell someone else about Jesus.

I remember the first time I led a person to Christ. He was a fifteen-year-old boy. The next Sunday night he was baptized at church. When I saw him baptized, a fire started to burn in my heart. Celebration flooded my heart. That was more than forty-five years ago. The fire is still burning. I have to stir it up from time to time, but the fire to tell others about Jesus has never gone out.

How does the celebration of the Holy Spirit make you feel? It makes me feel like singing and praising. I feel like telling someone about Jesus. I feel like coming "again with rejoicing, bringing in the sheaves" (Ps. 126:6 KJV).

Look at Romans 6:17 one more time. The truth of God is received in the mind, and it is the truth of God that moves the emotions. The emotions stir the will to obedience. Genuine emotion, which is produced by the Holy Spirit, must be initiated by the truth of the Word of God and culminated in obedience to the will of God. For example, we read in the Bible that Jesus gave his all on the cross for us. Our hearts are overwhelmed with gratitude. Then we respond to his call to surrender our lives to a daily life of cross-bearing. We don't start or stop with the emotional aspect. Emotion that does not lead to positive, correct action is dangerous.

So how do you tell if your emotions are genuine and Holy Spirit-created? After the emotion has passed, are you obedient to God?

We need the emotional aspect of the Spirit's work in our lives. Eighteenth-century England was in a mess. Unbelief had almost taken over. Infidelity and immorality were everywhere. A man named John Wesley went into a little chapel on May 24, 1738. There he heard Luther's preface to Romans. Wesley said, "I felt my heart strangely warmed." He was converted. Methodism was born. The course of a nation was changed because one man had a warming of the heart.

> Set us afire, Lord, stir us we pray;
> While the world perishes we go our way;
> Purposeless, passionless, day after day—
> Set us afire, Lord, stir us we pray.

**Stirring the Flame**

1. Begin a daily devotion time. If you already have one, renew your efforts to let the truths of the Bible grip your heart and motivate your actions for the day.

2. In every circumstance of life when your emotions come into play, look for the presence of the Holy Spirit in the situation. Claim the promises that he will be with you in the situation, providing love, joy, and peace.

3. Take a spiritual "getaway." Devote some special time to your relationship with the Holy Spirit. Seek a new intimacy with him. Fully express your love for him, the Lord Jesus and the heavenly Father.

4. And above all, *enjoy.*

## CHAPTER 15

# YOU, WORSHIP!

The worship service is beginning at Bethesda Baptist Church. The senior adults call it "Ole BeThursde." There are two amen sections: men to the right, women to the left. Most of the congregation is sitting in front of the pulpit. The pianist plays with a slow pace. Brother Bill lumbers to the pulpit and announces the hymn. We all stand to sing:

> Brethren, we have met to worship
> And adore the Lord our God.
> Will you pray with all your power
> While we try to preach the Word?
> All is vain unless the Spirit
> Of the Holy One comes down.
> Brethren, pray and holy manna
> Will be showered around.[1]

Now fast forward forty years to First Baptist Church, Jacksonville, Florida. The minister of music leads choir, orchestra, and congregation in a rousing rendition of "There's a feeling in the air, that God is everywhere." Things have certainly changed from "Ole BeThursde" to First Baptist Church, Jacksonville.

Worship is important to Christians. "There are many good definitions of *worship*. Worship is the believer's response of all that he is—mind, emotion, will, and body—to all that God is and says and does."[2] There is something so true about the old hymn we used to sing when I was pastor of Bethesda Baptist Church. Indeed, "All *is* vain" unless the Spirit of the Holy One comes down.

In John 4, Jesus gives the woman at the well important lessons about worship. He pointed out to her that worship is not so much a place as a person. He also indicated that true worship must be "in spirit and in truth." Here Jesus gave two very important guidelines for our worship. Worship must be "in Spirit"—spiritual. It must also be "in truth"—scriptural.

Romans 12:1 shows a beautiful picture of our total life being an act of worship. The believer offers himself or herself totally to God. That is what some translate as "spiritual worship." We go to church, but that's not all there is to it. Our entire lives should be acts of worship. Worship should be our constant attitude and activity. What we have been doing privately all week long, we should do publicly as we gather with God's people in God's house on God's day.

I have learned much about public worship from my Charismatic friends. Their worship has a relaxed, informal style. The sense of excitement and joy before the Lord is desirable. Too much worship in too many churches is cold, stiff, lifeless, and formal.

So there are differences of styles of worship. I don't know why, but churches tend to go to extremes. All the way from formalism to fanaticism, freeze or fry! Sometimes I watch visitors in our services. Those who come from Charismatic churches find it dull. Others from more formal churches look like they are bungee jumping. Actually, no specific style is mandated in the Bible. Just because you can't worship a certain way doesn't mean others cannot. The way you worship may not be suitable for everyone. The New Testament does not give specifics on forms of worship. No specific style of worship is part of any end-time restoration that will usher in the return of Christ.

This chapter will deal with some of the ingredients of worship from a New Testament perspective. Throughout this book, I have emphasized the culmination principle in studying Scripture. It means following a subject throughout the Bible, understanding that there is a progressive unfolding of truth in the Scriptures. With that in mind, it is surprising how little is said about public worship in the New Testament. With the New Testament suggestions to assist us, let's examine what is involved when God's people gather for public worship.

First, let's talk about certain physical activities. I have noted that Charismatics express themselves physically in their worship—lifting of hands, dancing, swinging with the music, prostrating, etc. They feel this deepens their worship. Clapping is mentioned in the Bible, but not much. Psalm 47:1 is one of the few references to clapping which seems to be connected to public worship. The clapping mentioned here seems to be different from the clapping in worship services today. I have seen clapping become a part of the worship services since I have been a pastor. Frankly, I didn't like it at first. It seemed irreverent to me. Clapping seems to be more an expression of pleasure at some musical presentation and agreement with the preacher's message. People do not necessarily worship the Lord by clapping. There is also rhythmic clapping to music which has been going on much longer. Before churches had orchestras, especially in rural areas, people would clap the rhythm to the music. Orchestras have rendered this unnecessary, though some worshipers still do it.

Shouting seems to have been a part of worship. The King James Version of Psalm 132:9 says, "And let thy saints shout for joy." I have known many saints of God through the years who have shouted. What about dancing? Passages in the Old Testament indicate dancing as a part of worship (see Pss. 149:3; 150:4; 2 Sam. 6:14). Lifting of hands is also mentioned in the Bible (see Pss. 28:2; 63:4; 119:48; 134:2; 141:2). When Jesus returned to heaven, we are told, "He lifted up his hands and blessed them" (Luke 24:50). First Timothy 2:8 mentions it: "I want men everywhere to lift up holy hands in prayer, without anger or disputing." The lifting up of hands here is connected to prayer. In the Old Testament it was common for people to pray with hands uplifted.

Most of the references to these various expressions in worship come from the Old Testament. They just aren't a big deal in the New Testament. A whole book in the Old Testament (Psalms) mentions some of these in a worship setting. But what about the New Testament? Various physical expressions are not the primary focus of New Testament worship. How are Christians to view them today?

I'll give you my personal approach to these matters. In the church I serve as pastor, we don't make a big deal out of them either way. We don't encourage, and we don't discourage. I do, however, discourage manipulation. If worship is genuinely of the Spirit, no one will have to "whip it up." Christians should be very respectful and sensitive to others and not be obnoxious. They should never distract from the preaching of the Word. I don't believe Christians should put pressure or impose their ways of worship on others. Keep in mind that what we do should be done decently and in order (see 1 Cor. 14:33, 40).

It is biblical to say "amen" but even this should not be done to get attention. It is proper for people to respond in praise to the Lord. When blessed by the Word, some believers weep. Others may respond with clapping or shouting. I don't think these matters should become points of contention.

Let's clarify. The pastor is the worship leader of his congregation. He is responsible to God to see that the worship is done decently and in order and that it follows the spiritual/scriptural pattern Jesus established. I believe that forms and methods of worship are secondary. Christians need not argue about them. If the form of worship at your church is not suitable to you, seek a church where it is. Don't become a source of irritation or a stifling force at your church.

So what is involved in New Testament worship? What ingredients are present when worship is conducted in the power of and with the blessing of the Holy Spirit? Grudem rightly says, "Worship is a spiritual activity and it must be empowered by the Holy Spirit working within us. This means that we must pray that the Holy Spirit will enable us to worship rightly."[3] Here are a few ingredients for successful public worship.

## Attending

Studying the New Testament church at worship reveals interesting terminology. New Testament Christians did gather for worship. They congregated. Paul declared in Galatians 3:28 that we are "all one in Christ Jesus." What a miracle! Because Jesus is alive and coming again and because we have been made alive in Jesus, we come together on the Lord's day.

Worship in the New Testament is often called a gathering or coming together. In Acts 14:27, the church was gathered together so Paul and his party could tell what God had done in the salvation of the Gentiles. Acts 12:12 mentions they gathered together for prayer. In Acts 15:30, they gathered together to read certain letters. Sometimes they even gathered for discipline (see 1 Cor. 5:4). Check out these other references: 1 Corinthians 11:17–18, 20, 33–34; 14:23, 26. Second Thessalonians 2:1 refers to "our being gathered to him." This is a reference to the second coming of Jesus. The church gathers together periodically in our local church meeting, but one day all God's people will gather together with him in that meeting in the air.

The Troas service is mentioned in Acts 20:7–12. The passage talks about "when the disciples came together" (KJV) and some of what went on. The gathering took place on the first day of the week to break bread. Whether it was the Lord's Supper or just a fellowship meal, it indicates fellowship with the Lord Jesus Christ. Paul preached to them, apparently until midnight. A young man named Eutychus went to sleep and fell out of the third floor. Paul went to Eutychus, embraced him, and evidently revived him from the dead. Then Paul preached until daylight! So much for services beginning and ending promptly.

Sometimes when New Testament believers met for worship, it was called assembling. In Hebrews 12:22, the church is called the "assembly." Our Assembly of God friends have chosen a good Bible name for their churches. The word *assembly* is a Greek word *ekklesia*, which means "to call out." Believers are those who have been called out from the world and gathered together around Jesus Christ.

Look at some of the references to assembling in the King James Version. John 20:19 talks about the disciples being assembled together in the upper room after the resurrection of Jesus. Acts 1:4 mentions the assembling together of the disciples awaiting the coming of the Holy Spirit on the day of Pentecost. Acts 4:31 talks of their assembling together after the arrest of Peter and John. While assembled, they prayed, the place was shaken, they were all filled with the Holy Spirit, and they spoke God's Word with boldness. Acts 11:26 mentions Paul and Barnabas assembling together with the church in Antioch for a whole year. Acts 15:25 mentions the church assembling together and making a decision to send Barnabas and Paul with the message of gospel liberty to Gentile believers.

What's the point of all this? Basically, if you want to be involved in genuine New Testament worship, you must attend. This is the first step. You can't participate in public worship if you aren't there. When I first started preaching, people said to me, "Preacher, I can't be there Sunday, but I'll be with you in spirit." That always sounded spooky to me. If you want to participate in public worship, you must gather with God's people. You must assemble with the saints. Hebrews 10:25 says, "Let us not give up meeting together, as some are in the habit of doing, but let us encourage one another—and all the more as you see the Day approaching." I believe the Christian has a responsibility to attend the scheduled services of his or her church. It is a matter of faithfulness and commitment.

Just coming to the services is a testimony to people. When your family gets in the car and heads to church, you are telling everyone who sees you how important worship is.

I believe there should be preparation before coming to the worship service. Too many Christians just come to the public worship services. Some may even think they can dine with the devil on Saturday night, then dine with the Lord on Sunday. The bar on Saturday night and Sunday school on Sunday morning? I don't think so. Some believers try to dine at both tables. Saturday night is a good time to pray and prepare our hearts for worship on the Lord's day.

The Bible even has something to say about our appearance for worship. First Corinthians 11 is fascinating. Remember the context. The local flavor and the eastern culture are reflected in the chapter. But the truths have universal applications. The chapter teaches that attitude and apparel in worship are extremely important.

I'm a big Alabama football fan. I recently went to the annual Alabama vs. Auburn game. My preacher buddy Fred Wolfe and I bought some hats as we went into the stadium. He looked really goofy. When I got back in the car and looked at myself in the mirror, I looked even goofier than he did. Now I know why the fans around me were laughing when they turned our direction. We were in a football mood. We were dressed for the game.

Paul talked about women with veils off and men with hats on. He wasn't happy. In the Eastern culture, women never appeared in public without a veil, which was a symbol of modesty and submission. In Corinth temple prostitutes, with uncovered heads and short haircuts, moved through the city. Today it would be like a pastor's wife coming to the service in a micro-mini skirt. What is the point? We should come before the Lord in our best. If you were going to visit the president at the White House, how would you dress? Certainly not like you were going to a tennis game. You would want to be dressed in your very best.

When we come to worship, we are coming into the presence of God. We should have on our very best, and it should be clean.

When we attend public services, we should also greet one another. Paul says, "Greet one another with a holy kiss" (2 Cor. 13:12). Phillips paraphrases it well, "A handshake all around, please!" It is a good thing to greet, pray, and hug one another when God's people gather for worship.

When we attend the services, we should always be ready to give our testimony. First Corinthians 14:26 indicates that we should be willing to share with others what God is doing in our lives. The King James Version of Psalm 107:2 says, "Let the redeemed of the Lord say so."

When we attend services, we witness the baptism in Christ of new believers. Or we periodically gather together to observe the Lord's Supper, remembering what he did for us on the cross, examining our relationship to him, and anticipating his return.

We should also participate in the service through the offerings. First Corinthians 16:1–2 is the best passage in the New Testament on the matter of giving. We bring our offering on the first day of the week, and we give as God has prospered us. Of course, there is more to giving than just money. We offer Him "a sacrifice of praise—the fruit of lips that confess his name" (Heb. 13:15).

In Romans 15:16, Paul talked about winning Gentiles to Christ. His statement in the King James Version is filled with words taken directly from worship: "ministering," "offering up," "acceptable," "being sanctified by the Holy Ghost." Paul was laying before the Lord those souls he had won to Christ. Do you want to make your worship service mean even more when you attend? Bring with you some person you have won to Christ. At the invitation time, walk down the aisle with him or her. In your own heart, offer that person up to the Lord as an act of worship. This will give your worship a new dimension.

## Singing

First Corinthians 14:15 says that when we come together we should have a psalm. Ephesians 5:19 and Colossians 3:16 tell us that we speak to ourselves, teach and admonish one another in psalms and hymns and spiritual songs. Let's talk about singing in our worship services. It's all about expressing thanksgiving, love, and adoration. When we congregate, we should celebrate. No more "services as usual." But we don't want a religious show. Music is vital to public worship.

Actually, music is important to our lives. At home, in the car, and at work, we're in an "ocean" of music. Music expresses every emotion—joy, sorrow, love, hate, war, peace. This is another reason you don't want to go to hell. There will be no music in hell. Here you would never hear the song of the little canary again or the anthems of a great choir. Only the curses and cries of the damned. No thank you!

God loves music. Music began when the morning stars sang together (Job 38:7) at the cloud where the angels stood to celebrate the creation. God has filled all creation with music. Silence is just a pause in God's great symphony. Do you hear it? The wind playing in the leaves, the insects humming in the summer. Why does a bumblebee hum? Maybe because it doesn't know the words? Hear the quail cooing in the woods or the rush of waves on the beach. Think about the beautiful music of the human voice. God has so wonderfully built our voices with distinct muscles that they are capable of more than 170 million different sounds. God has given us the skill to build instruments of music—piano, organ, flute, harp, and trumpet.

Music has power. Music of the flesh can drag a soul down to hell. Music of the Spirit can lift a soul into the presence of God.

Do you want to stir up some talk at your church? Just talk about music. Almost everyone has a strong opinion about it because music affects the total being. It instructs the mind, stimulates the emotions, and prompts the will. All of us have preferences in church music. Some people hear a song, and it turns them off. Others hear the same song, and they are blessed by it. Just because you don't like some music doesn't necessarily mean it is of the devil. There are many styles of music. Traditional. Formal. Contemporary. Southern Gospel. Evangelistic. And more.

How do we deal with this at our church? I tell our music ministers that we operate within a rectangular box. Some music outside that box is unacceptable for the purposes of our worship services. Most "high church" music is unacceptable for our purpose to minister to common people. I started off as a music minor in college. I sang in the university choir. For four years we sang an anthem entitled, "Awake the Harp." In four years, the harp never woke up! High church music threatens to turn into a melody but never does. The lyrics are normally Old Testament with no gospel. That's never a part of the worship services I lead.

Below the box is music that seems satanic to me. Its beat is raw. The words are bad news, not good news. Music like this is never used in our worship services.

But inside the rectangular box we try to have something in every service for everyone. Our desire is for people to find music to bless them and to build them up. It is a mistake for a church to adopt only one style of music. People can be taught to be tolerant and appreciative of the musical tastes of other people. Our people do it very well. We strive for the same twofold balance in music that Jesus gave us: Truth—music with scripturally correct words and spirit—music that moves the heart. We emphasize what I call gospel music and Jesus music. The music always points to Jesus.

What about choruses? They are very popular in our churches. They might fit in the category of spiritual songs. There is a valid place for choruses, but it is a mistake for churches to desert the great hymns. There is major power in some of those hymns. They are fragrant with the flowers of devotion throughout the ages. Think of these words.

> Amazing grace, how sweet the sound
> That saved a wretch like me.
> I once was lost, but now am found.
> Was blind but now I see.[4]

Or, "There is power, power, power in the blood of the lamb."[5] How often have God's people come to church loaded down with problems and depression. Through the singing of sweet hymns, these people seem to lose their burdens. Augustine said, "When sung, these sacred words stir my mind to greater religious fervor and kindle in me a more ardent flame of piety."[6] Many of the hymns I learned as a child are with me today. The words often come to mind with fresh blessing and power.

But what about choruses? Actually, churches have been using choruses all along. Some churches, however, use nothing but praise choruses. Some say God is doing a new thing. You don't put new wine in old wineskins, so to speak. So they eliminate hymns with the hint that God did not work in other years as he is working today. The fact is that the Holy Spirit has been working nonstop since the day of Pentecost. The great hymns of the faith give testimony to his work. To those who say people today don't know the hymns, I say *teach them!*

But I do believe there is a place for choruses. Just be sure about the words. Some choruses I hear are like cotton candy: sweet to the taste but soon gone with no remaining substance. I think there is also a danger in repetitive choruses. Donald Hustad, former professor at Southern Baptist Theological Seminary and organist for the Billy Graham Crusades, says, "Thirty minutes of singing songs in one music style, with much repetition of a few words of 'pure praise,' is an excessive invitation to emotional manipulation."[7]

What is our purpose in the music of worship? It is not to please the tastes of those among us. Actually, worship is for Christians. When our unsaved friends come, they should see and hear a difference between what goes on in church and in their world. Worship should prepare the hearts of the people to receive the Word of God. The heart of the preacher should likewise be prepared to preach the Word of God. Think of the prophet Elisha. When called upon to give a message from God, Elisha called for a minstrel (a musician who played upon a harp). When the minstrel played we are told "the hand of the Lord came upon Elisha" (2 Kings 3:15). Music and the ministry of the prophets were associated in the Old Testament (1 Sam. 10:5; 16:23). This is true in my own life. Often I have felt the hand of the Lord on me as some song was sung. I was ready to preach.

God's people are a singing people. Who knows what great music has done as God's people have gathered? King Richard I of England, on a journey to the Holy Land, was captured and thrown into a dungeon. He had a minstrel named Blondel. Blondel traveled from one dungeon to another, playing well-known tunes outside the dungeon windows, searching for the one hiding his king. At last his music was answered by the voice of the king. King Richard I was soon returned from exile and restored to the throne. How often some sweet gospel song has pulled us from a dungeon.

## Preaching

We also congregate to communicate. Acts 20:7, 1 Corinthians 14:19, and other passages emphasize the centrality of preaching in public worship services. Our church has a pulpit in the very center of the building. This is the focal point. The centrality of the pulpit in the building conveys that the preaching of God's Word is the center of the services. Charismatics often feel that united praise is the central part of the worship service. I believe that the preaching of the gospel is the central part. The pastor, therefore, is the worship leader. He is to monitor the music. He must be certain that the lyrics of the music do not contradict his message.

The preaching of the Word has first place in the worship services (see 1 Tim. 4:13; James 1:22; Col. 4:16). The Word must be proclaimed when we gather for worship. The preacher, with the anointing and power of the Holy Spirit, must explain God's truth to the people. The Holy Spirit helps the preacher explain it and helps the listeners understand it. Actually, when I preach, people hear more than me. God reveals his Son, the Lord Jesus, through the Bible by the power of the Holy Spirit. The truth of God's Word meets every need of the human soul. "Felt" needs are talked about today. The Bible speaks to "felt" needs and to unfelt ones as well. The Word is applied to our hearts by the Holy Spirit. The preacher has a responsibility to preach the Word. The people have a responsibility to hear the Word. The command of 2 Timothy 4:2 must be taken seriously by every preacher: "Preach the Word; be prepared in season and out of season; correct, rebuke and encourage—with great patience and careful instruction." When the preacher preaches in the power of the Holy Spirit, he will exalt the Lord Jesus Christ.

The purpose of the preaching is to bring the congregation face-to-face with the living God. First Thessalonians 2:13 says, "And we also thank God continually because, when you received the word of God, which you heard from us, you accepted it not as the word of men, but as it actually is, the word of God, which is at work in you who believe." What is the result of preaching? God works in the lives of people. He does it as the people respond in faith. Hebrews 4:2 says, "For we also have had the gospel preached to us, just as they did; but the message they heard was of no value to them, because those who heard did not combine it with faith." Many say people won't hear the Word of God. They will! I agree with Kent Hughes: "God's Word preached in the power of the Holy Spirit is invasive."[8]

## Responding

When God's people gather to worship the Lord, there must also be a response from the believers who are present. When we meet the God of the Word, we've just "gotta" do something! The truth of the Bible excites our emotions, and these emotions should result in decisions of our will. We should respond in obedience to God's revealed truth. True worship should also leave us at the feet of Jesus.

What happens with all of this? Often a response on the part of the unsaved. Though evangelism is not the primary purpose of our public worship services, an evangelistic factor is always involved. First Corinthians 14:23–25 is interesting. Get the picture—an unbeliever coming into a service where the church has come together for worship. The Word is preached. Christians share testimonies. It is indicated that "if an unbeliever or someone who does not understand comes in while everybody is prophesying, he will be convinced by all that he is a sinner and will be judged by all, and the secrets of his heart will be laid bare. So he will fall down and worship God, exclaiming, 'God is really among you.'"

Jim Cymbala says, "If meetings are governed by the Holy Spirit, when a visitor comes in there should be such a mixture of God's truth and God's presence that the person's heart is x-rayed, the futility of his life is exposed, and he crumbles in repentance."[9]

Yes, at "Ole BeThursde" we sang, "All is vain unless the Spirit of the Holy One comes down." Has worship really changed? We still have singing and praising and preaching and responding.

We better get tuned up in worship down here now. We will worship in heaven. I think about the two great praise scenes in Revelation 4–5. One of the joys of heaven will be the magnificent praising of the Lamb. What a choir! What worshipful sounds! The tide of praise rolls on, gathering power, force, and volume. Can't you hear the corners of the universe reverberating with praise to the Lamb? Not one discord or off-key sound. All are in tune. Heaven's music subsides. All creation repeats, "Amen, Amen." As the worship ends, all are bowed with faces on the ground at Jesus' feet. That's Holy Spirit worship.

### Some Tips for Worship

1. If you are going to worship with God's people, you have to show up.

2. Sing. Give it your best shot. You may be surprised at how well you sing when you blend your voice with all the other saints.

3. Be ready to share your testimony with others. Be available to pray with and encourage some downhearted Christian.

4. Bring your Bible, open it, and listen with your head and your heart while the preacher proclaims the Word of God.

5. Respond to the truth that God has presented to you from his Word through his spokesman by his Spirit.

As you leave the worship, realize the service is just beginning.

# CHAPTER 16

# YOU, GO!

Is there a hell? Yes.

Is there a heaven? Absolutely!

Did Jesus die on the cross and rise again to keep people out of hell? You bet!

So basically our work as Christians is all about getting people to Jesus.

You have just read the irresistible logic of Christian witnessing. Charismatic Christians and other Christians actually agree on the matter of witnessing. Charismatics have a love for people and a desire to introduce them to Jesus Christ. I have seen many Charismatic churches witness to and reach some hard cases through the years. Alcoholics, drug addicts, and embezzlers—I've seen them come to Christ, thanks to Charismatic believers.

Someone said, "The mission of the Holy Spirit is the evangelization of the world." Just look at Acts. The theme of the book is stated in Acts 1:8: "But you will receive power when the Holy Spirit comes on you; and you will be my witnesses in Jerusalem, and in all Judea and Samaria, and to the ends of the earth." What about the rest of the book? It tells us people were filled with the Spirit, and as a result, they were bold witnesses for Jesus Christ.

One witnessing experience from the Book of Acts shows in particular this witnessing purpose. It's the Acts 8 passage about Philip, the deacon, and the

Ethiopian eunuch. Okay, I've stood it about as long as I can. I'm going to preach a little. I'm going to take a text and *go!*

Keep Acts in its overall context. Actually, Acts 8–10 fit together quite nicely. In these three consecutive chapters, we see the Spirit's work in witnessing to the main people groups of the human family. Ham, Shem, and Japheth are the Bible's division for the human race (see Gen. 10:1). Acts 8 shows the conversion of the descendant of Ham (the Ethiopian eunuch). Acts 9 recounts the conversion of a descendent of Shem (Paul). Acts 10 records the conversion of a descendent of Japheth (Cornelius). The impact of these three consecutive conversions is deep. God wants the whole world to hear the message of Jesus. The ultimate purpose of the Spirit's work is to bring people to Jesus Christ.

Why have I picked the conversion of the Ethiopian eunuch? Because all the essential components for the salvation of a soul are found here. I've also picked it because the Holy Spirit sets the stage here for one of those unusual experiences occasionally determined by the Father in heaven and worked out by the Holy Spirit on the earth. We find here several aspects of the Holy Spirit's work.

## The Holy Spirit's SaintWork

In Acts 8:26, it's obvious that God has a witness in mind for a special soul-winning project. His name is Philip, one of the original deacons (see Acts 6:5). The early verses of Acts 8 tell us that Philip had been in Samaria for a great city-wide crusade. Multitudes of people are being saved (verses 5–8). The angel of the Lord gives him a message from heaven: "Go south to the road—the desert road—that goes down from Jerusalem to Gaza." Keep in mind that the Book of Acts describes a transition period. All kinds of miraculous activities occur during this transition to authenticate the word and the witness of the early Christians. We know that angels still minister to God's saints today. Hebrews 1:14 teaches they are "ministering spirits sent to serve those who will inherit salvation."

Why did the angel tell Philip to go? Why didn't the angel go? Why didn't Philip say to the angel, "Go yourself, I'm busy"? Here's the reason: *God does not send angels to witness to people.* Angels have never known what it is like to be a guilty sinner or to experience the joy of salvation. Actually, angels can only look in awe at God's amazing salvation work (see 1 Pet. 1:21). "Holy, holy is what the angels sing./ And I expect to help them make the glad hosannas ring. / But when we sing redemption's story, angels fold their wings, /For angels never knew the joy that our salvation brings."

So Philip was to go down to Gaza, about sixty miles south of Jerusalem, near the Mediterranean coast. Today the area is called the Gaza Strip. The road was heavily traveled. Travelers used it as a trade route to Egypt and to the continent of Africa.

Have you ever heard a great speaker? Perhaps at a meeting or on television? Philip was a great crusade speaker. As he preached in Samaria, many came to Christ. He was also a faithful one-on-one witness for Christ. The angel said, according to the King James Version, "Arise, and go." Verse 27 says, "And he arose and went." This is impressive. Philip was willing to leave the great crowds and talk personally with a needy soul. He was not even told why he was headed to the desert. He must have wondered what was up. Remember, we walk "by faith, not by sight" (2 Cor. 5:7). There was no hesitation on Philip's part. Often we don't know all the details about the Lord's plans for us. We must be ready to go wherever he leads.

Verse 27 continues, "An important official." Suddenly, as Philip journeys into the desert, he sees a great caravan and a covered chariot in the distance.

There is a man! Verse 29 says, "The Spirit told Philip, 'Go to that chariot and stay near it.'" I don't know how the Holy Spirit spoke to him. Maybe it was through an impression in his heart or perhaps the Spirit spoke through the circumstances of the situation. Maybe it was just the opportunity itself. The same is true in our lives. The Holy Spirit leads us into the will of God in various ways.

Verse 30 says, "Then Philip ran." Notice that Philip didn't appoint a committee to study the matter. The Holy Spirit said, "Go," and Philip went. Instant obedience. The man to whom Philip was to witness was a man of considerable importance. Sometimes Christians are intimidated by persons of influence, affluence, and celebrity. Think about the testimony of Psalm 119:46:

> I will speak of your statutes before kings
> and will not be put to shame.

Whatever his hesitations might have been, Philip was sensitive to the leading of the Holy Spirit. We should be, too.

So there's more to all this than just an angel. The Holy Spirit was at work. We see the Spirit's work in witnessing. He led a faithful witness to the right person at the right time. You may not have an angel to nudge you, but you can have leading and direction from the Holy Spirit. Jesus promised in Matthew 10:20, "For it will not be you speaking, but the Spirit of your Father speaking through you."

Here's one man riding in a chariot down a dusty road. A soul winner is sent to witness to him. God cares for one person. Jesus preached his great sermon on the new birth to one person—Nicodemus. Jesus preached his marvelous message about the water of life to one person—the woman at the well. Jesus told one of his most important parables about the importance of one—the one lost sheep.

It was no accident that this soul-winner Philip came at just the right time to the right person at the right place. The circumstances surrounding our witnessing opportunities are not coincidental. They are providential. That's how the SpiritWorks!

### The Holy Spirit's SinnerWork

So what about this "man of Ethiopia" in verse 27 (KJV)? He was a VIP (very important person). He was probably from somewhere south of Egypt. The

Ethiopia mentioned here may be today's Sudan. He was a "eunuch." In oriental courts, eunuchs often held important offices. This guy was a man of great authority. He held a very responsible position. He worked for Candace, queen of the Ethiopians, "keeping charge of all the treasury." In other words, he was secretary of the treasury in her administration. We are not given his name, but these statements tell us he was a man of authority, responsibility, and importance. But he was also a lost man. None of the things which made him great on earth prepared him for heaven.

I am concerned about the creeping universalism in Christian circles. The idea that all people are ultimately going to be saved is gaining ground in some Christian groups. The truth is that all people are lost and desperately need a Savior. The eunuch needed a Savior, too.

So we have a man in a chariot. Some chariot. He had his own private chauffeur. Perhaps a canopy shielded him from the sun. Undoubtedly, a large party traveled with him. Verse 27 says, "This man had gone to Jerusalem to worship."

He was also a VRP (very religious person). Evidently, he was what would be known then as a "God-fearer." While he was not a full-fledged member of the Jewish faith because of his physical condition (see Deut. 23:1), he was concerned about spiritual matters. He had journeyed over two hundred miles to visit Jerusalem, the religious center of that day. He must have been eager to get there.

But something had gone wrong. Verse 28 says that he was "on his way home." What did he find in Jerusalem? Elaborate buildings, an impressive ceremony, a large group of worshipers—but a religion as dry, dull, and dead as King Tut's tomb. What a disappointment. Perhaps he saw all the crass materialism, the pompous hypocrisy, and the racial intolerance. This sounds a lot like today. He left disappointed and disillusioned with the same hungry heart. He had gone seeking the water of life, and he returned still thirsty. He had gone looking for the bread of life, and he returned still hungry.

Do you ever wonder what people find when they come to our churches? Is the eunuch typical? Do they find monotonous messages and music exalting the musicians and not the Lord Jesus? Too many of our churches have settled for "having a form of godliness but denying its power" (2 Tim. 3:5). When people come to our services, is their spiritual hunger fed? Are they aware they are in the presence of God? A statement of Jesus often comes to my mind as I stand to preach to people. Jesus said, "Give them something to eat" (Mark 6:37). I want people to be spiritually fed at my services.

This man was also a VPP (very prepared person). Verse 28 says that he was "reading the book of Isaiah the prophet." This must be another evidence of the providential work of the Holy Spirit. Somehow, he got Isaiah! There he was sitting in a chariot, riding down a dusty desert road, reading the Bible. I don't think we would expect him to be reading a Bible. Well, we might be surprised who reads the Bible and seeks the truth of God. All human beings have a need for God. I read an article recently about the large number of Bible study groups in Washington, D.C. God's Word is being read and studied in strange places. Don't underestimate the power of God. The Holy Spirit goes into unusual places, preparing hungry hearts.

The eunuch was already divinely prepared. When the Holy Spirit sends us to witness, he wants us to follow where he has already been. Think about Jesus and the woman at the well. At the moment Jesus was at Jacob's well, here came this woman. The Holy Spirit is at work in many places.

God has provided at least three gifts to help get sinners to Christ: the Word of God, which brings light to dark hearts; the Spirit of God, which convicts people of their need of Christ; and the child of God. God gives Christians the ability to explain and to apply the Scriptures with the help of the Spirit of God.

Here was this eunuch with the scroll of Isaiah, opened to chapter 53, spread out in his lap. A soul-winner approached him. Philip had been in Samaria doing mass evangelism. Now, he sat by one man and kindly talked to him from the Scriptures about Jesus. That's how the SpiritWorks!

## The Holy Spirit's ScriptureWork

Verse 28 describes the eunuch reading from the scroll of Isaiah. Where did he get the scroll? We don't know. He was examining it, looking for something to satisfy his soul. He was searching for some solution to his heart's needs.

Philip saw that he was reading the Scriptures. We should be observant, too. Look for opportunities to witness to others about Christ. We stumble over people every day with hungry hearts. As a teenager, I learned the chorus, "Lead me to some soul today. Teach me, Lord, just what to say." Look for some chariots today.

Philip asked the eunuch if he understood his reading. The eunuch told Philip he needed a guide. He requested that Philip come up into the chariot and sit with him. Verses 32–33 indicate that the eunuch was reading from Isaiah 53:7–8.

In many ways, the Book of Isaiah is a miniature Bible. I know the chapter verses are not a part of inspired Scripture, but it is interesting to look at the chapter divisions in Isaiah. Isaiah has sixty-six chapters. Our Bible has sixty-six books. Isaiah's chapters are divided like the Bible. The first thirty-nine chapters have to do with judgment. Our Old Testament has thirty-nine books, ending in a curse (see Mal. 3:6). The last twenty-seven chapters of Isaiah are about grace. Our New Testament has twenty-seven books, all about the grace of our Lord Jesus Christ (Rev. 22:21).

At the moment Philip met the eunuch, he was reading from the central chapter of the last section of Isaiah. He was reading perhaps the clearest portrait of Jesus in the entire Old Testament. This encounter with Philip had to be divinely planned.

The Holy Spirit uses the Bible in witnessing. The Spirit of God never works apart from or in contradiction to the Word of God. The eunuch needed someone to guide him. The Holy Spirit dealt with it then and deals with it today by giving us teachers who are gifted to explain the Bible to people who need to understand it. The Holy Spirit was preparing the mind of the eunuch to understand the Bible story of Jesus. This is what I call evidence that the Holy Spirit was working in his heart.

Meanwhile, the eunuch raised the burning religious question of the day. "The eunuch asked Philip, 'Tell me, please, who is the prophet talking about, himself or someone else?'" (v. 34). A question like that begs for a sermon. Verse 35 says, "Then Philip began with that very passage of Scripture and told him the good news about Jesus." It's amazing to me that many modern scholars have a problem finding Jesus in the Old Testament. Philip didn't. Neither did Jesus. Luke 24:27 says, "And beginning with Moses and all the Prophets, he explained to them what was said in all the Scriptures concerning himself."

Jesus is the central person of the Bible. He's on every page. The Old Testament anticipates him. The New Testament announces him. The Old Testament predicts him. The New Testament presents him. If you had to write a paper for your English class discussing the theme of the Bible, no problem: It's Jesus.

Philip took the eunuch, by way of Isaiah, to the foot of the cross. Through Isaiah's eyes, the eunuch saw Jesus in his humiliation, crucifixion, and exaltation. He saw his virtuous life, his vicarious death, his victorious resurrection, and his visible return. That's how the SpiritWorks!

## The Holy Spirit's SalvationWork

Romans 10:17 teaches us that "faith comes from hearing the message, and the message is heard through the word of Christ." The Holy Spirit had this eunuch ready. As the chariot approached water, the eunuch said, "Look, here is water. Why shouldn't I be baptized?" (v. 36). The Holy Spirit had been preparing him all his life for this one moment.

Verse 37 is not in all New Testament manuscripts. Yet all agree that the statement here is thoroughly biblical. Philips translated it, "If you believe with all your heart, you may." This is it—the essence of the salvation message. Romans 10:9 puts it this way: Salvation is a heart experience. The Holy Spirit convinces the mind with the Word of God. He convicts the conscience. The Holy Spirit enables the will to decide for Christ. The eunuch did something about it, and he made a decision. He declared, "I believe that Jesus Christ is the Son of God." That's power evangelism. For the gospel is indeed the power of God unto salvation to everyone who believes (Rom. 1:16). Stop the chariot! We're talking born again. The Holy Spirit came to dwell within him. He was baptized by the Spirit into the body (the church); he was sealed by the Holy Spirit; and he received the down payment of the Holy Spirit in his heart. All this happened before he was baptized in water.

Philip and the eunuch went down into the water. Perhaps slaves gathered around. I think about some of my own baptismal experiences. Years ago, as pastor of rural churches, I baptized people in lakes and streams. On many Sunday afternoons, I have seen a lakeshore circled by family and friends watching me baptize new believers in Christ. Baptism is a wonderful outward expression of an inward experience.

They emerged from the water. Up came the eunuch, spewing water, dripping wet. "Hallelujah!" He turned to thank Philip, but he was gone! Verse 39 says, "The Spirit of the Lord suddenly took Philip away, and the eunuch did not see him again." The word for "took away" is the same word used for the Rapture in 1 Thessalonians 4:17. Philip experienced a rapture before the Rapture! Here's another miracle. Philip had been going, going. Now he's gone!

You may not have an experience like that. You may not be miraculously caught away. But to win a soul to Christ will get you flying pretty high.

Although the eunuch saw Philip no more, he "went on his way rejoicing." That chariot may have been turned into a gospel buggy bouncing joyfully down that dusty desert road. He sees a man in the distance. He pulls over. Want a ride? Then the eunuch shares from the Bible with the walker. "Would you like to invite Jesus into your heart?" You bet! Stop the chariot! Another baptism. Another time of Holy Spirit joy. As the eunuch pulls away in his chariot, a bumper sticker on the back reads, "Honk if you love Jesus." Holy Spirit joy is always an evidence that the Holy Spirit is at work. So this eunuch is now on his way to start the first church of Ethiopia. Perhaps his queen will be another convert.

Because Philip was willing to leave a city, he reached a continent. Who knew? God did. The Holy Spirit prepared the heart of the eunuch with the Word of God. The Holy Spirit led Philip to the desert for witnessing. The Holy Spirit glorified Jesus, and the Holy Spirit filled both Philip and the eunuch with joy. The Holy Spirit put a desire to witness in their hearts. And that is how the SpiritWorks!

## You, Go!

1. The Holy Spirit is interested in getting the story of Jesus to people. You, go!

2. The Holy Spirit will give you the words to say and will use you to tell someone about Christ. You, go!

3. As you share with lost people the way of salvation from the Bible, the Holy Spirit will use it. You go!

4. As you tell people from the Bible the old, old story of Jesus, the Holy Spirit will exalt Christ and draw the lost person to him. You, go!

5. It is time for us to get into the SpiritWorks. You, go!

# Epilogue

I unfurled my flag early. You knew I was Baptist from the beginning of the book. I am a Southern Baptist pastor. I have served Baptist churches for more than forty years. I don't think this makes me a better Christian or that I have a corner on the truth. But it does mean I have an understanding of Christian faith and practice, and this makes me different in some ways from Christians of other persuasions.

Noncharismatic Christians and Charismatic Christians are not the same. Our conclusions in several areas of Christian doctrine are different. Sincere Christians study the same Bible, and they emerge with different convictions. These differences are clearly seen in several areas of the Holy Spirit's work.

I have sought to explore and to delineate these differences without harshness or aggression. No Christian's sincerity or motives are attacked. If at any point I have failed to demonstrate a Christlike spirit, I ask your forgiveness.

Most of the disagreements aren't tests of fellowship. Good Christians differ. This is why there are Baptist churches, Charismatic churches, Presbyterian churches, Luthern churches, etc. Just because there are many churches doesn't mean we have failed to fulfill the prayer of Jesus that we might be one. I feel a real sense of oneness with all those who affirm love for Jesus Christ and commitment to his Holy Word.

In reality, there are levels where Christians of various beliefs should cooperate. We share common moral concerns, like the sanctity of life and religious liberty. We can work together to seek moral improvement in our nation and to preserve the right of every person to worship God according to his or her understanding of faith.

There are other areas where Christians must be faithful to truth as they know it and see it. Certain doctrines identify a particular Christian group. It's a fact I'm a Baptist. Baptists emphasize the person and work of Jesus Christ, and we acknowledge the power and work of the Holy Spirit. We believe that the Spirit's principal work is to magnify Christ. I'm not saying that everything about my denomination is completely scripturally based. Groups can become so cautious about excesses that the person and work of the Spirit can be deemphasized. But in matters concerning the work of the Holy Spirit, Baptists have a long history of faith and practice. Since earliest days, whether Anabaptists of South Germany and Switzerland, British Baptists, or Baptists of America, certain Charismatic practices have not been a part of our faith and practice.

In August 1654, the South Wales Baptist Association published this statement on the matter of tongues: "Item 6: Diversities of tongues, for the further publishing and confirmation of the gospel, by those primitive and extraordinary

Apostles, Prophets and Evangelists. All those offices and gifts were extraordinary, and therefore are now ceased."[1] I am not saying the statement is totally biblically correct. I am saying that Baptists have been clear on certain Charismatic practices for a long time. I defend Charismatic groups to hold their particular beliefs. Baptists also have the right to hold theirs.

Lastly, I mention matters of integrity. Churches have a certain integrity of name. The sign over a church door should be a true indication of the faith and practice of the Christians who meet there for worship. If my First Baptist Church in Jacksonville should become more Charismatic than Baptist in matters of faith and practice, integrity would demand a name change. Should I become more Charismatic than Baptist in my personal beliefs, I should let my church know it. If they want to change their convictions, fine. If not, I should quietly resign as pastor and seek a group of Christians who believe similarly. Unfortunately, to do anything else in a situation like that creates disharmony, confusion, and chaos.

We have come to the end of an interesting journey. I do not claim that all of my conclusions are 100 percent correct. Surely we all agree that our limited minds, encountering the unlimited mind of God in the written Word, can gain only imperfect understanding of truth. However, we should be seeking daily to understand God's truth more completely. And, whatever our differences in the interpretation of Scripture relative to the person and work of the Holy Spirit, we all surely agree that we want to know more about how the SpiritWorks!

# ENDNOTES

## Introduction

1. *Newsweek*, 13 April 1998, 51.
2. Ibid., 56.
3. Ibid.
4. Chuck Lawless, "The Relationship Between Evangelism and Spiritual Warfare in the North American Spiritual Warfare Movement, 1986-1997" (Doctoral dissertation at Southern Seminary, Louisville, Kentucky, 1977), 92).
5. *Newsweek*, 27 December 1993.
6. *Macleans*, 4 September 1995, 39.
7. *Florida Times-Union*, 6 December 1993.
8. *Newsweek*, 13 April 1998, 58.
9. Ibid., 59.
10. Frederick Bruner, *A Theology of the Holy Spirit* (Grand Rapids: William B. Eerdmans, 1970), 33.
11. *Florida Times-Union*.
12. Ibid.

## Chapter 1

1. John White, *When the Spirit Comes with Power* (Downers Grove, Ill.: InterVarsity Press, 1988), 55.
2. Richard Mayhue, "Cutting It Straight," *Moody Monthly*, 85:1 1984, 36. Quoted in Ron Dunn, *Will God Heal Me?*
3. *Florida Times-Union*, Jacksonville, Florida, 28 July 1998.

## Chapter 2

1. Bruner, 279.
2. John Phillips, *Exploring the Gospel of John* (Neptune, N.J.: Loizeaux Brothers, 1988), 308.
3. Quoted by J. Oswald Sanders, *The Holy Spirit and His Gifts* (Grand Rapids: Zondervan Publishing House, 1940), 73.
4. Phillips, 193.
5. J. Sidlow Baxter, *Awake My Heart* (Grand Rapids: Zondervan Publishing House, 1960), 170.
6. James A. Beverley, *Holy Laughter and the Toronto Blessing* (Grand Rapids: Zondervan Publishing House, 1995), 193.

7. Stanley M. Burgess and Gary B. McGee, eds., *Dictionary of Pentecostal and Charismatic Movements* (Grand Rapids: Zondervan Publishing House, 1988), 481.

## Chapter 3
1. Bruner, 184.
2. Lawrence W. Wood, "Third Wave of the Spirit, Pentecostalization of American Christianity: A Wesleyan Critique," *Wesleyan Theological Journal*, 37:1 (spring 1996), 115.
3. Ibid., 112.
4. Ibid., 130.
5. Ibid., 138.

## Chatper 4
1. Beverly, 95–96.
2. W. R. Moody, *The Life of D. L. Moody* (New York: Fleming H. Revell, 1900), 149.
3. Roy Fish, from a taped sermon preached at Cottage Hill Baptist Church, 27 August 1997.
4. Beverly, 54.
5. Beverly, 72.
6. Roy Fish, taped sermon preached at Cottage Hill Baptist Church, 8 August 1997.

## Chapter 5
1. Tenets of Faith, the Brownsville Revival.
2. Wayne A. Grudem, *Systematic Theology* (Grand Rapids: Zondervan Publishing House, 1994), 782.
3. Ibid.

## Chapter 6
1. F. Angus, *The Mystery Religions and Christianity* (New York: Dover, 1975), 100–01.
2. Grudem, *Systematic Theology*, 382.
3. Burgess and McGee, 340.

4. John P. Kildahl, "Psychological Observations," 124, in Hamilton, ed. *Charismatic Movements*, 124–25. Refer to the *Greek Orthodox Theological Review*, 28:2 (Summer 1983).

5. William J. Samaran, *Tongues of Men and Angels* (New York: Macmillan, 1972), 227.

6. Neil Babcox, *A Search for Charismatic Reality* (Portland: Multnomah Press, 1985), 65.

## Chapter 7

1. Burgess and McGee, 345.

2. Kenneth Hagin, *The Healing Anointing* (Tulsa: Faith Library Publications, 1997), 69–70.

3. Ibid., 24.

4. Ibid., 77.

5. Benny Hinn, *Good Morning, Holy Spirit*, 132.

6. Ibid., 119.

7. Hagin, *The Healing Anointing*, 163.

8. Bruner, 160.

## Chapter 8

1. Jerry Spencer, *Fires of Revival*, 28:1 (Jan. 1998), 1.

2. C. S. Johnson, *Frontier Camp Meeting* (Dallas: SMU Press, 1955), 57.

3. Peter Marshall and Don Manuel, *From Sea to Shining Sea* (Old Tappan, N.J.: Fleming H. Revell Co., 1986), 63–66.

4. Warren Smith, "Holy Laughter or Strong Delusion?" *SCP Newsletter*, 19:2 (fall 1994).

5. Ibid., 5.

6. White, 94.

7. Burgess and McGee, 790.

8. *Christianity Today*, 11 Sept. 1995, 27.

9. Smith, 14.

10. Ibid.

11. Watchman Nee, *Latent Power of the Soul* (New York: Christian Fellowship Publishers, 1972), 32-33.

12. Baptist Press article, 3 March 1995.

## Chapter 9

1. John Wimber, *Power Evangelism* (San Francisco: Harper and Row, 1986), 35.
2. Robert Menzies, "A Pentecostal Perspective on Signs and Wonders," *Pneuma*, 17:2 (fall 1995), 276.
3. Peter Wagner, *What Happens When You See Jesus?* 73.
4. *Florida Times-Union*, 20 Sept. 1998.
5. Ron Ritchie, "How to Interpret Signs and Wonders," *Wesleyan Theological Journal*, 31.

## Chapter 10

1. Peter Wagner, *Wrestling with Dark Angels* (Ventura, Calif.: Regal Books, 1990), 74.
2. Peter Wagner, "Territorial Spirits and World Missions," *Evangelical Missions Quarterly*, 25:3 (July 1989), 279.
3. Ibid., 284.
4. Mike Wakely, "A Critical Look at a New 'Key' to Evangelization," *Evangelical Missions Quarterly*, 31:2 (April 1995), 15ff.
5. Robert A. Guelich, "Spiritual Warfare: Jesus, Paul and Peretti," *Pneuma*, 13:1 (spring 1991), 28, n. 152.
6. Wagner, "Territorial Spirits and World Missions," 280.
7. *Pentecostal Evangel*, 26 Oct. 1997, 16.
8. George Otis, *Last of Giants* (Tarrytown: Chosen Books), 99.
9. Jim Cymbala, *Fresh Wind, Fresh Fire* (Grand Rapids: Zondervan Publishing House, 1997), 107.

## Chapter 11

1. Burgess and McGee, 236.
2. Ibid., 689.
3. Paul Wohlgemoth, "Praise Singing," *The Hymn*, January 1987, 19–20.
4. Donald P. Hustad, *Jubilate II* (Carol Stream: Hope Publishing Co., 1989), 289.
5. Ibid.
6. John Phillips, *Exploring the Psalms*, vol. 5 (Neptune, N.J.: Loizeaux Brothers, 1988), 271.
7. Merrill Tenney, ed., *Zondervan Pictorial Bible Dictionary*, Grand Rapids: Zondervan Publishing House, 1963), 196.

8. Ibid.

9. Keil, Delitzsch, *Old Testament Commentaries: Ezekiel 25–Malachi* (Grand Rapids: Associated Publishers and Authors), 1042.

10. Jack W. Hayford, *The Spirit-Filled Bible*, 1238.

11. *The New Brown, Driver, Briggs, Gesenius Hebrew and English Lexicon* (Peabody: Hendrickson Publishing, 1979), 697.

12. Hustad, 295.

13. Burgess and McGee, 534

## Chapter 12

1. Ken Hagin, *New Thresholds of Faith* (Tulsa: Faith Library, 1980), 54-55.

2. Jerry Sevelle, *Living in Divine Prosperity* (Tulsa: Harrison House, 1982), 77.

3. Dennis Hollinger, "Enjoying God Forever," *Trinity Journal*, 9:1 (spring 1988), 135.

4. H. Terris Neuman, "Cultic Origins of Word Faith Theology within the Charismatic Movement," *Pneuma*, 12:1 (spring 1990), 32.

5. John Avanzini, *TBN*, 15 September 1988; 20 Jan. 1991.

6. Fritz Rienecker, *A Linguistic Key to the Greek New Testament* (Grand Rapids: Zondervan Publishing House, 1976), 799.

7. John Avanzini, *TBN*, 1 Aug. 1989.

8. Position paper of the Assemblies of God, approved by the General Presbytery, 19 August 1980.

9. EP, "Former PTL Leader Jim Bakker Rejects "'Prosperity Gospel,'" Hendersonville, N.C.

10. A. T. Robertson, *A Short Grammar of the Greek New Testament* (New York: Harper and Brothers Publishers, 1931), 227–80.

11. Ken Hagin, *How God Taught Me about Prosperity* (Tulsa: Faith Library, 1985), 1.

12. D. L. McConnell, *A Different Gospel* (Peabody: Hendrickson Publishers, 1988), 3–14.

13. Earl Paulk, *Satan Unmasked* (Atlanta: Kingdom, 1985), 97.

14. Robert Tilton, quoted in Burgess and McGee, 719.

15. Ibid.

16. Neuman, 32.

17. McConnell, xvi.

## Chapter 13

1. Burgess and McGee, 96; Richard M Riss, *20th Century Revival Movements* (Hendrickson Publishers, 1987), 106; paper prepared by Elisbeth Lindeman, "New Religious Movements," spring 1996, Billy Graham School of Missions, Southern Baptist Theological Seminary.
2. James Ryle, *Sons of Thunder* (Longmont, Colo.: Boulder Valley Vineyard Tape Ministry), 1 July 1990.
3. David Cannistraci, *The Gift of Apostle* (Ventura, Calif.: Regal Books, 1996), 15.
4. Peter Wagner, *The New Apostolic Churches* (Ventura, Calif.: Regal Books, 1998).
5. *What Is the First Baptist Church of Homossa Springs About?*
6. Lindeman, op cit.
7. Neil Babcox, *A Search for Charismatic Reality* (Portland: Multnomah Press, 1985).
8. Assemblies of God Position Paper, 20 April 1949.
9. Williston Walker, *A History of the Christian Church* (New York: Charles Scribner's Sons, 1959), 55–56

## Chapter 14

1. J. I. Packer, *Keep in Step with the Spirit* (Grand Rapids: Fleming H. Revell, 1984), 192.
2. Cymbala, 144.

## Chapter 15

1. Hymn #379, *The Baptist Hymnal* (Nashville: Convention Press, 1991).
2. Warren Wiersbe, *Real Worship* (Nashville: Nelson, 1986), 27.
3. Grudem, 1010.
4. Hymn #330, *Baptist Hymnal.*
5. Hymn #132, *Baptist Hymnal.*
6. Mortimer J. Adler, ed., *Great Books of the Western World*, vol. 16, (Chicago: Encyclopedia Britannica Inc., 1990), 105.
7. Hustad, 295.
8. R. Kent Hughes, *The Coming Evangelical Crisis*, ed. John H. Armstrong (Chicago: Moody Press, 1996), 102.
9. Cymbala, 134

## Epilogue

1. H. Leon McBeth, *A Sourcebook for Baptist Heritage* (Nashville: Broadman Press, 1990), 61.